Наталья
Александровна
Бонк

Английский для международного сотрудничества.

English for international cooperation.

СП«ПРИН–ДИ», МОСКВА, 1992 г.

Н.А.Бонк

Английский для международного сотрудничества.

Книга представляет собой продолжение учебника "Английский язык. Курс для начинающих" Н.А. Бонк и И.И. Левиной.

Учебник предназначен для лиц, изучающих английский язык для использования в сфере международного сотрудничества. Может быть использован в стационарных учебных заведениях, на курсах, а также для самостоятельного изучения английского языка.

Дозированное введение обильного грамматического материала, современная тематика текстов, тщательно разработанный словарь и рациональная система упражнений делают учебник эффективным и легким для усвоения.

Редактор Бонк И.А.
Верстка Григорьев В.Д., Павлов К.Б.
Отв. за набор Жукова Т.Н.
Художник Гурович И.В.

Издание СП "Прин–Ди",1992

Набор и верстка издательской

службы газеты "Горожане",

Зеленоград

ISBN 5–88533–001–8

Содержание

Содержание

Предисловие

Предлагаемый учебник представляет собой продолжение курса для начинающих English. Course book for Beginners, Н.А. Бонк и И.И.Левиной.

Учебник рассчитан на 200 - 220 часов аудиторного времени и примерно столько же часов самостоятельной работы и предназначен для широкого круга лиц, изучающих английский язык для использования его в области международного сотрудничества, то есть в качестве составной части своей профессии.

Этим определяется тщательный подход к объяснению грамматических явлений и лексики, предлагаемой для активного усвоения, внимательное отношение к фонетике, отбор речевой тематики и речевая направленность системы упражнений.

Грамматика. Грамматический материал дается в объеме, обычно рассчитанным на гораздо больший срок обучения. Продолжается и завершается овладение системой видо-временных форм английского глагола, подробно проходится пассивный залог, различные способы выражения будущего действия, способы выражения долженствования, степени сравнения прилагательных и наречий, согласование времен, прямая и косвенная речь, сложное дополнение после глаголов желания и восприятия и ряд других явлений, необходимых для повседневного устного общения, чтения и письма. Таким образом, курс практически охватывает все наиболее существенные грамматические структуры английского языка.

Лексика. Для активного усвоения отбирались слова и словосочетания нейтрального разговорного стиля, характерные для речи современных носителей английского языка. По своему объему словарный запас, накопленный обучающимися по прохождении обоих учебников, дает возможность объясниться в любой жизненной ситуации, не относящейся к какой-либо узко-специальной области, однако самостоятельное накопление словаря должно всячески поощряться при условии, что новая единица воспринята адекватно в соответствующих границах употребления. Иначе говоря, на этой стадии обучающийся должен приучиться пользоваться словарями, как двуязычными, так и толковыми, если они имеются в его распоряжении. Поскольку скорее всего будет иметься возможность работать с отечественными словарями, в учебнике используется транскрипция, принятая в этих изданиях.

Среди лексических единиц особое место занимают формулы речи, необходимые в деловом и повседневном общении при ведении дискуссии и т.п.

Структура учебника и рекомендации по работе с ним.

Для удобства работы с учебником материал расположен линейно, то есть в той последовательности, которая наиболее целесообразна для его прохождения.

Новые грамматические явления в совокупности с речевой темой или ситуацией общения объединяются в урок-комплекс — UNIT.

Под *темой* автор имеет в виду те сферы жизни современного человека, по поводу которых может возникнуть желание что-либо рассказать или обсудить, чем-либо поделиться, выразить свое мнение, поспорить.

В качестве примеров можно привести такие темы, как планы на будущее, роль телевидения в жизни современного человека, значение планирования в организации рабочего дня, спорт в современной жизни и т.п.

Высказывания по поводу таких тем или проблем отличаются разнообразием и носят непредсказуемый характер, в них проявляется речевое творчество говорящего, и они не могут быть поэтому втиснуты в рамки готовых штампов. Речевое же общение при знакомстве, встрече, прощании, необходимости извиниться, спросить дорогу и т.п. носит совершенно иной характер по цели, содержанию, эмоциональной окраске. Это не речевая тема, а скорее *ситуация общения*, в которой речь чаще всего укладывается в рамки принятых клише, соответствующего речевого этикета. Здесь возможно известное разнообразие форм, которые надо понимать, но не обязательно использовать в своей речи во всем многообразии, ибо и на родном языке человек, как правило, не пользуется всей палитрой извинений, приветствий и т.п., а избирает одну-две формы по своему вкусу.

Для общения на иностранном языке такие формы должны быть рекомендованы и выучены, но речевого творчества здесь не потребуется. Эта разница между темой и ситуацией общения и предопределяет различный характер системы упражнений для того или иного учебного текста.

Между грамматической и лексической частью урока-комплекса нет резкой грани, так как и грамматика, и лексика рассматриваются как средства решения рече-мыслительных проблем, то есть по существу решают *одну* методическую задачу. Поэтому в разделе GRAMMAR имеются тексты как диалогического, так и монологического характера, которые содержат новую лексику, подлежащую активному усвоению и служат базой для речевой работы уже на этапе закрепления новой грамматики. Этот сравнительно короткий текстовой материал, не содержащий много новых слов, чередуется с тематическими текстами раздела TOPICS FOR DISCUSSION AND NEW WORDS, гораздо большими по объему и вводящими обильный новый вокабуляр. Главная цель этого раздела — накопление словаря и создание базы для серьезных речевых упражнений.

Как показала экспериментальная проверка учебника в Академии внешней торговли, такой плавный переход грамматического раздела в лексический является более гибким и удобным, чем жесткое деление материала на грамматический, не содержащий новой лексики, и лексический.

Предлагаемая система овладения иностранным языком исходит из того, что, обучая взрослого человека, мы имеем дело со зрелым носителем родного (в данном случае русского) языка, свободно пользующимся средствами этого языка как при устном общении, так и во всех других случаях, когда решение возникшей проблемной ситуации возможно только при помощи речи.

Задача, следовательно, заключается в том, чтобы овладеть новым кодом (средствами *изучаемого* языка) для решения того же круга проблем, которые человек решает в повседневной жизни с опорой на родной язык.

В условиях обучения многоязычной аудитории способность взрослого человека свободно пользоваться родным языком вряд ли может быть существенным подспорьем в преподавании иностранного языка. Однако при обучении аудитории *одноязычной* пренебречь возможностью опоры на родной язык значило бы упустить возможность огромной экономии времени и усилий и, следовательно, значительной интенсификации учебного процесса. Опора на родной язык отнюдь не предполагает переложения одного языка на другой, перенесения норм родного языка на язык иностранный или неизбежности опосредования родным языком иностранного языка для выражения мысли. Речь идет об использовании весьма эффективной возможности осмыслить способы решения рече-мыслительных проблем средствами иностранного языка, прибегая и к аналогиям, и к противопоставлениям, и к предупреждениям возможных недоразумений, вызванных интерференцией родного языка. Попутно хотелось бы заметить, что профилактика ошибок и система тренировки, направленная на то, чтобы обучающийся испытывал интерес и уважение к нормам чужого языка и получал удовольствие от того, что он овладевает этими нормами и говорит именно то, что хочет сказать, гораздо экономичнее и эффективнее, чем бесконечная мучительная коррекция устоявшихся ложных представлений и неправильных навыков.

Уместно было бы вспомнить, что грамотное владение иностранным языком и хорошее произношение традиционнно считались в России престижными, и в отечественной методике немало было сделано для разработки способов достижения этих целей.

Система упражнений.

Освоение средств изучаемого языка, будь то грамматическая структура, слово или словосочетание начинается с обильной иллюстрации уже на этапе введения. В грамматике это примеры, иллюстрирующие правило, в словаре — примеры, дающие представление об особенностях и границах употребления слова.

В системе упражнений эта иллюстрация значительно расширяется специальными упражнениями (см. упр. 1 стр. 5, упр. 3 стр. 25), построенными на отдельных предложениях. Работая над отдельными предложениями, следует иметь в виду, что они могут быть более ситуативными, чем длинные диалоги или связные тексты, поэтому эффективность упражнения повысится, если мобилизовать свое воображение и представить себе, где и когда эту фразу можно употребить или услышать. При выполнении этого условия будет как произвольно, так и непроизвольно происходить отбор и накопление того, что войдет в языковый арсенал обучающегося, причем отбор этот будет определяться не только типичностью и необходимостью фразы, но и личными склонностями говорящего.

Работая над диалогами, на этом этапе можно вполне рассчитывать на то, что они с легкостью будут выучены наизусть, однако на точном их воспроизведении настаивать не следует, надо лишь следить за грамотностью и адекватностью реплик и естественностью общения. Над диалогами удобнее всего работать, разбив группу на пары.

Если в группе нечетное число обучающихся, преподавателю следует по очереди разыгрывать диалог с каждым, ибо в игре всегда хорошо иметь более сильного партнера, к тому же именно такое соотношение сил будет и в реальном общении с естественным носителем языка, и обучающегося надо к этому подготовить.

Аналогичную рекомендацию можно дать и в отношении разыгрывания эпизодов по заданному сценарию (см. напр., упр. 9 стр. 29). Эта игра иногда носит характер полилога, причем задание легко модифицировать так, чтобы в игре участвовала вся группа. Надо дать участникам возможность продумать игру и свою роль в ней, обсудить все соображения предварительно (разумеется, на английском языке) с тем, чтобы в процессе самой игры они имели широкую возможность импровизации.

Среди упражнений, помогающих овладеть речевыми функциями (согласие, возражение, извинение, приглашение и т.п.) можно указать выбор подходящей ответной реплики с последующим развитием мысли (см. напр., упр.7 стр.28).

Несмотря на то, что в системе упражнений довольно большое место занимают тренировочные и предречевые виды работы, обеспечение обильной речевой практики на уроке легко достижимо. Речевая работа обеспечивается отбором тематики, стимулирующей дискуссию, обильным диалогическим материалом, подкрепляющимся инсценированием аналогичных ситуаций и ролевыми играми по заданному сценарию, лексико-грамматическим наполнением уроков-комплексов, обеспечивающим возможность решить эти задачи. Кроме того, к этому времени обучающиеся уже владеют достаточными языковыми средствами для обсуждения текущих событий и других тем, которые могут вызвать интерес и желание высказаться.

Упражнения, которые рекомендуется выполнять с использованием звукозаписи, помечены знаком 🔲 . Упражнения для письменных домашних заданий помечены знаком ✎ . Однако распределение видов работы может, резумеется, варьироваться по усмотрению преподавателя.

Учебник не был задуман как самоучитель, но он может с успехом использоваться лицами, изучающими язык самостоятельно.

Кроме начинающих, он может быть рекомендован лицам, ранее изучавшим язык, но основательно его забывшим и

Предисловие

нуждающимся в восстановлении утраченных знаний и приобретении устойчивых речевых навыков.

Автор выражает глубокую благодарность к.ф.н., доценту Изадоре Ильиничне Левиной, для которой английский язык является родным, оказавшей неоценимую помощь в стилистическом редактировании английского текстового материала, а также Ирине Анатольевне Бонк, которая отредактировала рукопись и подготовила ее к изданию.

Н.Бонк

СПИСОК ИСПОЛЬЗОВАННОЙ СПРАВОЧНОЙ ЛИТЕРАТУРЫ.

1. *A.J.Thomson, A.V. Martinet. A Practical English Grammar fourth edition. Oxford University Press, 1986*

2. *R.Murphy. English Grammar in Use. Cambridge University Press, 1990*

3. *J.Eastwood, R.Mackin. A Basic English Grammar. Oxford University Press, 1984*

4. *M.Swan. Practical English Usage. Oxford University Press, 1980*

5. *J.B.Heaton, N.D.Turnton. Longman Dictionary of Common Errors. Longman Group Ltd., 1987*

6. *A.S.Hornby (with A.P.Cowie and A.C.Gimson). Oxford Advanced Learner's Dictionary of Current English. Oxford University Press, 1987*

7. *A Dictionary of American English. Longman Inc., 1983*

8. *Longman Dictionary of Contemporary English. Longman Group Ltd.1978*

9. *Active Study Dictionary of English. Longman Group Ltd., 1983*

10. *E.A.M.Wilson. The Modern Russian Dictionary for English Speakers. Pergamon Press, "Русский язык" М., 1982*

11. *R.Courtney. London Dictionary of Phrasal Verbs. Longman Group Ltd., 1983*

Список сокращений, используемых в поурочных словарях

n (noun)	существительное (может быть исчисляемым и неисчисляемым)
n c (noun countable)	исчисляемое существительное
n u (noun uncountable)	неисчисляемое существительное
v (verb)	глагол
adj (adjective)	прилагательное
adv (adverb)	наречие
prep (preposition)	предлог
conj (conjuction)	союз
pl (plural)	множественное число
pron (pronoun)	местоимение
etc (etcetera)	и так далее
sb (somebody)	кто-либо
sth (something)	что-либо
one	местоимение, условно заменяющее любое лицо
one's	притяжательная форма, условно заменяющая любую притяжательную форму

Unit 1

GRAMMAR

1. Оборот **be going** + инифинитив с частицей to как один из способов выражения будущего действия.

1.1. В английском языке имеется несколько способов выражения будущего действия. Одним из этих способов является оборот **be going** + **инфинитив с частицей to**. Он употребляется, когда говорящий связывает будущее действие с тем, что уже происходит в настоящем. Эта связь с настоящим проявляется в д в у х случаях:

a. Говорящий высказывается о будущем действии как вытекающем из уже имеющихся у с л о в и й или п р и з н а к о в того, что действие произойдет:

Please hold me! I'm going to fall!

Держите меня, пожалуйста!
Я сейчас упаду!

It's going to be a long and difficult way!

Это будет долгий и трудный путь!

He's going to be a great pianist, isn't he?

Он будет великим пианистом, не правда ли?

б. Говорящий высказывается о будущем действии как вытекающем из принятого р е ш е н и я или имеющегося н а м е р е н и я : — 2 —

I'm going to say a few words about our new work.

Я скажу несколько слов о нашей новой работе.

How long are you going to stay?

Сколько времени вы пробудете?

He isn't going to give up tennis!

Он не собирается бросать теннис!

Как видно из примеров, оборот be going + инфинитив может переводиться на русский язык несколькими способами: сочетанием будущего времени со словом *сейчас*, сочетанием неопределенной формы глагола с глаголом *собираться (намереваться)* и просто будущим временем.

1.2.

1.2. Глаголы **go** и **come** реже других сочетаются с оборотом **be going**. Для выражения действия, запланированного и подготовленного для совершения в будущем, они чаще употребляются в форме **Continuous**:

1. We're **going** to the theatre tonight.	Мы идем сегодня в театр.
2. A Canadian hockey team's **coming** to Moscow.	В Москву приезжает Канадская хоккейная команда.

– 3 –

Обратите внимание на то, что и в русских предложениях глагол стоит в н а с т о я щ е м времени, хотя речь идет о будущем действии.

1.3. Частица **to** может заменить в обороте **be going** ранее упомянутый глагол, если из контекста ясно, о каком действии идет речь:

I haven't spoken to him about it yet, but I'm going to.	Я еще не поговорил с ним об этом, но собираюсь.

1.4. Оборот **be going** может употребляться и в прошедшем времени:

I was just going to call you when you came.	Я как раз собирался вам позвонить, когда вы пришли.

1.5. Слово **just** в сочетании **just going to** может означать *только, как раз, сейчас, сию минуту, очень скоро*:

1. Wait a bit! I'm just going to make a call.	Подождите немного. Я только позвоню.
2. I was just going to explain it	Я как раз собирался это объяснить.
3. I'm just coming!	Я сейчас (сию минуту, очень скоро) приду.

1.6. В высказываниях о будущих действиях и состояниях могут быть употреблены следующие обстоятельства времени:

this afternoon	сегодня днем, сегодня во второй половине дня, после обеда
this evening	сегодня вечером
tonight	1. сегодня вечером 2. сегодня ночью (предстоящей ночью)
tomorrow	завтра
tomorrow morning (afternoon, evening, night)	завтра утром (днем, вечером, ночью)
the day after tomorrow	послезавтра
in a few minutes (hours, days, etc.)	через несколько минут (часов, дней и т.д.)
in a week (in a week's time)	через неделю
in two months (in two months' time)	через два месяца
in a year (in a year's time)	через год
next week (month, year, etc)	на будущей неделе (в следующем месяце, на будущий год и т.д.)
next time	в следующий раз
soon	скоро, вскоре
some day	когда-нибудь (в будущем)
some time next week (month, year, etc.)	как-нибудь (где-нибудь) на следующей неделе, в следующем месяце, на будущий год и т.д.
in the next few days, (weeks, months, etc.)	в ближайшие несколько дней (недель, месяцев и т.д.)
in the near future	в ближайшем будущем

one of these days на днях (по отношению к будущему)

Сравните: **the other day** на днях по отношению к прошлому

EXERCISES

| 1 |

Прочитайте примеры вслух и представьте себе ситуации, в которых их можно употребить.

a. 1. I'm going to say a few words about it.
  2. We're going to give a party the day after tomorrow.
  3. They're going to finish their work in the next few days.
  4. I'm going to see you about it one of these days.
  5. We're going to meet again some time next month.
  6. They're going to solve the problem in the near future.

b. 1. Is it going to be cold next week?
  2. When are we going to see you again?
  3. What are we going to do next?
  4. They're going to settle all the problems in the next few weeks, aren't they?

c. 1. I'm not going to stay long.
  2. I'm not going to discuss it again.
  3. We aren't going to have any important work to do in the next few days.
  4. They aren't going to settle it in the near future.

d. 1. We're going there for the weekend.
  2. They're coming tomorrow, aren't they?
  3. Aren't you going out tonight?
  4. Where are you going for your holiday?

| 2 |

Повторите, используя подсказанные слова.

Дано: I'm going to see about the tickets

  (• to say a few words about it •)

Требуется: I'm going to say a few words about it.

  1. I'm going to **see about the tickets**.

— 5 —

•arrange a visit to the factory• ask the manager a few questions•
ask him to lunch•

2. Are you going to **read the English translation**?

•look through those catalogues•collect some information on the
subject• have another look at some of the models•

3. We're going to arrange it **next week**

•some time next week• in the next few days• in the near future•
one of these days•.

4. I'm just going to **say a few words about it**

•tell you a few things about the exhibition•explain our new ideas•
make a few calls• leave him a message •.

5. Aren't they **going to the theatre tonight?**

• coming tomorrow night • going to the country with us • coming
to Moscow next week •

6. They were just going to **leave the house** when I came

•have a coffee break•begin the discussion•finish work•

3

Какие вопросы нужно задать, чтобы получить эти ответы.

1. We're going to ask **ten** people to lunch.
2. The job's going to take them **a month**.
3. It's going to take **a week**.
4. She's going to spend the weekend with **her friends**.
5. I'm going **to the country** for my holiday.
6. Mr Smith's coming **tomorrow afternoon**.
7. They're going to talk about **classical music** today.

4

Прочитайте диалоги вслух и разыграйте их.

1

A. Have you seen "Good–bye to Love" yet?

B. No, not yet, but I'm going to. They say it's very interesting. Have you
seen it?

A. No, I haven't, either. Let's go together, shall we?

B. That's a good idea! But what about the seats?

A. That's all right! I'm going to see about them.

B. Oh, it's very kind of you, thank you very much.

A. Not at all.

2

A. You've seen "Good—bye to Love", haven't you?

B. No, I haven't and I'm not going to. The say it's very dull. Have you seen it?

A. Yes, I have, and I found it quite interesting.

B. Oh, did you? Then I must go and see it too.

— 7 —

Прочитайте рассказ вслух, обращая внимание на употребление времен. Перескажите его:
а) от лица миссис Дадли;
б) от лица собаки.

1

Mrs Dudley's asked some friends to tea, and she's making a cake. She's an excellent cook, so it's going to be a marvellous cake. Her dog Patch is watching her carefully. He always watches her when she cooks.

2

Mrs Dudley finished making the cake half an hour ago. She's put the tea things on the table. Her friends are coming any minute.

3

She was just going to give Patch his usual meal when the doorbell rang, and she went to open the door. You can't see her because she's talking to her guests in the hall. But you can see Patch, can't you?
What's he going to do?

7

Дайте ответы на вопросы. Суммируйте их в кратких сообщениях.

a. How many lectures do you usually have a day? How many (lectures) did you have yesterday? How many are you going to have today?

b. What time do you usually have lunch? Where do you usually have it? Have you had lunch today? If not, how soon are you going to have it? Who are you going to have it with? What are you going to have for lunch (today) ?

c. What do you usually do at the weekend? What are you going to do this weekend? Do you sometimes go to the country for the weekend? When did you last go to the country? Who did you go with?

d. Do you usually stay at home in the evenings or do you go out? When did you go out last? Where did you go? Did you have a good time? What are you going to do this eveninvg? And tomorrow evening?

e. When do you usually have a holiday? When are you going to have your next holiday? This year? Is it going to be a long holiday? Where are you going to spend it? What are you going to do in your holiday?

f. How often do you go to the theatre ? Do you usually go on weekdays or at the weekend? When are you going next? Who are you going with? What are you going to see?

8 ✎

Переведите на английский язык.

1. Не посылайте им письмо. Я как раз (just) собираюсь послать им телекс.
2. Какие вопросы мы будем обсуждать сегодня? Сколько времени займет обсуждение?
3. Что вы собираетесь делать днем? Вы будете очень заняты?
4. — Они собираются в Лондон на будущей неделе.– Да? Сколько народу едет?
5. — Вы идете с нами? – Боюсь, что нет. У меня совсем нет времени.
6. — Когда вы собираетесь пойти домой? – Через полтора часа.
7. — Вы идете сегодня в кино? – Нет, я не собираюсь выходить сегодня вечером. Я очень устал и хочу отдохнуть дома.
8. — Разве вы не читали его новую статью? – Нет, и не собираюсь. Мне совсем не нравятся его статьи. Они очень скучные.
9. Я как раз собирался выйти из дому, когда вы позвонили.
10. Я только скажу несколько слов о моих новых идеях.

GRAMMAR

2. Употребление настоящего времени группы **Continuous** для выражения будущего действия

Прочитайте следующие примеры и сравните с переводом на русский язык:

1. I'm leaving the house in five minutes.

Я выхожу из дома через пять минут.

2. "What are you doing tonight?"
"I'm going to the theatre."

– Что вы делаете сегодня вечером?
–Я иду в театр.

3. I'm meeting a friend tomorrow. He's coming for the weekend.

Завтра я встречаю приятеля. Он приезжает на субботу и воскресенье.

4. So we're playing tennis on Sunday, aren't we?

Итак, в воскресенье мы играем в теннис, да?

Как видно из примеров, **настоящее время группы Continuous (Present Continuous)** может употребляться для выражения будущего действия не только с глаголами **go** и **come**, но и с некоторыми другими глаголами, примерно в тех же случаях, когда в русском языке употребляют *настоящее* время в значении *будущего*. Эта форма выражения будущего действия близка по значению обороту **be going to** и отличается от него большей подготовленностью будущего действия, большей определенностью плана (*ср. русск:* Я **ухожу** в отпуск на следующей неделе). Поскольку эта глагольная форма способна выразить как настоящее, так и будущее действие, употребляя ее, для ясности часто добавляют соответствующее обстоятельство времени:

1. The delegation's arriving **tomorrow.**

Делегация прибывает завтра.

2. We're starting work **next week**.

Мы начинаем работать на будущей неделе.

3. What are you doing **tonight**?

Что вы делаете сегодня вечером?

EXERCISES

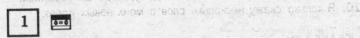

1

Прочитайте вслух и переведите.

1. What time are we meeting tomorrow?
2. My friend's coming here for a holiday soon.
3. They're giving a party next week.
4. They're arranging a visit to the factory next Thursday.
5. When are you going there?
6. Which of them's giving a talk tomorrow?
7. We're going to the new ballet next Saturday.
8. My colleagues are going abroad on business.
9. They're coming any minute.

2

Прочитайте диалоги вслух и разыграйте их.

1

A. What are you doing at the weekend?

B. At the weekend? I haven't thought of it yet.

A. Would you like to go to a football match with me?

B. Oh, I'd love to. Who's playing?

A. Two very good teams. They're both in very good form, so the match is going to be interesting.

B. Thank you ever so much. I haven't seen a good game for a very long time.

2

A. So we're playing tennis this evening, aren't we?

B. No, I'm afraid not. Not this evening.

A. Why? Didn't you **promise** to come and have a game with me?

B. Well, yes, but my people are going away on holiday, and I must see them off. The train's at seven fifteen p.m. I only found out an hour ago.

A. It's a pity we can't have a game this evening. What about the day after tomorrow then?

B. O'kay.

___

promise [ˈprɔmɪs] v   обещать

3

Guide: Tomorrow we're visiting Kuskovo.

Tourist: Are we going by bus?

G. Yes, as usual.

T. What time's the bus leaving?

G. At exactly eight. Please be in  time. And don't forget to take your cameras. You can take lots of beautiful photos there, and make films, too.

Turists: Splendid!
Lovely!
Marvellous!

T. Excuse me, what time are we getting back?

G. At seven o'clock in the evening.

GRAMMAR

3. <u>Определительные придаточные предложения, в которых относительное местоимение является подлежащим.</u>

3.1. Определительные придаточные, в которых речь идет о *людях*, вводятся относительным местоимением **who**, а определительные придаточные, в которых говорится о *неодушевленных предметах или животных*, вводятся относительным местоимением **which**.

1. The man **who** rang you this morning didn't leave any message.	Человек, который звонил вам утром, ничего не передавал.
2. The cable **which** has just arrived is very important.	Телеграмма, которая только что прибыла, очень важная.

ПРИМЕЧАНИЯ:

1. Определительные придаточные могут также вводиться относительным местоимением **that**, которое чаще употребляется, когда речь идет о неодушевленных предметах.

1. The fax that (which) arrived in the morning is in your file.	Факс, который прибыл утром, находится в вашей папке.
2. The air hostess who's (that's) going to help tne passenger find his seat speaks both English and Spanish.	Бортпроводница, которая собирается помочь пассажиру найти свое место, говорит по–английски и по–испански.

2. Обратите внимание на то, что в приведенных примерах определительное придаточное не отделяется от главного запятой.

3.2. Как и в русском языке, сказуемое определительного придаточного предложения согласуется в числе с тем существительным, к которому относится это придаточное:

1. The **girl** who usually **works** at this desk is on holiday now.	*Девушка*, которая обычно *работает* за этим столом, находится сейчас в отпуске.
2. All the **girls** who **work** at our exhibition as guides speak several foreign languages.	Все *девушки*, которые *работают* гидами на нашей выставке, говорят на нескольких иностранных языках.
3. The **shops** which **are** open on Sundays only work till three.	*Магазины*, которые *бывают* открытыми по воскресеньям, работают только до трех.
4. I know a **shop** which **is** sometimes open on Sundays.	Я знаю *магазин*, который иногда *бывает* открытым по воскресеньям.

3.3. Перед существительным, к которому относится определительное придаточное предложение, может стоять как определенный, так и неопределенный артикль (или местоимения some, any), по общему правилу употребления артиклей:

1. I know **a man** who speaks five foreign languages.	Я знаю человека, который говорит на пяти иностранных языках. (*одного* человека, *такого* человека, который ...)

2. I know **the man** who wrote that article.	Я знаю человека, который написал эту статью (*того самого* человека, который ...)

ПРИМЕЧАНИЕ. В английском языке, как и в русском, имеются также *описательные* определительные придаточные, содержащие *дополнительные* сведения о слове, к которому они относятся:

1. My business partner, *who is in London now*, is coming back tomorrow	Мой деловой партнер, который сейчас находится в Лондоне, возвращается завтра.
2. The explanation, *which only took a few minutes*, was very useful.	Объяснение, которое заняло всего несколько минут, было очень полезным.

— 14 —

Описательные определительные придаточные в английском языке отделяются от главного предложения запятой. Поскольку они содержат лишь дополнительную информацию, их можно опустить, не нарушив основного смысла высказывания. Такие придаточные характерны для книжно-письменной речи. В повседневной разговорной речи им предпочитают более короткие отдельные предложения или сложносочиненные предложения с союзами and или but:

1. My business partner is in London now. He's coming tomorrow.
2. The explanation only took a few minutes, but it was very useful.

EXERCISES

Прочитайте вслух и переведите.

a. 1. The policeman's just stopped a careless driver who went through the red light. "A driver who thinks the traffic rules are not for him must pay a fine!" the policeman says.
2. There's a garage which opens at eight in this street.
3. The man who's going to give us the next lecture has travelled a lot.
4. "Can you see the car that has stopped over there?" "Yes, it's got a flat tyre."

5. All the actors who played in that film were just marvellous.

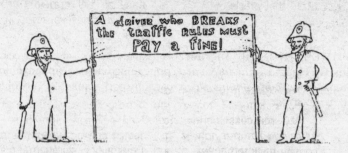

A driver who BREAKS the traffic rules must pay a fine!

b. 1. His partner, who's still a strong man at seventy, isn't going to give up his job.
2. The air hostesses, who were all young and pretty, showed the passengers to their seats.
3. The hotel, which was out of town, was very comfortable.

2

Заполните пропуски словами **WHO, WHICH** или **THAT**.

1. This is a letter from a friend, ... lives in Glasgow.
2. This is a letter from a company, ... sells computers.
3. The boy, ... is only fourteen, is going to be a splendid athlete.
4. When are you going to look through the telexes ... came this morning?
5. I can't find the the telephone bill ... was here a few minutes ago!
6. We must catch the train ... leaves at exactly ten.

3

Заполните пропуски артиклями.

1. Have you seen ... mail which arrived yesteday afternoon?
2. Have you ever met ... seaman who doesn't love the sea?
3. ... man who's just finished reading his paper is a friend of mine.
4. Let's listen to ... man who's going to speak next, shall we?
5. Can I speak to a representative of ... firm which sells these cassette recorders?
6. ... talk, which was very interesting, took an hour and a half.
7. I can't sit through ... talk that takes over two hours. Can you?
8. They live in ... district which is one of the best in the city.

Переведите на английский язык.

1. Мы все пойдем на выставку, которая открывается (opens) в понедельник утром.
2. Мне бы хотелось пойти на некоторые выставки, которые открываются (open) на следующей неделе.
3. Врач, который только что осмотрел ребенка, говорит, что ребенок совершенно здоров.
4. Врачи, которые только что осмотрели этого человека, говорят, что он немедленно должен лечь в больницу.
5. Можно подержать эту книгу еще одну неделю? Я еще не прочитал некоторых статей, которые я хочу использовать в своей работе.
6. У вас не уйдет много времени на то, чтобы перевести статью, которую я положил в вашу папку. Она совсем не трудная.
7. Лаборант, который обычно здесь работает, сейчас в отпуске. Он приезжает через неделю.
8. Все экскурсоводы, которые работают в этом музее, очень хорошо знают свой предмет.
9. Вы можете купить массу полезных вещей в этом магазине, который, кстати, всегда открыт по воскресеньям.
10. — Что вы ищете? — Мою записную книжку, которая была здесь минуту назад. Я всегда ее теряю и потом нахожу снова!

TOPICS FOR DISCUSSION AND NEW WORDS

Discussing Plans for the Future

1

A Television Interview

Alexei Nikitin's a young film **director** who has just **taken part** in a film **festival** abroad. His film has **won** a prize, and he's going to give an **interview** on television. The **interviewer's** a TV **reporter**.

Interviewer: I'd like to **congratulate** you on your **recent success**, Mr. Nikitin.

Nikitin: Thank you very much.

I. Have you got any **definite** plans for the **future**?

N. Oh, yes. I'm going to make a television **serial** about pop singers. It's going to be a **screen version** of a novel which is a great **success** with the reading **public** just now.

I. Are you going to work with the same team?

N. Yes, it's going to be the same team, **actually**. We're all **interested in** making another film together.

I. And when are you starting work on the film?

N. We have actually started. We spent a month interviewing different singers, but that's only a **beginning**, of course. We've got to do a lot in the next few months.

I. Well, that was all very interesting. You've made great **progress these last few years**, and I **wish** you every success with your new film. Good luck!

N. Thanks.

2

At an Industrial Exhibition

Boris Antonov is an engineer from a Moscow factory which is taking part in an industrial exhibition in Sokolniki Park.
Mr Bennett, a businessman from Canada, is talking to Antonov, who's working at the exhibition as a guide.

Bennett: Have you seen our new model, Boris?

Antonov: Yes, and I must say it's a very **up-to-date** design. My congratulations!

B. Thanks. I'm happy to hear that.

A. We're interested in buying some of these machines for our factories.

B. Are you? How many would you like to buy?

A. I can't give you a definite answer now, I think it may be quite a big **order**. Would you like to visit the factory and talk to the Director General?

B. I'd love to if you could arrange it soon, because I'm leaving Moscow next Saturday.

A. No problem, Mr Bennett.

B.   Good. Thank you ever so much.

3

At an International Conference

Mr Clark, a British scientist, is talking to
Oleg Smirnov, his Russian counterpart,
at an international conference during a
break.

Clark: Your recent **experiments** have been a great success, Mr Smir-
       nov. Congratulations!

Smirnov: Thank you very much. You've read my last article, then, haven't
         you?

C.   Of course I have. I'm very interested in your research, and I hardly
     ever miss your **publications**. By the way, when are you going to give
     a talk on your work?

S.   Some time next week at the Research Centre, but I can't tell you
     definitely yet.

C.   Could you ring me up and **let me know**?

S.   Certainly.

C.   Thank you ever so.

Learn these words:

1

director [dɪˈrektə, daɪˈrektə] *n*	1. директор, руководитель ор- ганизации, член совета ди- ректоров фирмы
	2. режиссер (театра, кино),
film director *n*	кинорежиссер
Director General	генеральный директор
take part (in)	принимать участие (в)
How many people are going to take part in tne discussion?	
festival [ˈfestɪvəl] *n*	фестиваль
win (won, won) [wʌn] *v*	выигрывать, побеждать

Ant.**lose (lost,lost)** *v*   терять, проигрывать

    Which team won the last match?

    Ben lost the game (to Nick).

prize *n*   приз, премия

    to win a prize   получить премию (приз)

    The Nobel prize [nəu´bel]   Нобелевская премия

interview [´ɪntəvju:] *n*   1. интервью

    a press interview   интервью для печати

    He gave a press interview (=He gave an interview to the press.)

                                                2. собеседование (часто при приеме на работу)

interview *v*   брать интервью (у) проводить собеседование (с)

    The TV people have just interviewed the delegation.

    The manager's going to interview the man the day after tomorrow.

interviewer [´ɪntəvju:ə] *n*   интервьюер

reporter [rɪ´pɔ:tə] *n*   репортер

    Syn. a newspaper man

congratulate [kən´grætjuleɪt] *v*   поздравлять, поздравить (с успехом, достижениями, результатами, событиями и т.п., но не с традиционными праздниками)

    Let me congratulate you **on** your excellent results

    Please congratulate him **for** me.

congratulations

    [kən,grætju´leɪʃnz] *n*   поздравления (обычно употребляется во множественном числе)

    (My) congratulations!   Поздравляю!

    (My) congratulations   Поздравляю с замужеством дочери!

    on your daughter's

    marriage!

    (My) congratulations   Поздравляю вас всех!

    to you all!

Give him my congratulations	Передайте ему мои поздравления!

Обычные формулы поздравления с праздниками:

Merry Christmas and (a) Happy New Year!	Поздравляю с Рождеством и с Новым годом!
The same to you!	И вас также!
Happy birthday to you! Many happy returns of the day!	С днем рождения!

---

recent [ˈriːsənt] adj	недавний, последний

a recent event (visit, discussion, decision, etc.)

recently adv	недавно, за (в) последнее время
I've seen him recently.	Я его недавно видел.
I haven't seen him recently.	Я его не видел в последнее время.
I saw him (quite) recently.	Я его видел (совсем) недавно.
success [səkˈses] n	успех, удача

We wish you (every) success in your new job.

He spoke about the recent successes of their research centre.

be a success	иметь успех, пользоваться успехом, быть удачным

The film was a great success with the public.

The young actress was a (great) success.

The party was a success.   Вечеринка удалась.

successful *adj*   успешный, удачный

Ant. **unsuccessful**

He's a successful businessman.

The plan was successful.

progress ['prəugrəs] *n u*   успехи, успешное продвиже-ние

make progress   делать успехи

You're making progress in your English.

Nelly's still in hospital, but she's making progress.   Нелли все еще в больнице, но она поправляется.

definite ['defɪnɪt] *adj*   определенный

Ant. **indefinite**

a definite answer, (plan, time, etc).

future ['fjuːtʃə] *n*   будущее

in the future   в будущем

The book's about flights to other planets in tne future.

in the near future   в ближайшем будущем

We're going to discuss it all again in the near future.

in future   в дальнейшем, впредь

In future be more careful with your money.

future *adj*   будущий (–ая, –ое)

serial ['sɪərɪəl] *n c*   многосерийный телефильм

screen *n c*   экран

version ['vəːʃn] *n c*   вариант, версия

a screen version (of)   экранизация

public ['pʌblɪk] *n u*   публика

public *adj*   общественный, публичный

a public park (library, etc.)

actually [ˈæktʃuəlɪ] adv фактически, на самом деле, действительно

Do you actually mean it? Вы и в самом деле так думаете?

interested [ˈɪntrɪstɪd] adj заинтересованный

be interested (in) быть заинтересованным (в), интересоваться

They are all interested in this project. Они все интересуются этим проектом.

We are interested in getting a definite answer.

beginning n c начало

They showed the beginning of the interview on TV.

Внимание: предлоги!

at the beginning в (самом) начале

at the beginning of the interview (the article, the story, etc.)

in (at) the beginning в начале, первое время (сначала, поначалу)

It was easy in the beginning (= **at first**), but in a few days we ran into difficulties.

from the beginning с (самого) начала

I knew from the beginning that the first prize was not for me.

from beginning to end от начала до конца

---

these last few years за эти последние несколько лет

Syn. in the last few years за последние годы

in the past few years за истекшие годы

wish v желать, пожелать кому–либо что–либо

We wish you all the best.	Мы желаем вам всего самого хорошего.
I wish you every success with your plans.	Желаю вам всяческих успехов в ваших планах.

wish *n* — желание, пожелание

Please give them my best wishes.	Передайте им мои наилучшие пожелания.
With best wishes ...	С наилучшими пожеланиями (например, в дарственной надписи)

2

up–to–date [ˌʌptəˈdeit] adj — современный, соответствующий современным требованиям

Сравните:

an up–to–date model (design etc.)	современная (отвечающая современным требованиям) модель, конструкция и т.п.
modern music (art, ideas, etc)	современная (относящаяся к новому времени) музыка, современное искусство, идеи и т.п.

---

order [ˈɔːdə] n — *зд. (коммерч.)* заказ

to make an order	сделать заказ

We're going to make an order for 10 machines.	Мы собираемся сделать заказ на 10 машин.

3

conference [ˈkɔnfrəns] n c	1. конференция
at a conference	на конференции
	2. совещание
to be in conference	быть (занятым) на совещании
Mr Bennett can't see you, because he's in conference just now.	— 24 —
experiment [ɪkˈsperɪmənt] n c	эксперимент, опыт
to make an experiment	поставить эксперимент
publication [ˌpʌbliˈkeiʃn] n c	публикация
definitely [ˈdefɪnɪtlɪ] adv	1. определенно, несомненно, безусловно
He's definitely going to win.	
You definitely didn't tell me about it.	
"Are you coming with us?" "Definitely!"	
I can't answer you definitely yet.	
let … know	сообщить (кому-либо), дать знать
Please let me know the date. We can let you know about it by fax.	Пожалуйста, сообщите мне дату Мы можем сообщить вам об этом по факсу.

EXERSISES

Прочитайте тексты вслух. Предварительно отработайте произношение следующих слов и словосочетаний.

congratulate	interview	prize
congratulations	interviewer	progress

won the first prize
with the same team

2

Ответьте на вопросы по текстам.

a. 1. What does Alexei Nikitin do?
  2. What is he doing abroad?
  3. Is he a successful film director?
  4. Does he know English?
  5. Has he got any definite plans for the future?
  6. Has he started work on his new film, or is he only going to?
  7. What's his new film going to be about?
  8. What kind of film's his team interested in making?
  9. Why did they spend a month interviewing pop singers?
 10. Why does Alexei say it's only a beginning?
 11. Why does the reporter say Alexei's made great progress these last few years?

b. 1. Why is Boris Antonov interested in the new model?
  2. How big's his order going to be?
  3. Why is Mr Bennett interested in visiting the factory?
  4. Is it difficult for Antonov to arrange Mr. Bennett's visit to the factory?

c. 1. What was Smirnov's last article about?
  2. Why is Mr Clark interested in his publications?
  3. Why does Mr Clark want to attend his talk?

3

Прочитайте вслух и переведите.

1. Could you tell me the name of the team which won the last match?
2. The athlete who's won the first prize is only seventeen.
3. Jim's so lucky at cards! He hardly ever loses a game. He nearly always wins!
4. In 1812 the Russian people won the war against Napoleon [nəˈpɔuljən]
5. Let me congratulate all the people who've taken part in the work on their great success!
6. Give them all my congratulations!
7. Please give my congratulations to them all!
8. I'd like to thank you all for your warm congratulations!

9. Recent experiments have shown that the new method is very good.
10. We couldn't even think of it in the recent past.
11. The play's definitely a great success!
12. Your book's going to be a success.
13. You're making good progress in your English.
14. His progress is just marvellous.
15. He's definitely going to be a successful bussinessman.
16. The plan definitely has a great future.
17. In future don't give a definite answer so soon.
18. These experiments may be successful in the near future.
19. We may actually find it out in the near future.

4

Заполните пропуски предлогами.

1. ... his interview the chess player said, "I lost two games .. . the beginning, because I wasn't ... very good form ... an illness, but I was able to win four games ... the end."
2. There were a lot ... foreign visitors ... the recent song festival. They were all interested ... the new songs and the young singers who took part ... the festival.
3. ... the end ... the interview the manager ... the exhibition congratulated the representatives ... all the organizations which took part ... it.
4. The problem's very important ... all ... **us, and we're going to settle it** ... the near future. We simply have to!
5. Please give them my congratulations ... their recent success.
6. You've made good progress ... your experiments. My congratulations!
7. There's going to be a new underground line ... this district ... the near future.
8. There're going to be several new stations here ... the near future.

5

Дайте ответы на вопросы. Суммируйте ответы в кратких сообщениях.

a. 1. Which of you has seen a television interview recently?
   2. When was it?
   3. Who gave the interview?
   4. Who was the interviewer?

5. Who else took part in the interview?

b. 1. Do you like television serials?
    2. When did you last watch a serial?
    3. How interesting was it?
    4. Did you watch it from beginning to end or did you only watch it in bits?

c. 1. Which screen versions of books can you remember?
    2. Do people get interested in a book after they have seen a screen version?
    3. Are all screen versions of books successful? If not, why?
    4. Are they going to show any new serials on TV next week?
    5. Do you like watching the same films several times?

d. 1. Have you watched any interesting matches recently?
    2. Which team won the match?
    3. Did the players congratulate each other on their success after the match?
    4. Why did the other team lose?

e. 1. Are you interested in literature?
    2. What kind of books are you interested in?
    3. Do you read every book from beginning to end?
    4. Do you go on reading a book if it isn't very interesting at the beginning?
    5. What English (Russian) books are you going to read in the near future?

6

Заполните пропуски артиклями.

    1. ... friend of mine, who's ... very succesful film director, is definitely going to win ... prize for one of his recent films.
    2. ... experiment's definitely ... success.
    3. It was ... very successful experiment, wasn't it?
    4. Please let me know ... exact date of ... interview.
    5. ... athletes who have won ... first prizes in ... Games are giving ... press interview in ... few days.
    6. Let me congratulate you on your success at ... last festival.
    7. We can't give you ... definite answer yet.
    8. ... answer was "No!"

9. "There's going to be ... new serial on television some time next month." "Oh, is there? ... screen version of ... novel again?"

7

Подберите подходящие ответные реплики к высказываниям, данным в колонке слева.

1. My brother's got married!

2. How good you've called. It's my birthday today!

3. It's very kind of you. Thank you ever so much!

4. Could you let me know the time of the meeting?

5. I wish you every success in your future work.

6. Are you going to speak about your recent experiments in your lecture?

7. (A) Merry Christmas and (a) Happy New Year!

Not at all! (That's all right!)

The same to you!

Yes, definitely!

Oh, is it? Many happy returns of the day!

Thanks. (Thank you very much! Thank you ever so!)

Certainly!

Oh! Please give him my congratulations!

— 28 —

8

Прочитайте диалоги вслух и разыграйте их, заменяя выделенные слова словами, данными в скобках.

1

A. Your **lecture** was just marvellous. My congratulations!
B. I'm very glad you liked it. Thanks.
   (• talk • recent publication • last article • paper • public lecture •)

2

A. I find you've made very good progress in **your English** in the last few months.
B. Oh, do you? I'm very glad to hear that.
   (• your music • your Spanish • driving • tennis •)

3

A. I'm going to be very busy this week. Could you arrange the interview for **some time next week?**
B. Certainly. No problem.
A. Thank you very much.
B. Not at all.
   (• these next few days• the next few days •)

4

A. I was just going to ring you and let you know **the time of the conference.**
B. Oh, were you? So what is the time?
A. Eleven on Wednesday.
   (• the exact time of the interview •)

9

Прочитайте сценарии и разыграйте их.

1. **A Russian specialist is going to work in an international organization.**
   Mr Smith, a representative of the organization, interviews him. Mr Smith has looked through the candidate's papers carefully, but he's still got some questions to ask him.
   "So you've been a factory manager these last few years," he says. "How many people work under you?" His next questions are, "How do you like your work?" and "What can you say about it?" He also asks the candidate a few questions about his family, his hobbies and his interests. The specialist gives full and interesting answers to all the questions. They thank each other.

2. **A representative of a Russian firm talks to a British businessman at an industrial exhibition.**
   The Russian specialist has just seen some new machines Mr Robinson's firm is exhibiting. He thinks the designers have done a good job and congratulates Mr Robinson on the firm's success. Mr Robinson can arrange for the Russian specialist to visit the factory which makes the machines and talk to the designers. The Russian specialist asks Mr Harrison to arrange the visit for some time next week and let him know the exact date by phone.

3. An athlete who's recently won the first prize in an international match gives an interview to a TV man.

John Harris, the interviewer, congratulates Oleg Petrov, the athlete, on his success. Oleg thanks the interviewer. John Harris asks Oleg about his plans for the future. Oleg says he's a bit tired, and wants to have a rest, then he plans to begin preparing (training) for the international games. The interviewer says Oleg has made great progress in the last few years. He's still very young, and it's only a beginning.

Oleg says he's going to work very hard. The interviewer wishes him every success in the games.

4. An actor who's won a prize at an international film festival gives a press interview.

A reporter says the actor's done very well and congratulates him on his success. "How many films have you played in?" another reporter asks. The actor answers he's already played in several films, but this is his first big role." You've had to work very hard, haven't you?" is the next question. The actor says he had to work very hard, but it's all been very interesting. One of the newspaper men asks him about his plans for the future. The actor plans to play a test pilot in a television serial. He's very interested in this work. The reporters thank him and wish him good luck.

— 30 —

Переведите на английский язык.

1. Несколько певцов, которые только что вернулись из Польши, где они принимали участие в международном фестивале, дают интервью для печати: "Поездка (tour) была успешной от начала до конца", говорит один из них. "Мы немного устали, конечно, но мы очень счастливы" Мы собираемся принять участие еще в одном фестивале в ближайшем будущем." "Вы приготовили какие-нибудь новые песни для следующего фестиваля?" спрашивает один из репортеров. "Нет еще", отвечает певец, "но собираемся".

2. — Вся наша семья смотрела новый многосерийный фильм от начала до конца. А вы? — Да, по-моему (я думаю), он очень удачный.

3. Выставка, которая открылась в центре города на прошлой неделе, пользуется большим успехом. На ней побывало (have been to ...) очень много народу.

4. Джордж получил премию за свою новую (recent) конструкцию – Да? Передайте ему наши поздравления. – Спасибо. Ему пришлось много поработать. Он несомненно сделал большие успехи как конструктор за последние несколько лет.

5. – Мы очень интересуемся вашими последними (recent) экспериментами. Мы только что получили ваши публикации и внимательно их изучаем. Нам нравятся ваши идеи и мы собираемся их обсудить в ближайшем будущем. – Мне очень приятно это слышать. Когда у вас будет обсуждение? – Боюсь, что не могу сказать вам определенно пока, но я могу дать вам знать. Где–нибудь в следующем месяце, я думаю.

GRAMMAR

4. Определительные придаточные предложения, в которых относительные местоимения не являются подлежащим.

4.1. Если относительные местоимения **who (whom)**, **which**, **that** являются .в предложении не подлежащим, а д о п о л н е н и е м , они в разговорной речи обычно о п у с к а ю т с я :

1. Here's a photo of the machine *we saw at the exhibition yesterday* (a photo which/that we saw at the exhibition yesterday).	Вот фотография машины, которую мы вчера видели на выставке.
2. The specialist *I want to see about our new contract* is coming in a week (The specialist who(m) I want to see).	Специалист, которого я хочу повидать по поводу нашего нового контракта, приезжает через неделю.

– 32 –

ПРИМЕЧАНИЕ: Если относительные местоимения **who, which** и **that** являются п о д л е ж а щ и м и придаточного предложения, они не могут быть опущены (см. стр. 12).

Сравните:

which — подлежащее	**which — дополнение**
Have you seen the cable **which** came this morning?	Have you seen the cable we received this morning?

4.2. Если в определительном придаточном имеется предлог (с которым, о которых и т.п.), он стоит на том же месте, что и в самостоятельном предложении. Относительное местоимение в разговорной речи обычно опускается:

1. These are the documents we've just **looked through**. (We've just **looked through** these documents).	Это документы, которые мы только что просмотрели.
2. Here's the specialist I **talked to you about**. (I **talked to you about** this specialist).	Вот специалист, о котором я с вами говорил.

ПРИМЕЧАНИЕ: В официальной речи, особенно письменной, предлог может стоять *перед* относительными местоимениями which или whom, но для разговорной речи такой порядок слов не характерен:

Официальная речь:

There are some questions in your letter **to which** we cannot yet give definite answers.

Разговорная речь:

There are some questions in your letter we can't yet give definite answers **to**.

EXERCISES

Прочитайте вслух и переведите.

1. Here's the document you're looking for.

2. That's just the problem we have to solve.

3. What's the name of the book you're interested in?

4. Isn't it a screen version of the book you talked to me about?

5. I'm going to say a few words about a problem we must settle in the near future.

6. Here's an article you must all read from beginning to end.

7. He's going to speak about the progress his team's made in the past few years.

8. Let me read you the congratulations we've just received.

9. We're going to write an article about the experiments we've made recently.

10. The person you wanted to talk to is coming tomorrow.

11. The photos you wanted to look at are on my table.

12. Today we're finishing the job we all started a year ago.

13. Now I can give you a definite answer to the question you asked me last time.

14. Let me show you the models you're interested in.

15. I'm afraid they can't settle the problem you're talking about so soon.

2

Прочитайте эти предложения вслух и объясните, почему в некоторых их них нельзя опустить относительное местоимение.

1. The experiment, which took a year, is definitely a success.
2. The experiment I'm talking about is definitely a success.
3. Have you answered all the faxes that came this morning?
4. Have you answered all the faxes we received this morning?
5. Have you met the man you're going to work with?
6. Have you met the man who's going to work with you?
7. I'm sorry, but the person you're waiting for is in conference just now.
8. I'm sorry, but the person who can help you with your problem is in conference now. Can you wait?
9. I've read the article you told me about from beginning to end.
10. I've just read an article which is very important for the work I'm doing now.
11. The experiments, which started in the beginning of the year, went on till May.
12. Not all the experiments they have made recently are successful.
13. What's the name of the reporter who's going to interview the winners?
14. The reporter you all liked so much is definitely making progress in his job.

3

Переведите на английский.

1. Книга, которую он только что написал, будет определенно пользоваться успехом.

2. Его книга, которая пользуется большим успехом, интересна от начала до конца.

3. Эксперимент, о котором я собираюсь вам рассказать, начался в марте и продолжался до начала июня.

4. Эксперимент, который продолжался до конца прошлого года, был безусловно успешным.

5. Вот папка, которую вы ищете.

6. Разрешите мне поздравить всех спортсменов, которые приняли участие в играх.

7. Нам пришлось повторить эксперимент, который мы поставили (made) в конце прошлого месяца, потому что он был тогда неудачным.

8. Все машины, которые мы только что посмотрели на выставке, очень современны.

9. Экспонат, которым вы интересуетесь, находится в зале (room) №3.

10. Разрешите мне поблагодарить всех людей, которые организовали эту полезную встречу.

GRAMMAR

5. Неопределенное местоимение **one** как слово-заместитель.

5.1. Слово **one**, известное вам как числительное, может быть и неопределенным местоимением.

1. I've lost my pen, I'm afraid. Can you lend me **one** (a pen) for today?	Я, кажется, потерял свою ручку. Вы можете одолжить мне какую-нибудь на сегодня?
2. They've got very nice guidebooks in that shop. Let me go and buy **one** (a guidebook).	В этом магазине очень хорошие путеводители. Пойду куплю такой путеводитель.

Как видно из примеров, местоимение **one** употребляют, чтобы не повторять ранее упомянутое исчисляемое существительное, если его следовало бы повторить в *единственном числе с неопределенным* артиклем. В этой функции слово **one** не имеет фразового ударения.

5.2. Вам уже известны другие способы избежать повторения ранее упомянутого существительного. Давайте их вспомним.

а) Исчисляемые существительные во множественном числе и неисчисляемые существительные заменяются неопределенными местоимениями **some** и **any**:

1. If you haven't (got) any **books** on the subject, I can lend you **some**.	Если у вас нет книг по этому вопросу, я могу вам одолжить.
2. We haven't (got) any **paper**. Let me go and fetch **some**.	У нас нет бумаги. Давайте я пойду и принесу.

б) Если ранее упомянутое существительное следовало бы повторить с *определенным артиклем*, вместо него употребляется соответствующее *личное* местоимение:

1. The new serial's very successful. I watched **it** (**the** serial) from beginning to end.	Новый многосерийный фильм очень удачен. Я смотрел его от начала до конца.
2. You've got an excellent assistant. I've got **one** (**an** assistant), too, but **he** (**the** assistant) doesn't help me much.	У вас отличный помощник. У меня тоже есть помощник, но он не очень-то мне помогает.

в) Вместо существительного с предшествующим притяжательным местоимением употребляется п р и т я - ж а т е л ь н о е м е с т о и м е н и е в а б с о - л ю т н о й ф о р м е:

1. If you haven't got a dictionary, you can use **mine**.	Если у вас нет словаря, вы можете пользоваться моим.
2. Seats three and four are **yours**, and seats five and six are **ours**.	Места третье и четвертое ваши, а пятое и шестое — наши.

г) После существительного в притяжательной форме слово **one** н е у п о т р е б л я е т с я:

"Is that suitcase yours or another **passenger's**?" "It's **Mr Bennett's**."	— Этот чемодан ваш или другого пассажира? — Г-на Беннета.

EXERCISES

1

Прочитайте эти предложения вслух и скажите, вместо каких слов употребляются выделенные местоимения.

1. I haven't got a car yet, but I'm going to buy **one** in the near future.

2. "Can you see any taxis here?" "Oh, yes, I can see **one**. Let's take it. Hi, taxi!"

3. "Is there any interesting news in the paper today?" "Yes, there is **some**. Have a look!"

4. "If you're going to travel, you must take a camera with you!" "But I haven't got **one**." "Take **mine!**"

5. "Could you lend me some matches?" "I'm afraid I haven't got **any.**"

6. Haven't you read his recent publications? **They**'re very interesting.

7. "I like that design. It's very up–to–date. Is it **yours**?" "No, it's a friend's. He's the designer."

2

Употребите местоимение _one_ вместо выделенных слов.

1. I haven't got a pet, but I'd like to have **a pet**.
2. What a lovely cat! I've got **a cat**, too, but it isn't so pretty.
3. An answering machine is a very convenient thing. I'd like to have **an answering machine** at home.
4. If you want to buy a camera, you can buy **a camera** in a shop near here.
5. I know how to use a computer, but I haven't got **a computer** yet.

3

Выберите правильное слово.
ONE or IT?

1. It's a very useful article. Read (it, one) very carefully.
2. I'm looking for a coat for my daughter. I saw (it, one) in your shop window that I liked. Could I have (it, one)?
3. "Let's have a snack in a café today!" "Good idea! I know (it, one) round the corner. (it, one) is very nice."

4. It's so convenient to work with a computer. I'm going to buy (it, one) when I have enough money.

4

Заполните пропуски подходящим по смыслу местоимением.

1. We've got a language lab in our college, and ...'s quite up–to–date. Have you got ... in yours?
2. Your garden's so large and beautiful! We've got ... too, but ...'s very small.
3. If you haven't got a tennis racket, I can give you ... .
4. If you haven't got enough tennis balls, I can lend you ... .
5. I want a stamp for my letter. I must go and buy ... .
6. If you're interested in old stamps, I can show you ... from my collection.
7. I can't find my red felt pen. I think I've lost ... ! Could you lend me ... for a moment?
8. You've got an excellent secretary in your office. We've got ... , too, but ... doesn't speak any foreign lauguages.
9. If you haven't got enough money, I can lend you ... .
10. They say his recent films are very successful, but I haven't seen ... yet.

GRAMMAR

6. **One, ones** - <u>опорные слова в положении после</u> <u>прилагательного.</u>

6.1. Слово **one** часто заменяет исчисляемое существительное в единственном числе п о с л е п р и л а г а - т е л ь н о г о (a new one, the old one, his recent one, that blue one). В этом положении **one** имеет форму множественного числа **ones** (some new ones, the old ones, his recent ones, those blue ones).

Сравните с переводом на русский язык:

1. Don't read his old stories. Read his **new ones**. They're very good.	Не читайте его старых рассказов. Прочитайте *новые*. Они очень хороши.
2. We've got two tellies, **a big one** and **a small one**. The **big one**'s in the living room, and **the small one**'s in the kitchen.	У нас два телевизора — *большой* и *маленький*. *Большой* в общей комнате, а *маленький* на кухне.

Обратите внимание на то, что в приведенных примерах русское прилагательное заменяет существительное *самостоятельно*, а английское обязательно имеет после себя опорные слова **one** или **ones**.

6.2. Слово **one** заменяет исчисляемое существительное в е д и н с т в е н н о м числе в положении после указательных местоимений **this** и **that**:

"Would you like to have any of these photos?"

— Вам хотелось бы взять себе какие-нибудь из этих фотографий?

"Yes, **this one** and **that one**, if I may."

— Да, вот **эту** и **ту**, если можно.

6.3. Указательные местоимения **these** и **those** заменяют существительное во множественном числе с а м о - с т о я т е л ь н о , без опорного слова ones:

"They've got some excellent exhibits here — just look at **these**!" "Yes, and at **those**, too."

— У них здесь есть отличные экспонаты. Вы только посмотрите на **эти**! — Да, и на **те** тоже!

Сравните:

> Look at **this one**!   Look at **these**!
>
> Look at **that one**!   Look at **those**!

6.4. Определенный артикль может стоять непосредственно перед словами **one**, **ones**, если после них идут уточняющие слова. В этом положении слова **one**, **ones** произносятся с ударением:

1. I like the blue suit, **the one** *in the shop window*.

Мне нравится синий костюм, **тот**, *на витрине*.

2. I want to have a look at those models, **the ones** *with big screens*.

Я хочу посмотреть вон те модели. **Те**, *с большими экранами*.

EXERCISES

Прочитайте вслух и переведите.

1. Your car's too old. Aren't you going to buy **a new one**?

2. I've got two cassette recorders, **a small one**, and **a big one**. I use **the small one** for doing my English excercisises, and **the big one** for music.

3. Have you read all the articles in today's paper? There're **some very interesting ones**.

4. The reading public wasn't much interested in the writer's first novels, but his **recent ones** have been a great success. He's written some very **good ones** these last few years.

5. "Look! Isn't that house beautiful!" "**Which one**? The **tall one**?" "No, **the one next to the tall one**."

6. "We've got some very elegant ties today, sir. Have a look at + 40 — these." "Well, yes, let me have **this one**. And let me have a look at **that one**. No, no. Not **the red one**, **the brown one**."

7. It's a good question and **an important one**.

2

Замените выделенные слова местоимениями *one* или *ones*.

1. It's going to be a new screen version of that novel, quite a new **version** from beginning to end.
2. You know Fennell, the film director? Well, he has made several films in the last few years, and very good **films**, I must say!
3. Your old experiments were very successful, but we're interested in your recent **experiments**.
4. We've got an answer to the question you have asked, a very definite **answer**.
5. My friend isn't a reporter, he's a businessman, and a very successful **busenessman**.
6. Our teacher doesn't usually explain rules that are easy to understand, she only explains difficult **rules**.

3

Поставьте выделенные слова во множественное число и соответственно измените остальную часть высказывания.

1. **This** old **house** is very beautiful, and **that one**'s lovely, too!
2. We've got a lot of useful guide books. Look at **this one**, and let me fetch **that one** on that shelf.
3. I don't quite like this record. Could I listen to **this one**, and let me have a look at **that one** over there.

4. "I can't find the model I'm looking for in this catalogue, I'm afraid."
"Oh, can't you? Then have a look at **this one**, and let me look through **that one** on the table over there."

4 🖭

Прочитайте диалоги вслух и разыграйте их.

1

A. Have you got a small English–Russian dictionary or a big one?
B. I've got a big one. I don't like small dictionaries, do you?
A. No, I don't, either. Mine's small, but I'm going to buy a big one.
B. Are you? They sell some very good ones in a shop near here.
A. Do they? I must go and have a look then. Would you like to go with me?
B. Yes, let's go right away, shall we?
A. Yes, let's!

2

In a Shop

Shop assistant : Can I help you?
Customer. Could I have a look at that small TV set?
S.A. That one?
C. No, no, not that one. The one on the left, please.
S.A. This one?
C. Yes, that's right.
S.A. Just a moment. Let me put it here ... It's a very good one, isn't it? How do like it?
C. I think it's okay. Could I also have a look at those on the top shelf?
S.A. Just a second... Here you are!
C. They're all nice, but let me have the one I looked at first. Where do I pay?

3

A. Did you like the festival?
B. Oh, yes, there were some excellent films this time. The last one I saw was just marvellous.
A. Oh, was it? And were there any unsuccessful ones?

- 41 -

B. Of course, there were some. That's a usual thing at any festival, isn't it?

Разыграйте следующие эпизоды.

1. It's one of the students' birthday next Friday. Discuss what you are going to give him with the other students. (He's got several hobbies, is interested in jazz, can play the guitar).

2. You're in a shop buying a present to give your friend for his birthday. Ask the shop assistant to show you several things before you buy the right one.

— 42 —

3. You are at your friend's birthday party. Say happy birthday to him and give him the present you've bought him. You may tell each other funny stories, sing songs and discuss the things you're interested in (films, music, sports, etc.)

Переведите на английский язык.

1. — Мой фотоаппарат очень старый. Я должен купить новый перед отпуском. Я люблю фотографировать. — Да? Тогда у тебя прекрасное хобби и очень интересное.

2. — Давайте перекусим в кафе. На этой улице есть несколько очень хороших. — Да? Я никогда не бывал здесь раньше.

3. Мы приняли важное решение и очень полезное, не правда ли?

4. — Мне нравятся многие картины на этой выставке. Вот эта очень хороша, правда? — А мне нравится та, на той стене. — Которая? Та, что налево? — Да. Посмотрите на эти! Ну не великолепны ли они! И те тоже!

5. Вы смогли купить путеводитель? — Нет, не смог! — Тогда возьмите мой! — Спасибо!

GRAMMAR

7. Степени сравнения прилагательных

7.1. Как и в русском языке, качественные прилагательные имеют три степени сравнения — положительную, сравнительную и превосходную (Ср. *красивый — красивее*) или *более красивый — самый красивый*).

Способ образования степеней сравнения английского прилагательного зависит от того, является ли оно *коротким* словом или *длинным*.

7.2. **Короткие** прилагательные, состоящие из одного слога, образуют сравнительную степень при помощи суффикса —**er** (**colder** — *холоднее*), а превосходную — при помощи суффикса —**est** (**coldest** — *самый холодный*). Соблюдающиеся при этом правила орфографии видны из следующих примеров:

Положительная степень	Сравнительная степень	Превосходная степень
short	**shorter**	**(the) shortest**
nice	**nicer**	**(the) nicest**
big	**bigger**	**(the) biggest**

1. "This coat's too small, I'm afraid. I want a **larger** size."
   "Here's a **bigger** one. It's the **largest** size we've got."

2. What's the **shortest** way to the station?

3. This is the **biggest** library *in* the town.

4. Which is the **cheapest** *of* these models?

5. He's the **nicest** person *I've ever met*.

Обратите внимание на то, что после прилагательного в превосходной степени часто следует определительное придаточное со сказуемым в Present Perfect (пример 5).

7.3. Таким же способом образуют свои степени сравнения короткие двусложные прилагательные, оканчивающиеся на букву — **y** (easy, busy, happy) и некоторые другие короткие двусложные прилагательные (simple, idle);

easy – easier – (the) easiest
early – earlier – (the) earliest
simple – simpler – (the) simplest

1. "The nine o'clock flight's too late for me. I'd like to go by an **earlier** one."
   "But it's the **earliest** flight on Monday, I'm afraid. There are two flights on Tuesday, at 6 and 7 a.m."
   "The **earlier** one's okay."

2. It's the **luckiest** day of in my life! I'm the **happiest** man in the world!

3. He's the **luckiest** man I've ever met.

4. I've never seen a **lazier** student in my life!

7.4. Длинные прилагательные, состоящие из *нескольких* слогов, образуют свои формы степеней сравнения при помощи слов **more** и **most**.

Положительная степень	Сравнительная степень	Превосходная степень
beautiful	**more beautiful**	**(the) most beautiful**
expensive	**more expensive**	**(the) most expensive**
useful	**more useful**	**(the) most useful**

"Which is **the most convenient** day for our next meeting?"

"Wednesday, I think."

"Don't you think Thursday's **more convenient**?"

"No, Thursday's usually **the busiest** day of the week."

7.5. Таким же способом образуют обычно свои степени сравнения *более длинные двусложные* прилагательные.

careful — more careful — the most careful
modern — more modern — the most modern
tired — more tired — the most tired

1. You must be **more careful** when you drive in the rush hour.

2. Which design is **more modern**?

3. It's **the most useful book** I've ever read on the subject.

7.6. Слова **less** и **least** образуют с более длинными прилагательными степени сравнения с отрицательным значением:

less interesting	**the least interesting**
менее интересный	наименее интересный —

1. Don't let's discuss (the) **less important** problems today.

2. That was **the least interesting** of his recent publications, I'm afraid.

7.7. Запомните формы степеней сравнения прилагательных **good** и **bad**, которые образуются нестандартно:

good — **better** — **(the) best**
bad — **worse** — **(the) worst**

1. I have to buy a **better** car, I'm afraid. I just have to.

2. This is definitely **the best** machine on the world market at this price.

3. "Do you feel **worse** today?"
"No, no, doctor! I feel better, actually!"

4. Isn't it **the worst** room in this hotel!

5. Saturday's **the best** day of the week, and Monday's **the worst**!

7.8. Прилагательное **old** имеет по д в е формы степеней сравнения с разными значениями:

о членах одной семьи

older	**elder**
старше, более старый	старше (по возрасту)
(the) oldest	**(the) eldest**
самый старый	(самый) старший

1. He's one of my **oldest** friends.

2. This theatre is one of the **oldest** in the city.

3. My **elder** brother's a test pilot.

4. I'm the **eldest** in the family.

7.9. Перед сравнительной степенью прилагательных часто употребляются глаголы-связки, обозначающие п е р е х о д и з о д н о г о с о с т о я н и я (качества) в другое: **to get (got,got), to become (became, become), to grow** [grəu], (**grew** [gru:] **grown** [grɔun]).

1. The weather's **getting worse**. — Погода ухудшается (становится хуже).

2. The situation's definitely **getting better**. — Ситуация определенно улучшается.

3. He's **getting older**. — Он стареет.

4. It's **becoming more and more interesting** to learn English. — Изучать английский становиться все интересней.

5. It's **growing (getting)**   Темнеет.
dark.

Глагол-связка **to become** употребляется и перед превосходной степенью:

1. Jim has **become the best** athlete in his college.

2. He has **become** one of **the most successful** film directors in the last few years.

7.10. Степени сравнения от слов **many, much** — м н о г о и **little** — м а л о.

More означает б о л ь ш е п о к о л и ч е с т в у и употребляется как с исчисляемыми, так и с неисчисляемыми существительными: **more books, more time, more films, more bread.**

Less означает м е н ь ш е п о к о л и ч е с т в у и употребляется с неисчисляемыми существительными: **less time, less money.**
С исчисляемыми существительными в этом значении употребляется форма **fewer** (от прилагательного few): **fewer people, fewer times,** однако в современном языке допускается употребление **less: less students, less machines.**

1. You must eat more vegetables and less meat.   Вы должны есть больше овощей и меньше мяса.

2. You're making fewer and fewer mistakes (=less and less mistakes). Congratulations!   Вы делаете все меньше и меньше ошибок. Поздравляю!

Когда русские слова "больше" и "меньше" относяться не к количеству, а к р а з м е р у, они переводятся иначе:

This room's **larger (bigger)** and that one's **smaller.**   Эта комната больше, а та — меньше.

ПРИМЕЧАНИЕ. Слово **more** может соответствовать русскому слову е щ е в значении "больше по количеству."

1. I want **some more** soup.   Я хочу еще супу.

2. Let me have **five more** copies.

Дайте мне еще пять экземпляров.

3. I'm going to stay **one more** week (=another week).

Я собираюсь остаться еще на неделю.

7.11. Когда в предложении упоминаются о б а объекта сравнения, после прилагательного в сравнительной степени употребляется союз **than** [ðæn, ðən], который произносится без ударения в слабой форме. Особенности высказываний такого типа и их перевода на русский язык видны из следующих примеров.

1. London's bigger than Sheffield.

Лондон больше Шеффилда (больше, чем Шеффилд).

2. Italy's smaller than Spain.

Италия меньше Испании.

3. Russian grammar's more difficult than English grammar.

Русская граматика труднее английской грамматики.

4. Old things are sometimes dearer to us than new ones.

Старые вещи нам иногда дороже новых.

5. Your car's newer than mine.

Ваша машина более новая, чем моя.

6. This hotel's noisier than that (one).

Эта гостиница более шумная, чем та.

7. These models are more up-to-date than those.

Эти модели более современные, чем те.

8. His early films were less successful than the more recent ones.

Его ранние фильмы были менее успешными, чем более поздние.

7.12. Перед сравнительной степенью могут стоять усилительные слова **much**, **a lot** (разг.), **far** - *гораздо, намного*, **a little** - *немного*, **a bit** - *чуть, чуточку* (разг.).

1. Let's go by car. It's **much more convenient**.

... гораздо удобнее.

2. This model's **a little more expensive** than that one, but it's **a lot better**.

... немного дороже
... намного лучше

3. You **make far fewer** mistakes in your English now.

... гораздо меньше

7.13. Перед сравнительной степенью могут стоять уточняющие слова, перед которыми, в отличие от соответствующих русских предложений, н е т предлога:

1. He's **five years older** than his wife.

Он на пять лет старше своей жены.

2. This suit's **ten pounds more expensive** than that one.

Этот костюм на десять фунтов дороже, чем тот.

7.14. Если после союза **than** стоит личное местоимение, оно в разговорном стиле часто употребляется в косвенном падеже без последующего глагола.

Разговорный стиль

Нейтральный стиль

1. You're younger than **me**.

You are younger than **I am**.

2. I'm a more careful driver than **him (you, her)**.

I'am a more careful driver than **he is (you are, she is)**.

3. They've got more time than **us**.

They have more time than **we have**.

4. We're busier this week than **them**.

We're busier this week than **they are**.

EXERCISES

Прочитайте вслух и переведите:

a. 1. Let me have a larger suitcase, please.
2. Could I try on a size smaller?
3. It's deeper here. Be careful!
4. I'd like to go by an earlier train, if I can.
5. The picture's getting clearer.
6. It was getting colder.
7. I've never read a duller book in my life!

8. I've never heard a funnier story!
9. I hope you don't feel worse today.
10. Please have a better look at these documents.

b. 1. You must eat less bread and spend more time walking.
2. Would you like some more juice?
3. Shall I fetch you some more copies?
4. We've got fewer (less) people today, so we can work in a smaller room, can't we?
5. My family's bigger now, so we must think of a larger flat.
6. I don't use my car very often now, so less money goes on petrol.
7. That's more or less convenient.

8. "Is that okay?" "Well, more or less".

c. 1. I've never seen a more careless person in my life! Can't you be more careful?
2. Could we meet at a more convenient time?
3. Couldn't we try to find a less noisy room?
4. I've never eaten more delicious food in my life!
5. That's a less usual way of saying it in Russian, I'm afraid.

d. 1. This copy's neater than that one.
2. These slides are better than those.
3. The problem's more difficult than we thought.
4. Is their decision more important than ours?
5. They're more interested in our old models than in our recent ones.

e. 1. That is the most important problem today.
2. Which is the simplest way of solving the problem?
3. Their team's definitely the best in the world.
4. He's one of the best athletes of the year.
5. She's the loveliest girl I've ever seen!
6. It was the worst mistake I've ever made!

f. 1. The question was much longer than the answer.
2. The town we're going to visit is a little smaller than the one we've just been to, but it's a lot more interesting.
3. This fax machine's a bit more expensive than that one, but it's a lot better.

g. 1. My son's two years older than my daughter.
2. This road's about a mile longer than that one.

3. Model B's five hundred pounds cheaper than Model C, and Model D's a thousand pounds more expensive.

2

Напишите степени сравнения этих прилагательных:

angry, big, busy, cheap, clean, clear, close, cold, deep, fast, fat, dull, easy, early, funny, healthy, great, happy, heavy, hot, kind, lazy, light, long, lucky, neat, new, nice, poor, dear, pretty, quick, rich, sad, silly, simple, slim, slow, sure, tall, thick, thin, ugly, warm, young, large, small, many (much), little, good, bad, old, beautiful, careful, careless, comfortable, convenient, delicious, difficult, elegant, expensive, important, interesting, interested, peaceful, pleasant, pleased, useful, usual, definite, recent.

— 50 —

3

Сравните, как показано в образце:

1.

Дано: London, Leads (large, small).

Требуется: London's larger than Leads.
Leads is smaller than London.

2.

Дано: this hotel, that one (expensive).

Требуется: This hotel's more expensive than that one.
That hotel's less expensive than this one.

1. Europe, Asia (small, large).
2. France, England (big, small).
3. A journey by car, a journey by train (interesting).
4. A holiday in the country, a holiday in town (pleasant).
5. A meal in a restaurant, a meal in café (expensive, cheap).
6. The English language, the Japanese language (difficult).

4

Составьте предложения, как показано в образцах:

Дано: It, fast, plane, world.

Требуется: It's the fastest plane in the world.

1. This, beautiful, monument, Moscow.
2. The library of the British Museum, rich, England.

3. The Caspian Sea, large, lake (озеро), the world.
4. Peter, quick, player, team.
5. He, good, specialist, company.

Дано: Tuesday, busy, day, the week.
Требуется: Tuesday's the busiest day of the week.

1. January, cold, month, the year.
2. Spring, pleasant, time, the year.
3. Saturday, good, day, the week.
4. It was, happy, moment, his life.
5. It, successful, exhibition, the year.

Дано: This, clean, town, I, visit.
Требуется: This is the cleanest town I've ever visited.

1. She, nice, person, I, know
2. This, fast, car, I, drive
3. That, interesting, experiment, they, make
4. This silly, thing, he, do, his life
5. This, delicious, dish, I, eat
6. That, funny, film, I, see
7. It, least successful, novel, he, write
8. She, beautiful, girl, I, meet

5

Уточните сравнения, употребив перед прилагательным следующие слова: *much, a lot, a little, a bit, far.*

1. The problem's more important than you think.

2. Could you make your answer more definite?

3. John's older than his wife.

4. I spend less time on my homework if I work hard in class.

5. This watch is more expensive than that one, but it's better.

6. Anne's better at foreign languages than at other subjects.

7. Alex's more interested in football than in his lessons, I'm afraid.

8. My toothache's worse today!

9. This way's shorter and more convenient.

10. There are fewer (less) interesting museums in this big city than in the small town we visited yesterday.

6

Выберите правильное слово.

1. England is (less, smaller) than France.

2. I've got (less, smaller) time today than yesterday.

3. There're (less, fewer) people at the stadium on weekdays than at the weekend.

4. Don't we spend (less, fewer) time at the stadium than in front of our tellies?

5. We're going to do (larger, more) business with Brown and Co. in the near future.

6. (Larger and larger, more and more) companies in Great Britain do business with Russian counterparts.

7. "Isn't this exhibition a little (less, smaller, fewer) than the one we went to last Sunday?" "Yes, there are (less, smaller, fewer) pictures here, I think."

7

Переведите на английский язык:

1. Наша новая лаборатория **больше** старой и **гораздо удобнее**.

2. В этой книге **больше** информации по теме, которой я интересуюсь, чем в других книгах, которые я прочитал.

3. По пятницам у меня обычно **меньше** времени, чем по четвергам.

4. Наш стадион **немного меньше** вашего, но он находится в **более удобном** месте, поэтому сюда обычно приходит **больше** народу.

5. Не находите ли вы, что все и **меньше и меньше** народу ходит в театр? Не грустно ли это?

6. В нашем городе есть несколько хороших больниц, и скоро будет еще одна. Она будет **больше** других и **гораздо** современнее.

7. Этот магнитофон гораздо **дешевле** того, но он **хуже**.

8

Перефразируйте, как показано в образце.

Дано: Peter's taller than I am.
Требуется: Peter's taller than me.

1. My elder sister's two years older than I am.
2. Her husband's five years older than she is.
3. We were five minutes earlier than they were.
4. You were ten minutes later than we were.
5. You are a bit taller than he is.
6. Ann's much better at languages than I am.
7. Is Jane better at cooking than you are?
8. John's elder sister's a lot better at tennis than he is.

9

Ответьте на вопросы:

1. Which country is bigger, France or England (Spain or Italy, Sweden or Denmark, Holland or Finland)?

2. Which sea is deeper, the Black Sea or the Azov Sea?

3. Which sea is colder, the Black Sea or the Baltic Sea?

4. Which city is older, Moscow or St. Petersburg (London or Washington)?

5. Which is the best time for a holiday? Which is the worst?

6. Which month is shorter, July or August?

7. Which is the hottest month of the year, and which is the coldest?

8. Which is the busiest day of the week and why?

9. Who's the best athlete in your college? Who's the best student?

10. Are you better at English than at other subjects? Which subject is the easiest for you? Which is the most difficult? Which is the most interesting? Why are you more interested in it than in the other subjects?

10

Прочитайте рассказы вслух и обсудите их.

1

At an International Basketball Match

This is a match **between** a Finnish college team and a Spanish one. The Finnish players are taller than the Spanish. One of the Finns is taller than all the others in both teams. The shortest man's in the Spanish team, but he is definitely the quickest.

At the beginning the Finnish team was luckier, but later the **Spaniards** were more successful. They were quicker and **cleverer** with the ball.

Now they are winning 90 to 87, but they are a bit more tired than the Finns. There's only five minutes left. Which team's going to win the match? What do you think? Can only tall people play basketball? Are there any good basketball players **among** your friends?

— 54 —

Learn these words:

international [ˌɪntəˈnæʃnəl] *adj*   международный

between [bɪˈtwiːn] *prep*   между (двумя)

   between five and six o'clock
   between London and Paris

among [əˈmʌŋ] *prep*   между (более, чем двумя), среди

   He's among the best of our experts.

clever [ˈklevə] *adj*   1. умный

   a clever book (speech, student).
   How clever of you to think of the tickets!

                  2. умелый, искусный

He's clever with his hands.	У него умелые руки.
Are you clever with your needle?	Вы умеете обращаться с иглой (шить)?

Finn *n c*   финн

Spaniard [ˈspænɪəd] *n c*   испанец

2

At a Pop Music Festival

This French girl's the yougest singer at the festival. She's never taken part in such festivals before, but she's **doing** very well. She's definitely a success with the public.

Another singer, from Italy, is a bit older, but she's prettier and a better dancer. She's got a **beautiful** dress on. She's actually the most elegant girl at the festival.

This singer, who's Swedish is less beautiful than the other two, but she's got a more pleasant **voice**, and the songs she sings are more interesting.

Which of them is going to win the first prize? What do you think?

Learn these words:

voice [vɔɪs] n c   голос

to do well

преуспевать в чём–либо; успешно справляться с чём–либо; поправляться (о больном)

All the students are doing well **in** (their) English.

3

A Discussion.

The people you can see in this picture are discussing the design of a new machine.

A. The new version's more up–to–date, but it's definitely going to be more expensive. We must think of economy, mustn't we?

B. But **quality** isn't less important than economy, is it? The other versions were only a little cheaper,

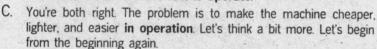

but the machine was going to be a lot heavier and less convenient to **operate**.

C. You're both right. The problem is to make the machine cheaper, lighter, and easier **in operation**. Let's think a bit more. Let's begin from the beginning again.

Are they going to solve the problem soon?
What do you think?

Learn these words:

quality ['kwɔlɪtɪ] *n u* качество

This watch is very good quality.
This is a high quality watch.

operate ['ɔpɔreɪt] зд. управлять, работать (с чем–либо)

The machine's easy to operate. Этой машиной легко управлять.

in operation [,ɔpɔ'reɪʃn] зд. в работе, в действии

Would you like to see the machine in operation?

✎

Переведите на английский язык:

1. Наша новая квартира гораздо больше и гораздо комфорта-
бельнее старой. Все комнаты больше и светлее, а кухня и
ванная более современные. Дом находится ближе к станции
метро, вокруг больше магазинов, чем на старом месте.

2. Мой сын только на полтора года младше дочери. Оба ребенка
уже ходят в школу, но они больше интересуются играми, чем
уроками. В будни жена проводит с детьми больше времени,
чем я, но по воскресеньям я провожу с ними весь день. Дети
любят задавать мне вопросы, которые становятся все труднее
и труднее. Гораздо проще читать им книгу или играть в
какую-нибудь игру, чем отвечать на их вопросы. Моя жена
определенно лучший учитель, чем я!

GRAMMAR

8. Прошедшее время группы **Continuous (Past Continuous).**

8.1. Прошедшее время группы Continuous употребляется,
когда говорящий рассказывает о действии, как о
неоконченном процессе, продолжавшемся в определенный момент или отрезок времени в прошлом. Этот
момент может быть у к а з а н (точное время), или
понятен из контекста.

1. I couldn't call you at two, because I was having lunch.	Я не мог позвонить тебе в два часа потому что я обе-дал.
2. We were playing tennis from five to seven.	Мы играли в теннис с пяти до семи.

Этот момент может быть также обозначен другим
к р а т к о в р е м е н н ы м действием.

When he came, we were just finishing the discussion.	Когда он пришел, мы как раз заканчивали обсужде-ние.

ПРИМЕЧАНИЕ: Когда речь идет о действиях, следовавших
одно за другим, употребляется прошедшее время группы
Simple:

He came, and we finished the discussion.	Он пришел, и мы закончили обсуждение.

8.2. **Past Continuous** употребляется также, когда речь идет о двух длительных действиях, происходивших параллельно. Придаточное предложение в этом случае часто вводится союзом **while** [waıl] - в т о в р е м я к а к , п о к а :

While the manager was talking on the phone, the secretary was getting the documents ready.	Пока управляющий разговаривал по телефону, секретарь готовил документы.

8.3. **Past Continuous** часто используется в описаниях, когда говорящий хочет воссоздать картину того, что происходило:

The square was full of people. Bands were playing. The people were singing and dancing ...	Площадь была полна народу. Играли оркестры, люди пели и танцевали ...

EXERCISES

Прочитайте вслух и переведите:

1. When I was going home, I met a friend.

2. Jane was looking through the mail when the telephone rang.

3. I didn't hear your question, because I was listening to a colleague.

4. This time last year he was living in London.

5. Who were you waiting for when I came?

6. So what were we talking about? (Итак, на чем мы остановились?)

7. The line was free from ten to eleven, I wasn't making any calls.

8. The weather was bad, and it was getting worse and worse.

9. While the gentlemen were discussing the recent events, the ladies were talking about the weather.

2 ✎

Какие вопросы нужно задать, чтобы получить эти ответы:

1. He was meeting his **British counterparts** when we saw him at the airport.
2. I was looking for **my key** when you came in.
3. John was looking through **the morning mail** when his boss called him.
4. I didn't answer the call, **because I was taking a shower.**
5. We were talking about **your proposal** when you came in.

– 59 –

3 🔲

Прочитайте рассказы вслух и перескажите их:
а) близко к тексту
б) от лица одного из персонажей

1

Alex wanted to talk to his wife Deb on the telephone during the lunch break, but he couldn't get through to her, because the line was busy.

"Who were you talking to on the phone at one o'clock?" Alex asked Deb when he got home.
"At one? Let me see... To Amy. Why?"
"How long were you talking?"
"Not very long, not more than five minutes."
"Five minutes? I was trying to get through to you till a quarter to two, but the line was busy all the time!"

"It was the worst moment I've ever had with him," Deb told Amy when

they were shopping together the next day.

2

These girls weren't working when the manager came in. One was talking to her boy friend on the telephone, two were looking at a **fashion magazine.** Another girl was reading a **detective** story.

The manager was very angry when he saw that. "What were you doing here? Why weren't you working?" he wanted to know. The girls couldn't explain, but they went on with their work at once.

Learn the new words:

fashion [ˈfæʃn]   *n u*   мода

   to be in (out of) fashion

   a fashion magazine   журнал мод
   [ˌmægəˈziːn]

Сравните:

magazine   *n c*   журнал, обычно содержащий рассказы, фотографии, рекламу и т.п.

journal [ˈdʒɜːnl]   *n c*   журнал, периодическое издание; газета,

detective [dɪˈtektɪv]   *n c*   сыщик

   a detective story   детектив (книга)
   a detective film   детектив (фильм)

4

Переведите на английский язык.

1. Когда мы обсуждали вчера мое сообщение, вы задали мне вопрос, на который я не мог ответить сразу. Сейчас я готов дать вам ответ.

2. — Просил ли г-н Браун что-нибудь мне передать, когда он разговаривал (spoke) вчера с вами по телефону? — Да, он передал сообщение (message). Вот оно.

3. Когда мы путешествовали по (round) Японии, я сделал много фотографий. Вы хотели бы посмотреть?

4. Когда я выходил из квартиры, зазвонил телефон, и мне пришлось вернуться и ответить на звонок.
5. Я не очень внимательно слушал преподавателя, когда он объяснял это правило, поэтому я сделал больше ошибок в переводе, чем другие студенты.
6. Когда он пришел, мы обсуждали очень интересный вопрос.
7. Когда он пришел, мы обсудили очень интересный вопрос.
8. Кто из вас поддержал (support) эту идею, когда мы ее обсуждали?

TOPICS FOR DISCUSSION AND NEW WORDS

Operating a Piece of Equipment

We are at an international exhibition of radio and **electronic equipment.**

In one of the rooms the visitors can see the **latest** models of radio and television sets, cassette recorders and players **made** in different countries. There are all kinds of exhibits here: colour television sets with larger and smaller screens, very small **portable** tellies, **video cassette recorders** and different types of **stereo** equipment.

The exhibition is a great success. **Most** visitors examine the exhibits with **interest** and often ask the stand **attendants** questions about the things they are interested in. One of the visitors, who is interested in a television set, is talking to the stand attendant about it.

Visitor: Excuse me, could you **switch on** that set, the one on your right?

Stand Attendant: Certainly!

(He switches it on. The **picture** is clear.)

V. Thanks. And how do I switch to another **channel?**

S.A. Just **press** this **button** on the **remote control unit.** This set is **extremely** easy to operate.

(The visitor presses the button and looks at the screen.)

V. I don't quite like the colour on this channel. How can I make it more **natural**?

S.A. You can **adjust** the picture with these buttons. Look! How do you like it now?

V. Oh, that's a lot better! It's very good **indeed**!

S.A. If you press this button twice, the picture becomes **slightly** different.

As they are talking, some other visitors come up to the stand. One of them is interested in a video cassette recorder, and the stand attendant shows him how it works.

S.A. First press this button to switch it on, and then press this one to **tune in to** the station you want. Let me do it for you first."

The attendant starts **tuning in. At first** there is no picture, but in a few seconds the picture **appears** on the screen. The visitor, who is very pleased, thanks the attendant and listens to the news for a short time.

"A high quality piece of equipment!" another visitor says. "I've got one at home and I'm very pleased with it. It's one of the most reliable VCRs I've ever had!"

The stand attendant **turns** the **sound down** a bit, and the visitors ask him some more questions to which he gives clear and full answers.

Learn these words:

equipment [ɪˈkwɪpmənt] *n u*	1. оборудование (машины, приборы и т.п.)
modern lab equipment	
fishing equipment	
	2. оборудование, процесс оснащения
The equipment of the new hospital took a year.	
electronic [ˌɪlekˈtrɔnɪk] *adj*	электронный
electronic equipment	электронное оборудование
latest *adj*	последний, новейший, свежий
the latest news	свежие новости, последние известия
in the latest fashion	по последней моде
the latest models	последние (новейшие) модели

Сравните: LATEST — LAST — RECENT

latest	последний по времени, новейший, самый свежий
last	последний по порядку
recent	последний, недавний
the latest events	самые последние события
a recent event	недавнее событие, одно из недавних событий
his last visit	его последний визит

made	сделанный, произведенный
made in Japan	
video cassette recorder [ˈviːdiəu kəˈset riˈkɔːdə] (**VCR** [ˈviːˈsiːˈɑː])	видеомагнитофон
portable [ˈpɔːtəbl] *adj*	переносной, портативный
stereo [ˈsteriəu, ˈstiriəu] *adj*	стерео-, стереофонический
stereo equipment	
most [məust] *adj*	1. большинство (об исчисл. сущ.)

Сравните:

Most children like toys.	Большинство детей (вообще) любят игрушки.
"Most **of** the children are doing well," said the teacher.	"Большинство детей (*из конкретного числа*) хорошо успевают", сказал учитель.
	2. бóльшая часть (о неисчисл. сущ.)
Most **of** the time went on discussions.	Большая часть времени ушла на дискуссии.
interest [ˈintrist] *n*	интерес

to do sth with interest	делать что–л. с интересом
to be of some (great) interest to sb	представлять некоторый (большой) интерес для кого–либо

This journal is of (great) interest to most of us.

to be of no interest to ...	не представлять интереса для ...
to be of little interest to...	не представлять большого интереса для ...

The work I've just looked through is of little interest to us, I'm afraid.

attendant [ə'tendənt] *n c* — обслуживающее лицо (контролер, билетер, служитель и т.п.)

   a stand attendant — стендист

switch on — включать

   Syn. turn on, put on

   Ant. switch off (turn off) — выключать

picture *n c* — зд. видимость, изображение

channel ['tʃænl] *n c* — 1. канал (пролив)

   the English Channel — Ла–Манш

2. канал (коммуникации, информации)

   through diplomatic channels

3. *зд* канал, программа

   Syn. programme (program) ['prougræm]
   on the first (second) channel (programme)

press *v* — нажимать

button ['bʌtn] *n c* — пуговица, кнопка

remote [rɪ'məut] *adj* — отдаленный

   remote control unit — дистанционное управление

extremely [ɪks'tri:mlɪ] *adv* — чрезвычайно, исключительно (усилительное наречие)

   Syn. very

extremely interesting (difficult, useful, etc)

natural [´næt∫ərl] *adj*

1. естественный, натуральный

Ant. unnatural

неестественный

It's quite natural to feel tired after such hard work.

2. естественный, природный

Ant. man—made, artificial
[ˌɑːtɪ´fɪ∫l]

сделанный человечески-
ми руками, искусственный

natural resources
[rɪ´sɔːsɪz]

естественные ресурсы

A channel is natural, and
a canal [kə´nɑːl] is
man—made.

Пролив создан природой,
а канал — человеческими
руками.

adjust [ə´dʒʌst]

регулировать, отрегулировать,
наладить

I must adjust my watch. It's fast.

indeed [ɪn´diːd] *adv*

действительно, в самом деле
(как усилитель после прилагательного или наречия, переводится по смыслу)

The equipment is very
good indeed.

Оборудование действи-
тельно очень хорошее.

Thank you very much
indeed.

Огромное вам спасибо.

as [æz, əz] *conj*

1. когда

Syn. when, while

As I was leaving the house, it began to rain

2. по мере того, как ...

We got more interested as the lecture went on.

tune in

настраиваться

tune in to a station
(a tune – мелодия)

настроиться на станцию

at first

сначала, первое время, вначале

Syn. at (in) the beginning

At first I read the book without interest, but as I went on, I liked it more and more (=better and better).

~~~~~~

Сравните: FIRST — AT FIRST

first *adv*	сначала, *в первую очередь, сперва*
at first	сначала, *первое время, поначалу*

Let me think **first**, and only then give an answer.

At first the film wasn't a success with the public, but as more people saw it, it became more and more popular.

~~~~~~

appear [ə´pɪə] *v*	появляться
Ant. disappear [͵dɪsə´pɪə]	исчезать
slight *adv*	незначительный, небольшой
a slight mistake	незначительная ошибка
a slight cold	легкая простуда
slightly *adj*	слегка, незначительно

Syn. a little, a bit
I feel slightly ill.

reliable [rɪ´laɪəbl] *adj*	надежный

reliable information, facts, etc.

turn down *v*	*зд.* приглушить, прикрутить

to turn down the light (the gas, the radio, etc.)

sound *n c*	звук

The sound's clear (good)

sound *v*	звучать

Does that sound natural in Russian?

That sounds nice, doesn't it?	Неплохо звучит? (т.е. производит неплохое впечатление)

2

An Hour before the Exhibition Opened

This is a photo a newspaper reporter took an hour before the exhibition opened. There were no visitors in the rooms **as yet.** The director of the exhibition was looking through the text of his opening speech. The managers were **giving last-minute instructions** to the stand attendants. A young girl was arranging some flowers on a little table near the electronic clocks and watches stand. The reporter liked the look of the girl and

decided to put her in the **foreground** of his picture.

When she saw that he was going to take a photo of her, she took the most beautiful flower out of the **vase** and smiled. So she was smiling and holding a flower in her hand when the reporter pressed the button of his camera.

Learn these words:

as yet	пока что
instructions [ɪnˈstrʌkʃnz] *n pl*	указания, инструкции (обычно во мн.ч.)

to give instructions
to get (receive) instructions
He got instructions to examine the equipment again.

last-minute *adj*	последние, происходящие в последнюю минуту перед чем-либо

last-minute instructions (preparations)

look	зд. (внешний) вид

I don't like the look of him.

Мне не нравится как он выглядит (смотрится)

foreground [ˈfɔːɡraʊnd] *n u*	передний план

Ant. background

задний план, фон

in the foreground
(background)

на переднем (заднем) плане

vase [vɑːz] *n c*   ваза

    a vase of flowers

smile *v*   улыбаться

smile *n c*   улыбка

EXERCISES

Прочитайте тексты вслух. Предварительно отработайте произношение следующих слов и словосочетаний.

[æ]	[əu]	[ʌ]
natural	most	adjust
international	stereo	button
channel	video	instructions

the colour on this channel

for a short time

2 ✎

Подберите в тексте английские эквиваленты.

последние модели • сделанные в разных странах • всевоз—можные экспонаты • различные типы оборудования • большинство посетителей • изображение хорошее • а как переключить на другую программу? • чрезвычайно легок в обращении • вы можете регулировать изображение этими кнопками • пока они разговаривают • сначала изображения нет • но через несколько секунд изображение появляется на экране • за день до открытия выставки • в залах еще не было посетителей • его речь по случаю открытия (выставки) • последние указания • стенд электронных часов • понравилось как смотрится девушка • на переднем плане.

3

Ответьте на вопросы.

a.1. Why is the first story called "Operating a Piece of Equipment"? (By the way, are you clever (good) at operating equipment?)

2. What kind of exhibition is the text about?

3. What can visitors see at the exhibition?

4. Why do you think the exhibition is of interest to most visitors?
5. Do you think it's a recent exhibition?
6. What kind of people visit these exhibitions?
7. Which exhibits are the visitors most interested in?
8. Does the visitor know how to operate the equipment?

b.1. Why did the reporter come to the exhibition an hour before it opened?
2. What were the people at the exhibition doing when the reporter arrived?
3. Why did the reporter decide to put the girl who was arranging flowers in the foreground of his picture?
4. What did the girl do when she saw that the reporter wanted to take a photo of her?
5. What was she doing when the reporter pressed the button of his camera?

Прочитайте вслух примеры на новые слова.

1. Does the company sell lab equipment?

2. We are interested in buying modern office equipment for a research institute.

3. We would like to have some more information about the equipment you make.

4. "How long is the equipment of the new hospital going to take?" "Not less than a year, I think."

5. "The last model on the list is your latest, isn't it?" "No, not the very latest, but a recent one."

6. You could see all the latest in electronic games at the last exhibition.

7. Most of his recent articles are of great interest to scientists.

8. Most people are interested in recent international events.

9. Most men like watching football and hockey on TV.

10. Most women are interested in fashions, aren't they?

11. Most of the women were dressed in the latest fashion.

12. The equipment is of no interest to most buyers, because it is out-of-date.

13. At first people watched the new serial with interest, but as it went on it became less and less interesting.

14. Let me read the article from beginning to end first, and then tell you what I think of it.

15. At first the boy worked hard at school and did very well, but soon he lost interest in his lessons and stopped making progress.

16. First study the instructions carefully, and only after that try to operate the machine.

17. The engineers got instructions to examine the equipment again before putting it into operation.

18. Did the manager give you any other instructions?

19. The manager was giving the last-minute instructions to his assistants when the TV people came to interview him.

20. The translation sounds slighly unnatural in Russian, I'm afraid.

Перефразируйте, как показано в образце.

Дано: turn the sound down
Требуется: How do I turn the sound down?

turn the sound up • turn it down a bit • switch the set on • turn it off • switch to another programme • adjust the picture • make the picture clearer • make the colour more natural • tune in to another station.

Составьте предложения, как показано в образце.

1. Дано: the book–economists
   Требуется: The book's of great interest to economists.

   his recent work – specialists
   the news – us all
   your latest catalogues — a lot of businessmen
   their recent publications — scientists
   the recent events – most of us

2. Дано: the interview — the public
   Требуется: The interview was of no interest to the public

the last match — those who were watching it
the equipment — the buyers
his last lecture — the students
the old models — the firm
the subject of the talk — most of the people

3. Дано: the discussion — those who took part in it
Требуется: The discussion wasn't of much interest to those
who took part in it

the recent fashion show — the public
the story — those who were listening
the screen version of the novel — those who knew the novel
most of his ideas — the specialists

7

Заполните пропуски предлогами.

1. My sister gave me a new TV set ... my last birthday, and I'm
very pleased ... it. It's a portable TV set much lighter than my
old one and a lot easier to operate. The picture's very clear, and
it isn't difficult to tune in. If you want to tune in ... a station you
are interested ..., you just press a button.

2. I usually listen ... the radio ... the morning ... breakfast. I don't
always have enough time to read the newspaper before I go ..
. work, so I'm very glad I can hear the morning news ... the
radio. I also enjoy listening ... music, and lectures and talks ...
different subjects.

3. There's a new musical ... the fourth channel ... nine thirty this
evening. I've seen it ... the theatre and enjoyed it ... beginning
... end.

4. A. I'm afraid I can't get a clear picture ... the fourth channel. What
can I do?
B. Let me come ... your place ... work and adjust it. I know all
about TV sets and radios.
A. Thanks so much. It's very kind ... you!

5. A guide was taking a group ... foreign tourists ... Moscow. ...
first the tourists only looked ... the sights and listened ... the
guide's explanations. Later they began to ask questions. The guide
gave full, interesting answers ... all their questions. "This is my
first visit ... Moscow," said one of the tourists. "And I'm enjoying
every minute ... it."

8

Выберите правильное слово.

1. (First, at first) we didn't quite like the new serial, but as the film went on, we got more and more interested.

2. "Let me (at first, first) adjust the picture, and then see to the sound," he said.

3. (First, at first) he wanted to be an actor, but then he got interested in medicine and decided to be a doctor.

4. (First, at first) most of his colleagues didn't like his new ideas, but after some extremely successful experiments he made, they saw he was right.

— 72 —

5. Have you heard the (last, latest, recent) news? Our team won the (last, latest, recent) match in Canada.

6. "Don't you think his (last, latest, recent) films are a little less interesting than his earlier ones?" "I thought so (first, at first), but now I think they are just slightly different in style.

7. He has only used (last, latest, recent) publications for his (last, latest, recent) talk on (modern, up–to–date) English literature.

8. Our (last, latest, recent) model is a bit more expensive than the others, but it's a lot more reliable and easier to operate. It's a very (modern, up–to–date) design.

9

Ответьте на вопросы. Суммируйте ответы в кратких сообщениях.

a. 1. You've got a radio–set, haven't you?
2. What kind of radio is it?
3. Is it the latest make?
4. Is it better than other models?
5. Is it reliable and easy to operate?
6. When did you buy it?
7. Are you pleased with it?

b. 1. Do you enjoy listening to the radio?
2. How regularly do you listen?
3. Which is more interesting, listening to the radio or watching television?

4. Do you usually switch on the radio when you are driving the car?

c. 1. What kind of TV set have you got?
   2. When did you buy it?
   3. Are you pleased with it?
   4. Would you like to buy another one?

d. 1. Have you got a cassette–recorder?
   2. Is it a portable model?
   3. Is it easy to operate?
   4. Is it one of latest models or is it a bit out–of–date?
   5. How often do you use it for your English?

e. 1. Which of you has got a colour TV set?
   2. Is it a high quality set?
   3. Are the colours natural?
   4. What can you do to make the colour more natural?
   5. Is the picture always clear? How can you make it clearer?
   6. What about the sound?

10

Придумайте короткие рассказы, используя данные слова.

1. recently; decide; a new radio set (TV set, cassette recorder, VCR); go to a shop; ask the shop assistant to show; several models; reliable; easy to operate; tune in to a lot of stations; at first; the picture; the sound; get clearer; the best ... I've ever seen

2. an English novel; at first; dull; not to give up reading; get more and more interested; recently; a screen version on TV; to be slightly different from the novel; successful; to watch from beginning to end; to enjoy

11

Разыграйте следующие эпизоды.

1. You are in a shop. You want to buy a portable cassette recorder. Ask the shop assistant to show you the latest models. You want a reliable one, easy to operate, and not very expensive. Ask the shop assistant how to operate the model you like best.

2. You are a guide at an exhibition of electronic equipment. Answer a visitor's questions about a TV set he is interested in. Show him how to adjust the picture and the sound; how to switch over to other channels, etc.

3. You are a visitor to an exhibition of TV sets and video cassette recorders. You are interested in a high quality VCR. Ask the stand attendant how to put in a cassette, how to make the picture clear, etc.

Прочитайте рассказы вслух и перескажите их.

1

A Clever Old Man

An Englishman was travelling in **Alaska**. In a village there he met an old man who was nearly one hundred years old. He could hardly read, and he couldn't write at all, but he knew a lot of interesting things about medicine, science and industry. As the old man told his stories, the Englishman grew more and more interested in him as a person. "And he has learnt all this without books, far from modern **civilization**! He's the cleverest man I've ever met!" he thought. "Could you tell me a few things about the near future?" he asked. "Certainly!" the old man answered. "It's going to get colder next week, some important visitors are coming to this country, and the president's going to give them an interview next Wednesday". "**Fantastic!**" the Englishman **exclaimed**. "How did you find all that out?" "I heard it on the radio," was the answer.

Learn these words:

Alaska [əˈlæskə]   Аляска

civilization [ˌsɪvɪlaɪˈzeɪʃn]   *n*   цивилизация

fantastic [fænˈtæstɪk]   *adj*   фантастический, зд. "Потряса—
 юще!"

exclaim [ɪks'kleɪm] v   воскликнуть

2

What does 'GB' Mean?

An Englishman, who couldn't drive, bought a car. As he had to learn to drive, he went to a driving school and took driving lessons. While he was learning, he had a large 'L' plate on the back of his car to show that he was a learner. After some time he took the driving test and passed it. He got a driving licence and was then able to drive without the 'L' plate. He decided to spend his holiday abroad, and so he had to **fix** a 'GB' plate on his car, because every car that leaves Great Britain must have a 'GB' plate on it.

One day his little son was playing with another boy, and they were discussing the new car. "Why did your father have an 'L' on the back of his car at first, and now a 'GB'? What does that mean?" the other boy asked. "Well," the car driver's son answered. "That's very simple: 'L' means learning, and 'GB' means getting better."

Learn these words

plate *n c*	табличка, номерной знак
an 'L' (learner) plate	знак "неопытный води- тель"
fix *v*	прикрепить

Переведите на английский язык.

1. Мы получили письма с заводов, которые интересуются Вашими машинами, г-н Беннетт, и сегодня я могу дать определенный ответ на Ваш вопрос о наших планах на будущее.

2. Цена этой машины немного выше цен других моделей, но ее качество гораздо выше. Это фактически самая лучшая модель, которую мы сделали за последние несколько лет. Конструкция современна, машина надежна и легка в эксплуатации.

3. — Мне не совсем нравится этот магнитофон, он очень тяжелый. Я хочу более легкий. — Одну минуту. Взгляните на этот. Он гораздо меньше и легче, но он немного дороже.

4. — Выставка чрезвычайно интересна, не правда ли? — Да, это самая удачная выставка, которая у нас была за последние несколько лет.

5. — Почему я не могу получить четкого изображения? — Давайте я Вам помогу. Вы нажимаете не на ту кнопку. Сейчас лучше? — Да, спасибо. А как переключиться на другую программу? — Нажмите эту кнопку.

6. У этого телевизора экран больше, но изображение не такое четкое.

7. Моя старая машина была меньше новой, и она была менее удобной, но она брала меньше бензина.

8. Завтра у меня будет меньше времени, чем сегодня. Завтра мы играем в баскетбол после занятий, а вечером я буду смотреть детектив по телевизору.

Unit 3

GRAMMAR

9. Степени сравнения наречий.

9.1. Степени сравнения имеют наречия, показывающие как, каким образом совершается действие.

Number 15's running very fast.

Number 18's running a little **faster** than Number 15.

Number 21's running a lot **faster** than all the other runners.
He's running **fastest** (of all).

9.2. Способ образования степеней сравнения наречий сходен со способом образования степеней сравнения прилагательных. Короткие наречия, совпадающие по форме с прилагательными, образуют степени сравнения при помощи суффиксов -er и -est:

hard	harder	hardest
high	higher	highest
early	earlier	earliest
fast	faster	fastest
late	later	latest

Dad gets up earlier than me, and Mum gets up earliest (of us all). (=Mum gets up earlier than all of us).

Более длинные наречия, оканчивающиеся на -ly образуют степени сравнения при помощи слов more и most.

lazily	more lazily	most lazily
carefully	more carefully	most carefully

1. Please say it more slowly!
2. I drive more carefully in the rush hour.

ПРИМЕЧАНИЯ:

1. В разговорном английском языке вместо формы more loudly *громче* обычно употребляется форма louder. Наряду с формой more quickly *быстрее* употребляется форма quicker.

1. Please say it **louder**.
2. Jane types **more quickly (quicker)** than Ruth.

2. В сочетаниях типа most successfully, most beautifully и т.п. слово most чаще всего имеет значение "весьма", "очень".

They use new ideas most successfully.   Они весьма успешно используют новые идеи.

9.3. Некоторые наречия образуют степени сравнения нестандартно:

well	better	best
badly	worse	worst

much	more	most
little	less	least

1. I work better after a holiday.	Я работаю лучше после отпуска.
2. Bill did worst in the last match.	Билл хуже всего выступил в последнем матче.
3. Most students usually work hardest before the exams.	Большинство студентов обычно усерднее всего занимаются перед экзаменами

9.4. После глагола like понятие "больше всего" чаще передается словом best, чем словом most.

1. He's good at many games, but he likes tennis **best**.	Он хорошо играет во многие игры, но больше всего ему нравится теннис.
2. I like this idea **best** (best of all).	Эта идея мне нравится больше всего.

9.5. Русскому обороту типа: "чем скорее, тем лучше" соответствует английский оборот типа "the sooner the better", в котором слово the, совпадающее по форме с определенным артиклем, является наречием степени:

1. The longer I look at this picture the more I like it.	Чем дольше я смотрю на эту картину, тем больше она мне нравится.
2. "When shall I come?"	Когда мне приехать?
"The sooner the better."	Чем скорее, тем лучше.

9.6. Если в сравнительной конструкции с наречием после союза than стоит личное местоимение, оно в разговорном стиле может употребляться в косвенном падеже без последующего глагола (ср.п.7.14, стр. 48).

Разговорный стиль	Нейтральный стиль
1. They arrived earlier than **us**.	1. They arrived earlier than **we did**.
2. She speaks English better than **him**.	2. She speaks English better than **he does**.

EXERCISES

1

Прочитайте вслух и переведите.

a. 1. Could you walk faster? We may be late!
2. Could you come a bit earlier tomorrow?
3. Let me explain it all a little later.
4. You must work harder if you want to make better progress in your English.

5. We're so sorry we couldn't give you a definite answer sooner.
6. Please speak louder! I can't hear you!
7. Could you do it more quickly?

b. 1. Could you speak more slowly, please?
2. Can't you write more neatly?
3. Please explain it more clearly!
4. Let me try to explain it more exactly.
5. The road's so bad today! You must drive more carefully!

c. 1. Jim works harder than Tom, but earns less.
2. Alice speaks French better than Nancy, but she writes worse.
3. You know it better than me (You know it better than I do).
4. They arrived earlier than us (They arrived earlier than we did).
5. I left the house later than them (I left the house later than they did).
6. The train left a little later than usual.
7. The team's doing better than usual today.
8. He sang worse than usual last night, didn't he?

e. 1. The sooner you come the better.
2. The longer we live the more we learn.
3. The less we eat the better we feel.

f. 1. Which of them worked hardest?
2. Which of the students is doing best?
3. Which of them's doing best of all?
4. "Which photo do you like best of all?" "I like that one best."

2

Перефразируйте, как показано в образце.

Дано: Could you give a more definite answer?

Требуется: Could you answer more definitely?

1. Women are more careful drivers than men.
2. John's a less careful driver than his wife.
3. Please try to give a more exact explanation.
4. His work's more successful now than before.
5. He gave a clearer explanation of the rule, didn't he?
6. I'm sure we can find an easier way of settling it all.

3

Прочитайте диалоги вслух и разыграйте их.

1

A. Good morning. The English Language Department.

B. Good morning. I'd like to know the exact time of tomorrow's exam.

A. So sorry, I can't hear you. Could you speak louder, please?

B. Can you hear me better now?

A. Yes, a bit better. Who's calling?

B. My name's Savelyev, a student from Moscow.

A. I'm sorry, I didn't quite catch the name. Could you say it more slowly, please?

B. Certainly. But I can hardly hear you now. Let me call back, Okay?

A. That's a good idea! Okay!

―――――――――――

department [dɪ'pɑːtmənt] *n c*   отдел, *зд.* кафедра

2

A. When do you feel better, in the morning or in the evening?

B. Well, I've never thought of that! Let me see ... In the afternoon. Yes, most definitely! I work much better in the afternoon than in the morning, I even try to leave the more important jobs for the afternoon. And you?

A. I work best in the morning. I like to begin working early, the earlier the better. I get tired more quickly in the afternoon than in the morning.

B. Do you go to bed late?

A. Oh, no! I have to go to bed not later than eleven o'clock so as not to feel sleepy the next morning.

4

Ответьте на вопросы.

1. Which of you did best at the last exam?
2. Which of you comes earliest of all?
3. Which of you comes later than all the others?
4. Which of you plays football (tennis, etc) better than the other students?
5. Who can dance best?
6. Which of you can sing best of all?
7. Who can play the guitar better than the others?
8. What kind of music (films, books) do you like best of all?

5

Переведите на английский язык.

1. — Пианист, который получил первую премию, играл лучше всех, на правда ли? – Мне больше понравился пианист, который получил вторую премию, но большинство (людей) думают как вы (like you или as you do).
2. Вы можете решить эту проблему более успешно, если (вы) обсудите ее с конструкторами машины.
3. Пожалуйста, говорите немного медленнее, мне трудно вас понимать, когда вы говорите так быстро.
4. В следующий раз будьте осторожнее.
5. В следующий раз ведите машину осторожнее.
6. Говорите громче! Я вас не слышу!
7. Я пою гораздо хуже него, но играю на гитаре немного лучше, чем он.
9. Вы могли бы прийти завтра немного раньше, чем обычно.
10. Он пришел раньше всех, как всегда.
11. Чем больше я слушаю эту музыку, тем лучше я ее понимаю.
12. Чем дольше я работаю с ним, тем больше он мне нравится.

GRAMMAR

10. Сравнительные конструкции **as...as...; not so ... as...**

10.1. При сравнении двух предметов (или лиц), или двух действий, обладающих одинаковой степенью качества,

употребляется конструкция с двойным союзом **as...as.
..** *так же как, такой же как ...* и прилагательным
или наречием в положительной степени:

1. It's as warm today as it was yesterday.	Сегодня так же тепло, как вчера.
2. He isn't as old as he looks.	Ему не столько лет, на сколько он выглядит.
3. Is ten o'clock as convenient for you as eleven?	Десять часов так же удобно вам, как одиннадцать?
4. He was running as quickly as he could.	Он бежал так быстро, как мог.

10.2. В отрицательных предложениях наряду с союзом **as.
..as** употребляется союз **so...as...** .

1. The traffic here isn't so heavy as in the city centre. (= The traffic here isn't as heavy as in the city centre).	Здесь движение не такое сильное, как в центре.
2. I can't come as early as all the others, I'm afraid. (=I can't come so early as all the others, I'm afraid).	Боюсь, что я не могу прийти так рано, как все остальные.

Запомните:

As far as I know ...	Насколько я знаю ... (насколько мне известно...)
As far as I remember...	Насколько я помню...

ПРИМЕЧАНИЕ: В английском языке широко употребляются
устойчивые сравнения при помощи союза **as...as**, в которых
после второго **as** стоит существительное:

as white as snow	белый как снег
as busy as a bee	занятый (трудолюбивый) как пчела
as black as coal	черный как уголь

Таких устойчивых сравнений очень много. Они являются принадлежностью разговорного языка и составляют его фольклорное богатство.

10.3. С конструкцией **as...as** могут употребляться слова **twice** *вдвое*, **three times** *втрое*, **four times** *вчетверо* и т.д.

1. Petrol's twice as expensive now as it was a few years ago.	Бензин теперь вдвое дороже, чем несколько лет назад.
2. Your garden's three times as large as ours, isn't it?	Ваш сад раза в три больше нашего, не правда ли?

10.4. Понятие *во столько-то раз больше по количеству* выражается сочетанием **as...as** со словами **many** и **much.**

1. This year there are twice as many exhibits as there were last year.	В этом году экспонатов вдвое больше, чем в прошлом.
2. You may have to spend three times as much time if you go by train.	Вам, возможно, придется потратить втрое больше времени, если поедете поездом.
3. He must read five times as much if he wants to make progress.	Ему надо читать в пять раз больше, если он хочет делать успехи.

EXERCISES

1

Прочитайте вслух и переведите.

1. This room's as large as that one, but it isn't so light.
2. His German's as good as his French.
3. The problem isn't as simple as we thought.
4. Please send us an answer as soon as you can.
5. Is the new model as reliable as the old one?
6. Is the screen version as successful as the book?
7. The problems we are going to discuss today are as important as the ones we've already solved.
8. This model looks as elegant as the one we've just seen, but it isn't so easy to operate, I'm afraid.

9. I'm sure the new method's ten times as economical as the old one.
10. I'm trying to finish this work as quickly as I can.

2

Составьте предложения, как показано в образце.

Дано: this design, that one, up–to–date
Требуется:

a. This design's as up–to–date as that one.

b. That design isn't as up–to–date as this one.

c. Is this design as up–to–date as that one?

1. his early films, his recent ones, successful
2. the novel, its screen version, interesting
3. Room Five, Room Six, convenient
4. a winter holiday, a summer holiday, healthy
5. classical music, modern music, difficult to understand
6. This make, that one, reliable
7. This company, that one, reliable.

3

Перефразируйте, как показано в образцах.

Дано: The new model's less expensive than the old one.
Требуется: The new model isn't as expensive as the old one (the new model isn't so expensive as the old one).

1. The traffic in the afternoon's often heavier than in the morning
2. The conference last spring was less successful than this one.
3. The old models were less convenient to operate than the recent ones.
4. The picture on this screen's worse than on that one.
5. The first singer's voice was less pleasant than this one's, wasn't it?

Дано: I play tennis worse than John (worse than he does).
Требуется: I don't play tennis as well as John (as well as he does).

1. I read less than he does.
2. He smokes more than I do.

3. I feel less tired today than yesterday.
4. He knows the subject better than I do.
5. The other students work harder than you do
6. His sister can play the piano better than him.

GRAMMAR

11. Оборот **used to**

11.1. Оборот **used to** [´juːst tə] + основная форма глагола (used to smoke, used to live) употребляется для обозначения действий, которые когда-то в прошлом совершались регулярно, часто, но в настоящем уже не совершаются.

— 86 —

1. I **used to go** to the stadium often, but now I haven't got enough time, I'm afraid.	Раньше я часто ходил на стадион, но сейчас у меня, к сожалению, слишком мало времени.
2. – Do you play tennis? – Not now, but I **used to.**	– Вы играете в теннис? – Сейчас нет, но когда-то играл.

11.2. Оборот **used to** употребляется также для обозначения состояний или фактов, которые имели место в прошлом, но более не существуют.

1. She **used to be** very beautiful when she was young.	Она была очень красива в молодости.
2. He **used to be** an army officer.	Когда-то он был военным.

ПРИМЕЧАНИЯ:

1. В силу своего значения этот оборот употребляется только в о д н о й временной форме - простом прошедшем времени.

2. Вопросительная и отрицательная формы употребляются реже, чем утвердительная.

Did he use to be an athlete?	Он раньше был спортсменом?
We didn't use to stay at home as often as now.	Мы не сидели раньше дома так часто как сейчас.

3. Как видно из примеров, в русском языке соответствующей грамматической формы нет, поэтому в переводе значение оборота **used to** передается лексическими средствами — словами *раньше*, *прежде*, *когда-то*, *в прошлом* и т.п.

EXERCISES

Прочитайте вслух и переведите.

1. We used to live in a village when we were little children.
2. Old John used to be a seaman.
3. "Ben used to be a good athlete." "Oh, did he?"
4. We don't go out as often as we used to, I'm afraid.
5. I can't speak German as well as I used to, I'm afraid.
6. Tom hasn't given up smoking, but he doesn't smoke as much as he used to.

Закончите предложения, как показано в образце.

Дано: John doesn't play tennis now, but he...
Требуется: John doesn't play tennis now, but he used to (...but
he used to be very good at tennis when
he was young).

1. Peter's too old to go skiing now, but he...
2. John's given up smoking, but he...
3. Mary's very fat now, but she...
4. Sally doesn't go out to work, but she...
5. Roy's a rich man now, but he...
6. I'm too old to dance, but I...

Дано: We don't go out as often...
Требуется: We don't go out as aften as we used to.

1. We don't give parties as often...
2. I don't smoke as much...
3. He doesn't work as hard...
4. I don't drive as carelessly as...

3

Придумайте собственные рассказы об этих людях.

I'm not so slim as I used to be!

— 88

They can't play tennis as well as they used to, but they still play well enough to enjoy an occasional game.

Granddad says that long ago people used to live without the telly. Isn't that funny!

This man used to be a heavy smoker. He gave up smoking when his doctor told him he was going to get ill **because of** that.

---

because of   из-за

TOPICS FOR DISCUSSION AND NEW WORDS

Television in Modern Life.

How do people usually answer to questions like "What are you going to do tonight?" or "What are you doing at the weekend?" In other words, how do people spend their free time?

Some twenty or thirty years ago the usual answers used to be:"We're going to the theatre (or the cinema)" or "We're going to a party" or "We're having some friends round". Now you very often hear: "We're going to stay at home and watch the telly."

A **first–rate** colour TV set has become an **ordinary** thing in the **household** today, and a video cassette recorder is quickly becoming one.

Modern television **offers** the **viewers** several programmes on different channels. **In addition** to **regular newscasts** you can see plays and films, operas and ballets, and watch all kinds of **contests**, **quizzes**, and **sporting events**. You can also get a lot of useful information on the **educational** channel. A good serial (perhaps, a detective story or a screen version of a classical novel) can keep the **whole** family in front of the telly for days, and don't we spend hours and hours watching our **favourite** football or hockey team in an important international event?

Television most definitely plays a very important part in people's lives. But is this a good thing or a bad one? Haven't we become lazier because of television? Don't we go out less often than we used to? Don't we read less?

Here's a discussion on the subject

Interviewer: How much time do you usually spend watching TV?

A. Me? Well, I've never thought of that, actually. Let me see ... The news... perhaps a film ... some pop music. Well, not less than three hours a day, I **suppose**.

Interviewer: And you?

B. As little as I can!

Interviewer: Why? Don't you like watching the telly at all?

B. Like it? I **hate** it! It's the silliest thing you can spend your time on! And the programmes are getting worse and worse! My **own opinion** is that ...

A. Excuse me for **interrupting** you, but how do you know the programmes are as bad as all that if you hardly ever watch them?

B. I'm not saying I don't watch the telly at all. I only mean there are a lot of far better things you can do than **waste** your time sitting in front of the box.

Interviewer: Do all of you agree that the programmes have become worse than they used to be?

C. No, **not really** ... Some have become better, actually, but it's **true** there are some that **leave a lot to be desired.**

A. And **yet** I think the telly's made life more interesting. We can see such a lot **thanks to** it, and it holds the family together, by the way!

Intervitwer: Are you sure?

A. **Absolutely!**

Interviewer: Do you also think so?

C. Well, yes and no ... **On the one hand** television can keep the whole family at home, but **on the other** it may **lead to** a family **quarrel**.

B. I quite agree with you! I couldn't agree more! And how do you like it when little **kids** stay up as long as the **adults** to watch things that aren't good for children at all!

A. I just don't **allow** my kids to watch any programme they like – **except for** special children's programmes, of course ... I

mean films, **cartoons**, that sort of thing, you know ...

B. And when you're away from home? Then it's a problem, isn't it?

A. Yes, that's so, I'm afraid, but what do you **suggest**? I can't give up my job because of that, can I?

B. What do I suggest? I suggest that you should sell your telly before it's too late!

A. Sell my telly? Never!

C. That's another problem. I suggest discussing it some other time.

Interviewer: Excuse me, which problem do you mean?

C. Children and television.

Interviewer: I see! Tnat's a good **suggestion**, isn't it?

B. And a very important one! People who make up TV programmes sometimes forget there are children in the viewers' families, eh?

Interviewer: That isn't the only thing the TV people have to think of when they make up pro- grammes, I'm afraid.

A. They've got to think of a lot of things, and the result isn't always successful, but in my opinion, they're doing a **wonderful** job **on the whole**, and television **does** us all **a lot of good**.

B. And a lot of **harm**, too!

Interviewer: Well, our time's up, I'm afraid. We've had a very useful discussion. Thanks for **joining** us!

Learn these words:

first–rate	*adj*	первоклассный

Syn. **first class**

ordinary [´ɔːdənrɪ]	*adj*	обычный, обыкновенный

an ordinary day's work

household [´haushəuld]	*n*	дом, хозяйство
offer [´ɔfə]	*v*	1. предлагать (кому–л. что–л.)

to offer sb (one's) help, money, a job, etc.

She offered us a cup of tea.

2. вызваться выполнить дей- ствие, предложить свои услу- ги в выполнении действия

He offered **to do** the job.
Он вызвался сделать эту работу.

He offered **to get** us tickets.
Он предложил достать нам билеты.

offer *n c*

предложение чего–л. конк- ретного (помощи, денег, то- вара и т.д.)

We thank you for your kind offer (of help).

suggest [sə'dʒest] *v*   предлагать (советовать, вы-
                                 двигать предложение, идею)

I suggest that you   Я предлагаю вам обсу-
(should [ʃud])   дить это немедленно
discuss it at once.   (исполнитель действия
(I suggest you   назван – you),
discuss it at once)
He suggests   Он предлагает обсудить
discussing it at   это немедленно (испол-
once.   нитель действия не на-
                                зван).

suggestion [sə'dʒetʃən] *n c*   предложение (идеи, дейст-
                                     вия)

to make a suggestion   внести предложение
What's your suggestion?
Have you got any (other) suggestions (to make)?

viewer (televiewer) ['vjuːə] *n c*   телезритель

audience ['ɔːdɪəns]   зрители (в театре, на концер-
                                 те), аудитория (на лекции)

in addition (to)   кроме, помимо, сверх того

Syn. **besides** [bɪ'saɪdz]

She does a lot of other work in addition to her lectures (=besides
her lectures).

regular ['regjulə] *adj*   регулярный, постоянный

regularly *adv*   регулярно, постоянно

newscast ['njuːzkɑːst] *n c*   радио или телепрограмма
                                    новостей

Syn. **news programme**

newscaster *n c*   диктор, читающий новости

Syn. **announcer** [ə'naunsə]   диктор

commentator ['kɔmənteɪtə]   комментатор

contest ['kɔntəst] *n c*   состязание, соревнование,
                                 конкурс

a musical contest, a beauty contest

quiz [kwɪz] *n c*   викторина

education [ˌedjuˈkeɪʃn] n   образование

    She has had a good education.

    a higher education   высшее образование

educational [ˌedjuˈkeɪʃənl] adj   учебный, образовательный

whole adj   весь, целый (употр. с исчисл. сущ)

    the whole world (=all the world)

    the whole day (=all the day, all day, all day long)

    We were busy the whole day (=all the day, all day long).

on the whole   в целом

    On the whole, I liked the programme.

    It was quite good, on the whole.

favourite [ˈfeɪvərɪt] adj   любимый, излюбленный

    my favourite game (book, writer, actor, announcer, commentator, etc)

part n c   зд. роль

suppose [səˈpəuz] v   зд. полагать

Syn. **think**

    I suppose he's right (He's right, I suppose).

hate   v   1. ненавидеть

Ant. **love**

    Why does he hate his mother–in–law?

    I hate getting up early.

    2. очень не хотеть что–л. делать (при выражении извинения)

    I hate to ask you to come again, but I have to.   Мне очень неловко просить вас прийти снова, но я вынужден это сделать.

own [əun]   adj   собственный

    I saw it with my own eyes.

opinion [əˈpɪnjən] n c   мнение

What's your opinion **of** the new project? (=What do you think of . ..)	Каково ваше мнение о новом проекте?
in my opinion	по моему мнению (по—моему)

In my opinion they're wrong.

My opinion is that he wasn't quite right.

interrupt [ˌintəˈrʌpt] *v* — прерывать

Excuse me for interrupting you, but ...	Извините, что я вас пре—рываю, но...

waste *v* — напрасно тратить что—л.

Let's not waste our time on this useless discussion!

I've wasted a lot of money on that old car!

waste *n* — 1. напрасная трата

It's a waste of time!

2. отходы, отбросы

industrial waste	промышленные отходы

agree [əˈgriː] *v* — соглашаться

a) to agree **with** a person or his opinion, point of view, etc.	согласиться с кем—л. (его мнением, точкой зрения и т.п.)

I quite agree with you, (your point of view, etc)

b) to agree **to** a price (a plan, etc.)	Согласиться на что—л. (цену, план и т.п.)

We can't agree to the prices because they are too high.

c) to agree about (on) a date (a place, etc.)	согласиться, договорить—ся о дате, месте и т.п.

Let's agree about the date and place of our meeting.

d) to agree to do sth.	согласиться, договорить—ся что—л. делать

They agreed to start work at once.

really [ˈrɪəlɪ] *adj* — действительно, на (в) самом деле

Really?	Да ну?

Not really   Не совсем, не особенно

"Are you hungry?" "No, not really."

true [truː] *adj*   правдивый, истинный, верный

a true story, a true friend

Is it true (that) ...?   Правда ли, что ...?

It's true, he's not an expert, but ...   Он, правда, не эксперт, но ...

truth [truːθ] *n*   правда

to tell the truth   говорить правду

to tell a lie (to tell lies, to lie)   солгать

desire [dɪˈzaɪə] *v*   желать

The quality leaves much (a lot) to be desired.   Качество оставляет желать много лучшего.

yet *conj*   однако, и все же

The film may be silly, yet most people like it.

thanks to *prep*   благодаря

thanks to you (your help, etc)

absolutely [ˌæbsəˈluːtlɪ] *adv*   совершенно, абсолютно

That's 'absolutely wrong!

on the one hand ...   с одной стороны ...
on the other (hand) ...   с другой стороны ...

lead (led, led) [liːd, led] *v*   вести

All roads lead to Rome.   Все дороги ведут в Рим.

lead to   приводить к чему-л., вызывать что-л.

An ordinary cold can lead to a bad chill.

quarrel [ˈkwɔrəl] *n c*   ссора

They had a bad quarrel about it.

quarrel *v*   ссориться

Have you quarrelled?

— 95 —

I don't want to quarrel about (over) such a silly thing!	Я не хочу ссориться по такому глупому поводу!

kid *n c* — ребенок

Syn. **child**

adult [ˈædʌlt, əˈdʌlt] *adj nc* — взрослый

Syn. **grown–up** [ˌɡrəunˈʌp]

allow [əˈlau] *v* — разрешать, позволять

Syn. **let ... do**

The doctors don't allow him to smoke at all.

except [ɪkˈsept] *prep conj* — за исключением, кроме

Syn. **except for, but**

Ant. **besides, in addition to**

I liked all the stories except for the last one (= but the last one)

special [ˈspeʃl] *adj* — специальный

cartoon [kəˈtuːn] *n c* — зд. мультфильм

only *adj* — зд. единственный

That was **the** only picture I really liked at that exhibition.

He's **an** only child.	Он единственный ребенок.

result [rɪˈzʌlt] *n* — результат

What was the result of the experiment?

They worked hard, but without much result.

As a result we quarelled.	В результате мы поссорились.

wonderful [ˈwʌndəfl] *adj* — чудесный, удивительный, замечательный

The weather's just wonderful!

You've done a wonderful job!

do good — приносить пользу

A holiday at the seaside always does me a lot of good.

do harm — наносить вред, вредить

This medicine can't do you any harm.	Это лекарство не может вам повредить.
join *v*	присоединиться к
Let me join you in five minutes.	Разрешите мне присоединиться к вам через пять минут.
Thanks for joining us!	Спасибо, что вы к нам пришли.

EXERCISES

Прочитайте текст вслух. Предварительно отработайте произношение следующих слов и словосочетаний.

In other words	On the one hand	regular
worse and worse	on the other ...	favourite
educational	I suggest that you should sell it.	
absolutely	That's a good suggestion.	
	That's absolutely natural.	

Найдите в тексте английские эквиваленты.

такие вопросы как• иначе говоря• как люди проводят свободное время• к нам собираются прийти друзья• обычная вещь в доме• по образовательной программе•детектив• совершенно определенно играет важную роль• сколько времени вы проводите у телевизора?• я никогда об этом не задумывалась, собственно говоря• я лично думаю, что ...• извините, что я вас перебиваю, но...• почти никогда• нет, не совсем• некоторые стали даже лучше• оставляют желать много лучшего• сплачивают семью• дети не ложаться спать• всякое такое• я предлагаю вам продать телевизор пока не поздно• предлагаю обсудить это как-нибудь в другой раз• в целом они делают замечательную работу• наше время истекло.

3

Ответьте на вопросы.

1. Is it true that a first rate colour TV set has become an ordinary thing in nearly every household today?
2. What about a video cassette recorder?
3. Have you got a video cassette recorder? If not, would you like to have one? Why not?
4. Do you find that all the programmes television offers are interesting or at least (по крайней мере) useful?
5. Which programmes do you watch regularly? Why?
6. What's your opinion of the educational programmes?
7. Do you like to watch TV quizzes? Which of those programmes is your favourite? Why?
8. Can you say that television plays an important part in your life?
9. Do you go out less often because of television?
10. How many people took park in the interview? (see text)
11. What kind of people are they? (Give each of them a name, speak about their jobs, age, etc).
12. Do you think there are many people who hate watching TV as B. does?
13. Do you agree that watching television is one of the silliest things you can spend your time on? What's your own opinion?
14. Is watching the telly a waste of time?
15. Is it true that some of the programmes leave a lot to be desired?
16. Do you agree that television has made life more interesting?
17. Do you allow your children to watch all the programmes they like?
18. Watching the telly doesn't do you any harm, does it?
19. On the whole the programmes television offers are not bad, are they?
20. Which programme (newscaster, commentator) is your favourite?

4

Прочитайте и переведите примеры на новые слова.

1. My opinion is that the new design's definitely first-rate.
2. When he was rich, he used to travel first class and live in first-rate hotels.
3. In my opinion he's just an ordinary writer.
4. My opinion is he's no ordinary writer.

5. He used to be an ordinary country doctor.
6. "It isn't an ordinary household, is it?" "Yes, it is. It's quite ordinary".
7. He couldn't go to the theatre, and offered me the tickets.
8. They offer us the machine at the price of $1,000.
9. Can I offer you a cup of coffee?
10. They offer their services ['sɔːvisiz] (услуги) at a lower price than other firms.
11. He offered to find us a taxi.
12. He suggested going by taxi.
13. He suggested that we should go by taxi.
14. They offered to take us to the country in their car.
15. They suggested going to the country for the weekend.

16. They suggested that we have another look at the machine.
17. Thank you for your kind offer of help.
18. Thank you for all your suggestions. They can really help our team to make the next programme more interesting.
19. Are you going to offer any new models in addition to those we can see in the catalogue?
20. Would you like to make any other suggestions in addition to those we've just heard?
21. Bennett and Co. aren't the only firm we've received an offer from. There are several other reliable companies who've sent us offers besides them.
22. We can agree to all the suggestions but the last one.
23. He answered all the questions except the last one.
24. Except for one old lady, the bus was empty.
25. I can't agree with you there, I'm afraid.
26. Let's agree about the date of our next meeting.
27. They agreed to interrupt the discussion and make a short break.
28. Excuse me for interrupting you, but we're wasting our time, I'm afraid.
29. "Is it true that the medicine you're talking about has already done a lot of harm?"
    "No, not really!"
30. It's true his English still leaves a lot to be desired, yet (и все-таки) he's making progress.
31. Is it true you've quarrelled over such an unimportant thing?
32. It's true his suggestion may lead to some difficultly, yet in my opinion it's the only way to solve the problem.
33. Both adults and children like cartoons.
34. Moscow television offers special programmes for language learners in several languages.

5

Заполните пропуски предлогами: *on, in, for, of, to, with, except, except for, because of.*

1. ... their letter, they thanked their counterparts ... their kind offer ... help.
2. The commentator could speak English nearly as well as a real Englishman, and he could speak two more foreign languages ... English.
3. I liked the programme ... the whole. All the singers did well ... ... the last one.
4. They couldn't skate as well as usual... ... the bad weather.
5. She's had a good musical education ... addition ... special training ... dancing.
6. How many pianists are going to take part ... the contest?
7. It's true! I heard it ... my own ears.
8. What's your opinion ... the new project?
9. ... the opinion ... most televiewers, the announcers who take part in children's programmes are doing a wonderful job.
10. Excuse me ...interrupting you, but I've got a very important suggestion to make.
11. I've wasted so much money ... that old cottage!
12. I quite agree ... your opinion ... that job. It was just a waste ... time!
13. I'm so happy we have agreed ... all the important things.
14. We can agree ... your new prices, I suppose.
15. ... the one hand his suggestion isn't bad at all, but ... the other it may lead ... new discussions and even quarrels.

6

Повторите, употребляя подсказанные слова.

Дано: We can offer you **a new model**.
  •the latest models•

Требуется: We can offer you the latest models.

1. We can offer you **a new model**.

   a portable model• our latest design• our help• another explanation• the most up–to–date equipment• our services at a lower price than other firms

2. I suggest that you should **go with us**.

look through the catalogue• give your own opinion• listen to some other opinions• begin your story from the beginning• test the set more carefully• work at your English twice as much

3. I suggest **going there together.**

having a short break• discussing the results more carefully• going to the country for the weekend• taking part in the next conference• discussing the project again• listening to the expert's opinion

Подберите подходящие ответные реплики к высказываниям, данным в колонке слева. Продолжите мысль.

1. Mothers who go out to work don't have enough time to look after their children.	Well, no, not really …
	On the whole, yes.
	I couldn't agree more
2. Buying cheap low quality things is just a waste of money.	Yes, that's so, but what do you suggest?
3. It isn't easy to under— stand another person's point of view if it's different from yours.	Well, I suppose so ….
	Well, yes and no. On the one hand … on the other (hand) …
4. The earlier in life one starts earning his own money the better.	That isn't quite so I'm afraid.
	My own opinion is …
5. Helping children with their homework doesn't do them much good.	I quite agree with you.
	I think so, too, but …
6. People don't go to see each other as often as they used to.	Well, I'm not absolutely sure …
7. Most people have hobbies in addition to their jobs.	No, they don't, and it's absolutely natural, because …
8. A hobby makes life more interesting.	What makes you think so?

9. Most hobbies are very silly. They're just a waste of time.

 8

Заполните пропуски артиклями и обсудите текст.

"Three out of each four televiewers in Great Britain dislike ... programmes British television offers them daily so much that they are ready to give up watching the box." That was what ... popular British newspaper wrote after its reporters had interviewed ... large group of people to find out what public opinion was on ... subject. In ... opinion of many viewers most of ... programmes left ... lot to be desired. Not all ... adult viewers ... interviewers talked to liked television. Some even hated it, very often because of ... harm it was doing to ... children. ... interview showed that ... kid in ... ordinary British family watched ... telly about twenty – five hours ... week. Most parents can't control it, because they have to stay away from home most of ... time, so ... little televiewers can sit in front of ... box as long as they like and watch all ... programmes they like.

 9

Прочитайте диалоги и инсценируйте их.

1

A. Our time's nearly up, I'm afraid.

B. Are you sure?

A. Absolutely. We can only stay in this room till twelve.

B. Oh, is that so? I've left my watch at home. Can you tell me the time?

A. Certainly. It's five to twelve. There's only five minutes left.

B. Oh, dear! And we haven't done so much!

A. No, we haven't! Well, what do you suggest?

B. I suggest that we should meet again. What about next Thursday?

A. Splendid! Thursday morning, say, at ten o'clock. Okay?

B. Okay! Till Thursday, then, Buy!

2

A. Is it true that the less you eat the better you feel?

B. Well, yes and no. On the one hand good food is certainly good for health, but on the other, too much food makes people fat, and this may lead to some very unpleasant things.

A. I see! Heavy food does you more harm than good, doesn't it?

B. Quite right.

3

A. I suggest reading the documents again from beginning to end before we **sign** them.

B. A very good suggestion.

A. Let's not waste our time, then. Let me begin reading.

sign [saɪn] *v*	подписать

10

Прочитайте рассказы вслух и перескажите их.

1

A Football Fan

A man spent his whole Sunday in front of the TV set watching one football game after another. His wife, who did not want to quarrel with him, let him watch the telly till he **fell asleep** in his armchair. After doing all her housework she went to bed and slept till morning. When she got up, she saw that her husband was still asleep in his armchair. "He may be late to work!" she thought and went to wake him up. "Get up, dear," she said. "It's five to seven!" The man woke up at once and said: "Five to seven? And who's leading?"

a fan	болельщик
to fall asleep	заснуть

2

Clever Dogs

Two men were speaking about their dogs. "My Spot's the cleverest dog I've ever seen," one of them said. "He switches on the telly and watches it, and then switches it off!" "That isn't news to me," the other man said, "I've

known it for a long time, actually." "Really? And who told you?" "My Patch!" was the answer.

11

Согласны ли вы со следующими высказываниями? Обоснуйте свою точку зрения.

1. People give parties more often than they used to. A dinner party is quite an ordinary thing in modern life. People even go to see each other on weekdays.
2. One doesn't have to prepare much food for a party. It's quite enough just to have some friends for a cup of coffee and cake and a friendly talk.

3. Television is really a very bad thing. When people get home after work, they don't discuss the news of the day or go out for a walk. They sit down in front of the box and watch it until they go to bed. Isn't it the silliest way of spending one's evenings? Just a waste of time!
4. Television interests both men and women. Men are usually interested in serials, musicals and educational programmes, while women usually watch sporting events.

12

Переведите на английский язык.

1. — Можно предложить вам чашечку кофе? — Да, спасибо.
2. Фирма, о которой я вам только что рассказал, предлагает различные виды оборудования для легкой промышленности.
3. Он предлагает отвезти нас за город на своей машине.
4. Я предлагаю просмотреть все документы еще раз.
5. Я предлагаю вам делать эти упражнения регулярно, не от случая к случаю.
6. Что вы предлагаете обсудить, кроме тех результатов, о которых мы уже говорили?
7. Я предлагаю вам посмотреть все фильмы, кроме двух последних. Я их уже смотрел и должен сказать, что это была напрасная трата времени.
8. Мы согласны со всеми вашими предложениями, кроме (all . . . but) последнего.
9. — Какого вы мнения о последней выставке? — В целом она мне понравилась, но некоторые картины оставляют желать много лучшего. Жаль, что в ней не приняли участия некоторые мои любимые художники.

10. Извините, что я вас прерываю, но я должен попрощаться и уйти.
11. В целом мы совершенно согласны с вашей точкой зрения, но по нашему мнению, обычный специалист не может работать с этим оборудованием. Для этого нужно (You must have) специальное образование.
12. Я предлагаю сейчас же договориться о дате следующей встречи.
13. Правда ли, что качество некоторых машин, которые мы получили в прошлом году, оставляет желать много лучшего?
14. Это единственное мнение, с которым мы не можем согласиться.
15. Мы не можем на это согласиться, потому что это определенно приводит к напрасной потере времени. Наш метод (method) не так прост как ваш, но он не требует (take) столько времени и (or) денег.

Unit 4

GRAMMAR

12. <u>Будущее время группы **Simple**.</u>

12.1. Утвердительная форма. Образование утвердительной формы будущего времени группы Simple хорошо видно из следующей схемы:

I
We } will (shall) come

He
She
It
They } will come

Как вы увидели, в первом лице единственного и множественного числа наряду со вспомогательным глаголом will (слабая форма 'll [l]) употребляется также вспомогательный глагол **shall** (слабая форма [ʃl]).

Однако в современном языке есть тенденция употреблять во всех лицах вспомогательный глагол will, который в утвердительном предложении не имеет ударения и поэтому в речи нормального темпа обычно употребляется в своей слабой, редуцированной форме 'll:

1. I'll do it.	Я это сделаю.
2. He'll be happy to hear it.	Он будет счастлив услышать это.
3. She'll call you tomorrow.	Она позвонит вам завтра.
4. I hope it'll be interesting.	Надеюсь, это будет интересно.
5. I'm sure they'll support [sə'pɔːt] your idea.	Я уверен, что они поддержат вашу идею.
6. They'll be here tomorrow.	Они будут здесь завтра.

12.2. В отличие от оборота **be going,** будущее время группы Simple н е подчеркивает связи будущего действия с тем, что происходит в настоящий момент, а лишь н а з ы в а е т действия, которые произойдут в будущем. Из этого общего значения будущего времени группы Simple вытекают следующие частные случаи употребления:

a. Говорящий высказывается о будущем действии или состоянии как о е с т е с т в е н н о м х о д е с о-б ы т и й :

My elder son will be seven in June, and he'll go to school this autumn.	Моему старшему сыну исполнится в июне семь лет этой осенью он пойдет в школу.

б. Говорящий высказывает свое м н е н и е (пред-п о л о ж е н и е) о том, что действие или состояние будет (или не будет) иметь место в будущем.

1. **I think** we'll go to the seaside for our holiday.	**Я думаю,** мы поедем в отпуск к морю.
2. **I hope** you'll enjoy your holiday.	**Я надеюсь,** вы получите удовольствие от отпуска.
3. **I think** there'll be a lot of people there.	**Мне кажется,** там будет много народу.
4. **I don't think** there'll be many people there.	**Я думаю,** там **не** будет много народу.
5. **Perhaps** the weather'll get better.	Погода, **может быть,** улучшится.
6. He'll **probably** [ˈprɔbəblɪ] take part in the conference.	Он, **вероятно,** примет участие в конференции
7. **Perhaps** they'll be interested.	**Возможно,** они заинтересуются.
8. **I suppose** it'll be useful.	**Полагаю,** что это будет полезно.

12.3. Будущее время группы **Simple** употребляется также, когда говорящий высказывается о будущем действии с оттенком обещания или заверения:

1. We'll be on time.	Мы будем точно в назначенное время.

2. He'll call you back later.　Он перезвонит вам попозже.

12.4.　Будущее время группы **Simple** может выражать решение, принятое в момент разговора:

Just a second! I'll put it down.　Одну секунду! Я это запишу.

So you really think it's important? I'll go there at once, then.　Значит вы действительно считаете это важным? Тогда я сейчас же туда поеду.

Сравните:

Решение, принятое *в момент разговора*	Решение, принятое *заранее*, намерение, сложившееся *до разговора*: *запланированное* действие:
1. Wait here! I'll go and get a taxi.	I'm going to the theatre next Saturday.
2. I'm hungry. I'll go and have a snack.	I'm going to have some friends round at the weekend.
3. I quite forgot to make an important call. I'll do it now.	We're playing tennis on Sunday.

12.5.　Модальные глаголы **can** и **must** формы будущего времени н е имеют.

Понятия *смогу, сумею, буду в состоянии* передаются эквивалентом глагола can **be able to.**

I hope we'll **be able to** settle it all in the near future.　Надеюсь, мы сможем все это урегулировать в ближайшем будущем.

Понятия *придется, должен буду, буду вынужден* передаются эквивалентом глагола must **have to.**

Perhaps they'll **have to** discuss these proposals again.　Возможно, им придется обсудить эти предложения еще раз.

ПРИМЕЧАНИЕ: Хотя модальные глаголы **can** и **must** не имеют формы будущего времени, они способны относить

действие к будущему, если в предложении имеется соответ-
свующее обстоятельство времени *(tomorrow, next week, in five
days, etc)*. Обратите внимание на то, что аналогичным образом
употребляются русские слова *могу*, и *должен*.

1. They **can give** a press interview **any time you like**.	Они *могут дать* интервью для прессы *в любое подходящее для вас время*.
2. We **must agree** about the prices **not later than next week**.	Мы должны согласовать цены *не позднее следующей недели*.

EXERCISES

Прочитайте предложения вслух и представьте себе ситуации,
в которых их можно употребить.

1. I'll call you back in fifteen minutes.

2. I'm afraid I'll be late.

3. We'll be happy to see you in Moscow again, Mr Clark.

4. I'll probably see them one of these days.

5. I'm sure the work'll be successful.

6. I hope it'll be a success.

7. We'll try to find it out tomorrow.

8. There'll be a new serial on the first channel next week.

9. It'll only do you good, I'm absolutely sure of it.

10. They'll give us a definite answer soon, I suppose.

11. Just a second, I'll switch it off.

12. Just a moment, I'll turn down the radio.

13. You'll only press the button.

14. Wait a bit, I'll go and find out.

15. I'm afraid we'll have to agree to their prices.

16. We'll have to spend two more days on this job.

17. I'm sure they'll be able to operate the equipment.

2

Скажите, что по вашему мнению произойдет в будущем.

Дано: He's always late. (I'm afraid).
Требуется: I'm afraid he'll be late.

1. They're interested in our suggestions. (I hope).
2. You have made good progress in your English. (I'm sure).
3. This style's (стиль) in fashion. (I think).
4. They allow us to watch their experiments. (I hope).
5. He can make very successful films. (I hope, be able).
6. We always have to wait for him. (I'm afraid).
7. It's a waste of time (I'm afraid).
8. His flight's late. (I'm afraid).

— 110 —

3

Прочитайте диалоги, обращая внимание на различные способы выражения будущего действия.

1

A. I think today's discussion will be very interesting. Are you staying?
B. I don't know. Actually, I've finished work, so I'll have to wait for nearly an hour. Are you staying?
A. Yes, I am, and I'm even going to speak.
B. Oh, are you? Then I think I'll stay, too.

2

On the Phone.

A. Hello! Is that Mr. Johnson's office?
B. Quite right. What can I do for you?
A. Could I speak to Mr. Johnson, please?
B. No, I'm afraid not. Not for the next two hours. Any message?
A. No, I'll call back in two hours' time. I hope he'll be able to talk to me then.
B. Yes, I think so. Your name, please?
A. Hailey. Frank Hailey.

B.   Just a second, I'll put it down... I'll tell Mr Johnson you rang him.
A.   Thank you, bye!
B.   Bye!

Переведите на английский язык, используя будущее время группы Simple.

1. Я полагаю, у нас будет достаточно времени, чтобы выслушать все мнения.

2. Надеюсь, что вы согласитесь со мной.

3. Сегодня вечером будет интересная лекция по образовательной программе. Надеюсь, что я смогу добраться домой во—время, чтобы послушать.

4. Я, может быть, зайду к вам как—нибудь на следующей неделе.

5. Они, может быть, предложат нам какие—нибудь другие модели, кроме этой, но я не совсем уверен.

6. Они, может быть, предложат нам принять участие в дискуссии.

7. Одну минуту. Я приглушу радио.

8. Подождите минутку, я посмотрю (look up) его номер телефона в моей записной книжке.

10. Это лекарство принесет вам только пользу. Я уверен, вы скоро поправитесь.

11. Боюсь, что мы только зря потратим время.

12. Боюсь, что нам придется прекратить работу (stop working) из—за этого шума.

Переведите на английский язык, используя различные способы выражения будущего действия.

1. Мы собираемся закончить нашу работу в ближайшие дни.

2. Я выхожу из дома через десять минут.

3. Они собираются урегулировать это в ближайшем будущем.

4. Подождите немного. Я только позвоню и присоединюсь к вам.

5. Сколько времени вы пробудете в Москве?

6. Мы уверены, что наша новая модель будет очень надежна в работе.

7. Они приезжают завтра в три часа дня.

GRAMMAR

(continued)

12.6. Отрицательная форма будущего времени группы **Simple**.

Образование отрицательной формы будущего времени группы **Simple** видно из следующей схемы:

$$\left.\begin{array}{l}\text{I}\\\text{We}\end{array}\right\}\text{ will (shall) not come}\qquad\left.\begin{array}{l}\text{I}\\\text{We}\end{array}\right\}\left\{\begin{array}{l}\text{won't come}\\\text{shan't come}\end{array}\right.$$

[wəunt]
[ʃɑːnt]

$$\left.\begin{array}{l}\text{He}\\\text{She}\\\text{It}\\\text{They}\end{array}\right\}\text{ will not come}\qquad\left.\begin{array}{l}\text{He}\\\text{She}\\\text{It}\\\text{They}\end{array}\right\}\text{ won't come}$$

В современном английском языке есть тенденция употреблять для всех лиц форму **won't**, которая всегда произносится с ударением.

1. I won't come tomorrow. — Я завтра не приду.

2. We won't be late. — Мы не опоздаем.

3. It won't take you long. — Это не займет у вас много времени.

4. You won't have to wait long. — Вам не придется долго ждать.

5. He won't be able to come soon. — Он не сможет прийти скоро.

6. There won't be many people there. — Там не будет много народу.

ПРИМЕЧАНИЕ. Обратите внимание на перевод русских высказываний, начинающихся со слов *думаю, мне кажется,* после которых идет о т р и ц а т е л ь н о е предложение:

1. Я думаю, он **не** придет. — I don't think he'll come.

2. Мне кажется, что времени **не** будет. — I don't think there'll be time.

| 3. Он думает, что **не** сможет это сделать в срок. | He doesn't think he'll be able to do it in time. |

EXERCISES

1

Прочитайте предложения вслух и представьте себе ситуации, в которых их можно употребить.

1. I won't forget it.

2. He probably won't remember.

3. I won't keep you long.

4. Perhaps it won't take us long.

5. You won't have to waste any time.

6. It won't do him any harm, I'm sure.

7. He won't be able to take part in the contest, I'm afraid.

8. I don't think they'll be interested.

9. He doesn't think the machine will be reliable.

10. We'll never forget it.

11. There won't be any problems.

12. I don't think there'll be any difficulty.

2

Начните высказывания со слов *I don't think.*

Дано: There won't be many people there.
Требуется: I don't think there'll be many people there.

1. The weather won't get any better.
2. The film won't be a success.
3. It won't be an ordinary event.
4. There won't be any news soon.
5. He won't offer us any help.
6. We won't be able to give a definite answer soon.
7. You won't have to stay from beginning to end.

3

Сделайте высказывания отрицательными.

1. They'll stay there the whole week.
2. The opera'll be an ordinary one.
3. My favourite actors will play this time.
4. I'll watch it from beginning to end.
5. It'll take us very long.
6. They'll support this idea.
7. They'll agree to it.
8. They'll agree with your opinion.
9. It'll be a waste of time.
10. We'll have to interrupt our work.
11. They'll be able to operate this equipment without any special instructions.

— 114 —

4

Переведите на английский язык.

1. Я уверен, что обсуждение не займет много времени.
2. Боюсь, что он опять опоздает.
3. Боюсь, что этот фильм не будет иметь успеха у публики.
4. Я не думаю, что будет много вопросов.
5. Вероятно, он не сможет дать интервью на этой неделе.
6. Он надеется, что нам не придется ждать долго (to wait long).
7. Я не уверен, что найду мои любимые книги в такой маленькой библиотеке.
8. Я не уверен, что все вы согласитесь с моим мнением.
9. Я думаю, что они не смогут работать на этой машине без специальных инструкций.
10. Мне кажется, что одна сигарета в день не принесет мне никакого вреда.
11. Я думаю, вам не придется понапрасну тратить свое время.
12. Я вас долго не задержу. Нам не понадобится много времени на то, чтобы решить все наши проблемы.

GRAMMAR

(continued)

12.7. Вопросительная форма будущего времени группы Simple.

Образование вопросительной формы видно из следующей схемы:

Will I (you he, she, it, they) arrive in time?

В современном английском языке есть тенденция употреблять в вопросительной форме будущего времени группы Simple вспомогательный глагол **will** для в с е х лиц:

1. Will I (we) go with you?	Я (мы) поеду (поедем) с вами?
2. When will he (she) be back?	Когда он (она) вернется ?
3. Will they be in time?	Они будут во–время?
4. Will it be convenient for you?	Это будет удобно для Вас?

ПРИМЕЧАНИЕ. Как вам уже известно, вопрос в первом лице, начинающийся с **shall** в большинстве случаев является вопросом о р а с п о р я ж е н и и и лишь иногда, в зависимости от контекста может выражать просто будущее действие.

Сравните, обращая внимание на ответы собеседника.

1. "Shall I explain it again?"	— Объяснить это еше раз? (Вопрос о распоряжении)
"Yes, please!"	— Да, пожалуйста.
2. Shall I have enough time?"	— У меня будет достаточно времени? (Будущее действие)
"Yes, you **will**."	— Да.

12.8. Вопрос, начинающийся с **will** и обращенный ко второму лицу, может в зависимости от контекста выражать либо просто будущее действие, либо в е ж л и в у ю п р о с ь б у .

Сравните, обращая внимание на ответ собеседника:

1. "Will you be at home to-night?"	— Вы будете дома сегодня вечером? (Вопрос о будущем)
"Yes, I will."	— Да.

2. "Will you turn down the
sound, please?"
"Certainly."

— Уменьшите, пожалуйста,
звук! (Вежливая просьба).
— Пожалуйста!

В вежливых просьбах наряду с **will** употребляется **would**
[wud].

1. Would you (please) come back later?
2. Open the window, would you?

12.9. Вопросительная или вопросительно-отрицательная форма вопроса, обращенного ко второму лицу, часто имеет
оттенок приглашения.

Сравните, обращая внимание на ответ собеседника:　　　

1. "Will you (won't you)
have some tea?"
"Yes, thank you".
("With pleasure [´pleʒə]")

— Не попьёте ли чайку?

— Спасибо.
— (С удовольствием)

2. "Will you (won't you)
have a snack?"
"No, thanks, I'm not hungry
yet."

— Не перекусите?

— Нет, спасибо. Я еще не
проголодался.

12.10. Глагол **will** может употребляться после повелительных
предложений для образования своеобразного присоеди-
ненного вопроса, выражающего полу-просьбу, полу-
приказание. В таких высказываниях иногда
употребляется слово *just*:

1. Just press this button,
will you?

— Нажмите эту кнопку, хо-
рошо?

2. Please switch off the
light before you leave, will
you?

— Пожалуйста, потушите
свет перед уходом, хоро-
шо?

ПРИМЕЧАНИЕ. Как вам уже известно, глагол shall употребляется для образования своеобразного вопроса после
побудительных предложений, начинающихся с Let me и Let's:

1. Let me turn the sound
down, shall I?

Давайте я приглушу звук,
хорошо?

2. Let's have a break,
shall we?

Сделаем перерыв, хоро-
шо?

EXERCISES

1 📼

Прочитайте примеры вслух и представьте себе ситуации, в которых их можно употребить.

a. **1.** Will it be convenient for you to begin at nine?
2. Will you be back in Moscow by that time?
3. Will they be in time for the interview?
4. When shall we meet again?
5. Which of you'll be able to join us?
6. How long shall we have to wait?
7. Which of them will be able to take part in the discussion?
8. Why won't he be able to operate the machine alone?

b. **1.** Will you have a cup coffee?
2. Won't you sit down?
3. Will you have a cigarette?
4. Will you join us?
5. Will you join me for lunch?

c. **1.** Please, switch it on, will you?
2. Just turn it off, will you?
3. Please close the window, will you?

d. **1.** Let's discuss it some other time, shall we?
2. Let's work out more definite instructions, shall we?
3. Let's listen to the specialist's opinion, shall we?

2

Какие вопросы нужно задать чтобы получить эти ответы.

1. He'll be **fifty** next month.

2. It'll take us **two hours** to discuss all the proposals.

3. Mr Fennell will be in his office **the whole day** tomorrow.

4. He'll be back **in a month.**

5. There'll be **an English film** on the educational channel tonight.

6. You'll have to wait for **an hour and a half.**

7. I won't be able to come, **because I'll be busy all day.**

8. He won't be able to give us any news, **just because there isn't any.**

9. I won't be able to give you a definite answer tomorrow, **because it's too soon.**

Перефразируйте просьбы.

Дано: Please press this button!
Требуется: 1. Will you press this button, please?
2. Just press this button, will you?
3. Would you press this buttom?

1. Please switch to another channel!
2. Please turn off the radio!
3. Please turn on the light!
4. Please switch off the telly!
5. Please turn down the sound!
6. Please see to the tickets!
7. Please test it again!
8. Please begin from the beginning!
9. Please turn up the sound!
10. Please fetch me some juice!

Выучите диалоги наизусть и инсценируйте их.

1

A.   Good morning, Mr Bennett.
B.   Good morning, Mr Antonov. It's so nice to see you in London again. Won't you sit down?
A.   Thank you.
B.   Have a cigarette?
A.   No, thank you. I don't smoke.
B.   Oh, don't you? You used to smoke, didn't you?
A.   Yes, I used to be a heavy smoker, but I've given it up, and I'm very happy about it!
B.   Oh, good! I don't smoke either, actually. A cup of coffee, then?
A.   With pleasure!
B.   I'll tell Mary to bring us the coffee, and then we'll

get down to business, shall we?

A. Okay!

Learn this:

to get down to business   приступить к делу

2

On the phone

A. 575 09 79
B. Hello! Is that Bailey and Co.?
A. Yes, it is. Can I help you?
B. I'd like to speak to Mr Bailey.
A. Mr Bailey? I'm not sure he's in. Will you hold on a moment? I'll go and find out.

(A few seconds later)

A. Are you there?
B. Yes, I'm with you.
A. Mr Bailey is out at the moment. Will you leave a message?
B. No, I think I'll call back. When will Mr Bailey be in?
A. In the afternoon. Will it be convenient for you to ring then?
B. Yes, quite. Perhaps I'll even come round. Do you think he'll be able to receive me?
A. I think so. Who shall I say was calling?
B. Lawson.
A. Will you repeat the name, please?
B. Let me spell it. L–a–w–s–o–n, Lawson.
A. Yes, thank you, Mr Lawson, I'll tell him you called. Bye!
B. Bye!

Переведите на аглийский язык.

1. — Вы скоро вернетесь? — Да, через десять минут.
2. — Вы будете смотреть всю программу от начала до конца?
   — Нет, думаю, что нет. У меня не будет времени.
3. Что сегодня будет по первой программе?
4. Что будет по образовательной программе днем?

5. — Какие предложения мы обсудим в первую очередь?
— Самые важные, конечно.

6. — Вы сможете решить эти проблемы в ближайшем будущем?
— Боюсь, что нет.

7. Много ли новой информации будет в его докладе? Будет ли эта информация представлять интерес для нас?

8. — Вы пойдете с нами (join us) пообедать ? — С удовольствием.

9. — Вы выпьете чашечку кофе? — Да, спасибо.

10. — Вы не приглушите звук? — Пожалуйста!

11. — Позаботьтесь, пожалуйста, о билетах, хорошо? — Конечно, позабочусь.

12. Давайте переключим на другую программу, хорошо? — Да, давайте. Эта не интересная.

13. Пожалуйста, выключите телевизор, хорошо? Здесь слишком шумно.

14. Разрешите мне внести еще одно предложение, хорошо?

TOPICS FOR DISCUSSION AND NEW WORDS

1

Making an Appointment

Victor Pavlov is a representative of a Russian company which is interested in buying Japanese equipment. The company has done business with Japanese firms before.

Victor has just come to Tokyo. He wants to make an appointment with his Japanese counterpart. Victor is learning Japanese, but he is afraid it will be difficult for him to speak Japanese on the phone. He knows that his counterpart's secretary speaks **fluent** English, so the whole **conversation** is in English:

Pavlov: Good morning! Is that Mr Fukuda's office?

Secretary: Good morning. Yes. What can I do for you?

P.   Victor Pavlov from Moscow here. Can I speak to Mr Fukuda, please?

S.   I'm sorry, not just now. Mr Fukuda's in conference.

P.   Oh, is he? When will he be free?

S.   In an hour and a half, I think. Will you leave a message?

P. No, I'll call back later.

Two hours later Pavlov calls back and makes an appointment with Fukuda for eleven o'clock the next day. Next morning Pavlov and Fukuda meet at the **appointed** time for **talks**. Here's the end of the talks:

P. I think we'll order ten of these machines now, and we'll probably buy some more in the near future.

F. I'm sure you won't have any **trouble** with them. It's really a first class model.

P. Could I see the machine in operation while I'm here?

F. Certainly! We can arrange a visit to a factory where they have just **installed** some. You'll be able to ask the engineers any questions you like. When would you like to go?

P. The sooner the better. How long do you think it'll take you to make the **arrangements?**

F. It won't take me long. I'll just have to let them know and **fix** the time. Will the day after tomorrow be too late for you?

P. Oh, no! I'm only going home in five days, so it'll **suit** me **perfectly**. Shall I give you a call tomorrow?

F. Yes, please. I think I'll be able to give you a definite answer **towards** the end of the day, and the day after tomorrow I'll call for you at your hotel and take you to the factory.

P. Splendid! Thank you very much! I'll give you a ring tomorrow afternoon, then.

2

Calling Off an Appointment

Nelly Stepanova, an **interpreter** with our **Embassy** in London, has an appointment with the dentist, but she has caught a bad cold, so she won't be able to go. She has rung up the dentist's office and is speaking to the nurse.

Nurse: Hello! Dr.Robertson's office.

Nelly: Good morning. My name's Stepanova. I've got an appointment for three o'clock this afternoon, but I won't be able to keep it, I'm afraid.

Nurse: I'm sorry, I didn't quite catch your name. Will you spell it, please?

Nelly: S–t–e–p–a–n–o–v–a, Stepanova.

Nurse: Ah, Stepanova. Yes. Let me have a look at the book... Yes... Miss Stepanova, three o'clock. Shall I **cancel** it?

Nelly:	I'd like to **put** it **off** till next Thursday, if I may. Sorry to **give** you so much **trouble**, but I've fallen ill.
Nurse:	Shall I **put** you **down** for Thursday at the same time then?
Nelly:	Yes, I think I'll be all right by then. Thank you very much.
Nurse:	Not at all. Thursday at three, then.

Learn these words:

appointment [ə´pɔɪntmənt]   1.встреча, свидание

I have (I've got) an appointment **with** the manager **for** five p.m.	У меня встреча с директором на пять часов вечера.
to make an appointment	назначить встречу, договориться о встрече

I'll make an appointment with my dentist for tomorrow.

to keep an appointment	встретиться (как было назначено)
to cancel (call off) an appointment	отменить встречу
	2. назначение (на должность)

Mr Bennett has received a new appointment, hasn't he?

appoint [ə´pɔɪnt] *v*   назначить

They appointed him (as) their representative.
Let's appoint the day of our next meeting, shall we?

appointed *adj*   назначенный

at the appointed time (hour)	
on the appointed day	
at the appointed place	

fluent [fluənt] *adj*   беглый (о речи)

He speaks fluent French (=He speaks French fluently).	Он бегло говорит по-французски.
He's fluent in several foreign languarges.	Он бегло говорит на нескольких иностранных языках.

conversation [ˌkɔnvə´seɪʃn] *n*   разговор, беседа

We've had several conversations on the subject.

talks *n pl* переговоры

to have talks вести переговоры

The manager's having talks with the British businessmen just now.

trouble [trʌbl] *n u* беспокойство, неприятности

to have trouble with ... испытывать трудности, неудобство с чем—либо. (по поводу чего—либо).

I've never had any trouble with my old car.

to give sb trouble причинять кому—л. беспокойство

"I'm sorry to give you so much trouble." Простите, что я причиняю вам столько беспокойства.

"Not at all" Ничего.

("It's no trouble at all.") Меня это совсем не затруднит.

install [ɪnˈstɔːl] *v* устанавливать (о машинах, оборудовании и т.п.)

arrangement [əˈreɪndʒmənt] *n* 1. договоренность

to make arrangements (for) договориться о чем—л., устроить что—л.

The secretary'll make arrangements for your visit to the factory (=He'll arrange your visit).

2. расположение, аранжировка

I hope you'll all like the arrangement of the exhibits.

fix *v* 1. прикрепить, закрепить

Please help me (to) fix the shelf on the wall, will you?

2. назначить, устоновить

to fix the time (date, price, etc.)

at fixed prices по твердым ценам

suit [sjuːt] *v* подходить, быть подходящим, устраивать

Will tomorrow suit you?

The arrangement doesn't quite suit us, I'm afraid.

The hat doesn't suit me at all!	Шляпа мне совсем не идет!

perfect [´pə:fəkt] *adj* — совершенный, безупречный, безукоризненный

He speaks perfect English.
The weather was perfect.

perfectly *adv* — совершенно, совсем, абсолютно

Syn. quite, absolutely
I'm perfectly all right (happy, well, etc)

towards [tɔːdz] *prep* — 1. по направлению к ..., в направлении

They were driving towards (=to) the seaside.

2. *(о времени)* ближе к ...

I think they'll be back towards evening.

interpreter [ın´tə:prətə] *n* — переводчик (устный)

Syn. translator — переводчик (письм. и устн.)

embassy [´embəsı] *n c* — посольство

the French embassy **in** Great Britain

ambassador [æm´bæsədə] *n c* — посол

the British ambassador **to** the United States

put off *v* — отложить (во времени)

We'll have to put it off **till** next Friday, I'm afraid.	Боюсь, что нам придется отложить это до следующей пятницы.

put down *v* — записать

Syn. write down
Just a moment, I'll put it down in my notebook.

EXERCISES

Прочитайте текст вслух. Предварительно отработайте произношение следующих слов и словосочетаний.

[ɜː]	[ɔː]	[ə-æ]
interpreter	talks	Embassy
surgery	order	ambassador
perfectly	install	cancel

to make an appointment
to make an arrangement
it'll suit me perfectly

2

Найдите в текстах английские эквиваленты:

компания вела торговлю с японскими фирмами • он хочет назначить встречу • бегло говорит по-английски • весь разговор происходит по-английски • г-н Ф. сейчас на совещании • когда он освободится? • я перезвоню попозже • через полчаса • в назначенное время • у вас не будет с ними никаких неприятностей • я мог бы посмотреть машину в работе, пока я нахожусь здесь? • чем скорее, тем лучше • как вы думаете, сколько времени вам понадобится, чтобы договориться? • я уезжаю домой только через пять дней • это вполне меня устроит; к концу дня • она назначена к зубному врачу • я назначена на три часа дня сегодня • я не совсем разобрала вашу фамилию • извините, что причиняю столько беспокойства • записать вас на четверг?

3

Ответьте на вопросы.

1. What can you say about the business relations between Mr Pavlov's company and the Japanese firm?
2. How well does Pavlov know Japanese?
3. Why can't Pavlov speak to Mr Fukuda when he makes his first call?
4. Why does he want to see the machine in operation?
5. Do you think he'll ask the factory people any questions?
6. Do you think he'll be pleased with his visit to the factory?
7. When do you think he'll make his next order?

8. What does Nelly Stepanova do?

9. Do you think she's fluent in more than one foreign language?

10. Why won't she be able to keep her appointment with the dentist?

11. Why do you think the nurse can't catch Nelly's surname first time?

12. What arrangement does she make with the nurse?

4 🔲

Прочитайте вслух и переведите примеры на новые слова.

1. I'm afraid I'll have to miss a class tomorrow, because I've got an appointment with the dentist.

2. I hope I'll be able to make an appointment with Mr Clark for an earlier hour.

3. I won't be able to keep the appointment, I'm afraid.

4. I'll have to call off my appointment with the factory manager tomorrow.

5. Please don't cancel my appointment, just put it off till next Monday.

6. I've got so many appointments for next week, that I'm afraid I won't be able to keep some of them.

7. I hear you've got a new appointment . My congratulations!

8. Let me congratulate you on your appointment as manager!

9. Is it true they've appointed Mr Parker manager?

10. "Let's appoint the day of our next meeting." "Yes, let's fix it now while we're all here."

11. You're far more fluent in Russian than you used to be, Mr Parker.

12. He's as fluent in Spanish as in Italian.

13. I had several conversations with Mr Bennett.

14. There'll be an international conference on the problem next month.

15. Let's appoint the day for the talks.

16. They're having talks just now. Will you leave a message.?

17. We're having some trouble with the machine we've just installed.

18. I'm absolutely sure you won't have any trouble with this piece of equipment. It's one of our best models.

19. Their son's a great trouble to them all!

20. The trouble is I haven't got enough time!

21. I'm nearly sure we won't be able to finish the work in time. That's the whole trouble!

22. "I'm sorry to give you so much trouble, but I have to put off our appointment. I really do !" "That's perfectly all right. No trouble at all. We can meet towards the end of the week."

23. I'll make arrangements for one of our people to meet you at the airport.

24. I've made all the arrangements for my journey.

25. "Let's fix the date for our next meeting, shall we?" "Yes, let's. Does next Friday suit you?"

26. It suits me perfectly.

27. Does the time suit you?

28. Does this arrangement suit you all?

29. It's perfect quality, isn't it?

30. The results are perfect, aren't they!

31. He's just been appointed ambassador to Italy.

32. The Embassy is in one of the most beautiful streets in London.

Прочитайте диалоги вслух и разыграйте их.

1

Secretary: 756 6109. Mr Johnson's office. Good morning.

Petrov: Good morning. Can I speak to Mr Johnson, please?

S. Just a moment. I'll put you through.

Johnson: Johnson here.

P. Good morning, Mr Johnson. This is Petrov from Moscow. We bought some machines from you a few months ago.

J. Yes, I remember. What can I do for you, Mr Petrov?

P. You see, Mr Johnson, we're having some trouble with one of the machines, and I'd like to see you about it.

J. When would you like to come?

P. The sooner the better. Will tomorrow morning be too early?

J. No, it's quite all right. Will 10 o'clock in the morning suit you?

P. Yes, perfectly. Till tomorrow, then. Good–bye.

J. Good–bye.

2

Next morning

P. Good morning. I've got an appointment with Mr Johnson for 10 o'clock. My name's Petrov.

S. Just a moment, Mr Petrov. I'll tell Mr Johnson you're here. Won't you sit down and wait a little?

P. Thank you.

3

S. Here's Mr Petrov to see you. He's got an appointment for exactly ten. It's a quarter to ten. He's a bit early.

J. That's perfectly all right. Please ask him to come in, will you?

S. Right!

4

J. Good morning, Mr Petrov. Pleased to meet you.

P. Nice to meet you, too.

J. Won't you sit down?

P. Thank you.

J. Will you have a cigarette?

P. No, thanks, I don't smoke.

J. A cup of coffee, then?

P. With pleasure.

J. (*presses a button*)
Mary, will you bring us some coffee, please?

. . .

J. So what exactly is the trouble, Mr Petrov? We tested all the machines very carefully, and your inspectors were here during the tests, weren't they?

P. Yes, that's true, and the machines operated normally for a time after we installed them at our factory. But towards the end of the first month we began to find some very funny **defects** in the **products**. I've got a list of them here. Will you have a look, please?

J.   Certainly.
(*He goes through the list.*)
Yes, I quite agree with you. It's more than funny. You see, we've never had any trouble with this model. I'm afraid you'll have to go to the factory and discuss it there.

P.   Yes, actually I've thought of that, too. But I'm only staying here a week, and I wouldn't like to put off my visit to the end of my stay. The sooner I go the better.

J.   No problem, Mr Petrov. It won't take me long to make arrangements. You'll be able to visit the factory tomorrow. How about that?

P.   Suits me perfectly! And how do I get to the factory?

J.   Just leave your telephone number with Mary. I'll ring you tomorrow morning, and we'll go there together.

P.   It's very kind of you, Mr Johnson. I'm really sorry to give you so much trouble.

J.   No trouble at all, Mr Petrov. I'm interested, too. Any more questions to ask me?

P.   No, that's all, thanks.

J.   Till tomorrow, then. Bye!

P.   Bye!

Learn this:

defect [dɪˈfekt]   дефект

product [ˈprɒdʌkt]   зд. изделие, продукция

Подберите подходящие ответные реплики к высказываниям, данным в колонке слева.

1. A cup of coffee?   Suits me perfectly.

2. I'm afraid I'll have to call off my appointment for today.   It's no trouble at all!

3. I'm sorry to give you so much trouble.   When do you think he'll be free?

4. Mr Bennett's in conference just now.   Shall I put you down for another day?

5. I'm a bit early, I'm afraid.	No, thanks, I don't smoke.
6. We can go there right away. How about that?	With pleasure.
7. Is that the Embassy?	Oh, has he? Give him my congratulations.
8. Fred's just got a new appointment!	Well, yes and no ...
9. Are you pleased with your new appointment?	Yes let's. Wednesday suits me perfectly.
10. Let's make an appointment for 11 o'clock next Wednesday.	Quite right. What can I do for you?
11. A cigarette?	That's perfectly all right.

7

Заполните пропуски предлогами.

1. I've got an appointment ... Dr Floyd ... three o'clock ... the afternoon, but I won't be able to keep it, I'm afraid. Can I put it off ... next Friday ... the same time, if I may?
2. The conference began ... the appointed time.
3. Mary's extremely good ... foreign languages. She's fluent ... Spanish, Italian and even Japanese.
4. If Mr Carter's ... conference now, I'll call back later.
5. I hope you won't have any trouble ... the new car.
6. Please make arrangements ... Mr Fennell's visit ... the exhibition ... Friday morning, will you?
7. I can't say I like the new arrangement of things ... the room.
8. Please put ... the address ... the Embassy.
9. He's been ambassador ... several countries ... Europe and Asia.
10. Don't put off ... tomorrow what you can do today.

8

Заполните пропуски артиклями

1. I suggest that we make ... appointment with ... production manager for Tuesday, not for Monday. Does ... day suit you all?
2. "What time will ... talks begin?" "At exactly eleven. Didn't Miss Gray tell you ... time?"

3. I fully support ... idea of ... special conference on ... subject, but I don't think this is ... right time for it. I suggest that we put it off till some time towards ... end of ... year.
4. Her English is perfect, and she never has any trouble with ... most difficult translations.
5. In my opinion Alan's ... best sports commentator we've ever had on television. It's always ... pleasure to listen to him, and besides, he's fluent in several foreign languages, so he interviews most foreign athletes without ... interpreter.
6. In my opinion ... talks were just ... waste of time. They did more harm than good and nearly led to ... quarrel.
7. On ... whole ... exhibition is ... success, but ... arrangement of ... exhibits leaves much to be desired.
8. ... trouble with ... engine started right after we installed ... machine and began to operate it.

Допишите недостающие реплики и разыграйте диалоги.

1

Making an Appointment

(You want to make an appointment with Mr Jackson, the production manager of a company you are doing business with)

Secretary: 708 99 66. Mr Jackson's office. Good morning!
You: This is .... Could I ....
S. Mr Jackson's in conference just now, but I think he'll be free soon. Shall I take a message?
Y. I'd like .... It's important.
S. Will you call back later or leave your telephone number?
Y. ...

2

The Trouble with the Engine

(You have come to Mr Jackson's office to discuss your problem)

Jackson: Good morning, Mr .... Won't you sit down?
You: ....

J. Isn't it cold today! Won't you have a hot cup of coffee?

Y. ...

J. Well, let's get down to business then. So what exactly is your problem?

Y. ...installed ... a month ago. At first ... normally, then ... funny noise in the engine ... defects ....

J. I'm very sorry to hear that. It's a new model, but it's selling well, and we're using it at our own factories, too.

Y. Are you? Could I ... and speak ...

J. Good idea! I'll make all the arrangements for you visit at once. When would you like to go?

Y. The sooner .... Say, ...

J. Very good. I'll call for you at your hotel and we'll go to the factory together.

Y. ...

10

Переведите на английский:

1. Извините, что я причиняю вам столько беспокойства, но мне хотелось бы встретиться с вами еще раз и обсудить некоторые вопросы.

2. Я уверен, что у вас не будет никаких неприятностей с этой машиной. Это одна из наиболее надежных машин на мировом рынке. Кстати, она не намного дороже других машин такого типа.

3. Боюсь, что мне придется отложить нашу встречу в понедельник, потому что я буду очень занят. — Ничего. Когда вы сможете прийти? — В среду утром, если это устраивает вас. — Вполне меня устраивает. — Отлично! Чем раньше мы начнем, тем лучше. До среды!

4. Г–н Феннел все еще на совещании. Тогда я перезвоню к концу дня.

5. Разрешите поздравить вас с новым назначением, мы все уверены, что ваша работа будет успешной как всегда.

6. Анна говорит по–французски так же хорошо, как по– английски. Кроме того, она знает испанский и итальянский. Ей очень хорошо даются иностранные языки. Она никогда не испытывает затруднений даже в самых трудных переводах.

7. Боюсь, что я недостаточно хорошо говорю по-английски, чтобы провести (to have) переговоры без переводчика.

8. Вы были недостаточно внимательны, когда устанавливали машину. В этом-то и вся беда.

Unit 5

GRAMMAR

13. <u>Местоимения производные от **some, any, no, every**.</u>

13.1. Местоимения **some, any, no** имеют следующие производные:

something	somebody	someone
[´sʌmθɪŋ]	[´sʌmbədɪ]	[´sʌmwən]
что–то	кто–то	
что–нибудь	кто–нибудь	

anything	anybody	anyone
[´enɪθɪŋ]	[´enɪbədɪ]	[´enɪwʌn]
что–то	кто–нибудь	
что–нибудь	кто–либо	

nothing	nobody	no one
[´nʌθɪŋ]	[´nəubədɪ]	[´nəuwʌn]
ничто	никто	
ничего	никого	

Правила употребления этих производных местоимений аналогичны правилам употребления местоимений **some, any, no.**

13.2. Местоимения **somebody, someone, something** употребляются в у т в е р д и т е л ь н ы х предложениях, а **anybody, anyone, anything** в в о п р о с и т е л ь – н ы х **и** о т р и ц а т е л ь н ы х предложениях:

1. **Something** interrupted their conversation.

Что–то прервало их разго– вор.

2. Did **anyone** ring me this morning?

Кто–нибудь звонил мне ут– ром?

3. I **can't** hear **anything**.

Я ничего не слышу.

4. We **didn't** find **anybody** (anyone) there.

Мы никого там не застали.

5. I **can't** see **anything**.

Мне ничего не видно.

Если говорящий хочет п о д ч е р к н у т ь отсутствие того, о чем идет речь, он употребляет отрицательные местоимения **nobody**, **no one**, **nothing** после сказуемого в у т в е р д и т е л ь н о й форме:

1. We **found nobody** there (We didn't find anybody there).
2. I **can** see **nothing** (I can't see anything).

— 135 —

Перед сказуемым (т.е. в функции подлежащего) в значении *никто,ничто* употребляются только производные от no - **nobody**, **no one**, **nothing** а не от **any**:

Nobody (no one) rang you.

Никто вам не звонил.

No one agreed to help.

Никто не согласился помочь.

Nothing interrupted our work.

Ничто не прерывало нашей работы.

ПРИМЕЧАНИЯ:

1. В специальных вопросах, а также в общих вопросах, содержащих просьбу или предложение, могут употребляться местоимения производные от **some**, а не от **any**:

1. Why didn't you ask **somebody** to call the factory manager and cancel the appointment? (Why didn't you ask **anybody?**)

Почему вы не попросили *кого–нибудь* позвонить директору завода и отменить встречу? (Почему вы *никого* не попросили ...)

2. Can you arrange **something** so as not to put off our appointment?

Вы можете *что–нибудь* устроить, чтобы не откладывать нашей встречи?

2. В условных придаточных предложениях после союза **if** чаще употребляются производные от **any**, а не от **some**:

If **anybody** has any questions to ask me, I'm ready to answer.

Если у кого–нибудь есть ко мне вопросы, я готов ответить.

3. Местоимения **anything, anybody** могут употребляться утвердительных предложениях в значениях *что угодно, кто угодно, любой.*

1. **Anybody** can do it.	Это может сделать кто угодно (любой).
2. You can buy **anything** you like there.	Вы там можете купить все, что угодно (все, что захотите).

13.3. После местоимений - производных от **some, any, no** часто стоит прилагательное:

something more definite	что–нибудь более определенное	— 136 —
nothing special	ничего особенного	
anything interesting	что–нибудь интересное	
nothing urgent [´ɔːdʒənt]	ничего срочного	

13.4. Местоимение **every** образует в сочетании с **–one, –body, –thing** следующие производные:

everybody [´evrɪbɔdɪ]	⎫
	⎬ все
everyone [´evrɪwʌn]	⎭
everything [´evrɪθɪŋ]	всё

Местоимения **everybody, everyone, everything** могут быть в предложении дополнением, подлежащим и именной частью сказуемого:

1. I'll arrange everything.	Я все устрою.
2. Everything's all right.	Все в порядке.
3. Music's everything to him.	Музыка для него все.

13.5. В функции п о д л е ж а щ е г о **everybody, everyone, everything** (как и другие местоимения, оканчивающиеся на **–one, –body, –thing**) согласуются со сказуемым в е д и н с т в е н н о м числе:

1. Everybody (everyone) **knows** about it.	Все об этом знают.
2. Not everybody **knows** about it.	Не все об этом знают.

3. Everybody **was** busy. (*Cp*. They **were** all busy)	Все были заняты.(*Cp*. Они все были заняты)
4. Everything **was** ready for the talks.	Все было готово к переговорам.

13.6. **Some, any, no, every** образуют с - **where** следующие производные наречия:

somewhere [ˊsʌmwɛə]	где–то, где–нибудь, куда–то, куда–нибудь
anywhere [ˊenıwɛə]	где–нибудь, куда–нибудь
nowhere [ˊnɔuwɛə]	нигде, никуда
everywhere [ˊevrıwɛə]	везде, всюду

Все эти наречия являются в предложении обстоятельством места:

1. I've left my telephone book somewhere!	Я где–то оставил свою книжку с телефонами.
2. I can't find their new address anywhere.	Я нигде не могу найти их новый адрес.
3. They sell it everywhere.	Это продается везде.

13.7. После местоимений и наречий-производных от **some, any, no, every** может стоять слово **else:**

1. Please ask somebody (someone) else.	Спросите кого–нибудь еще.
2. I don't know anything else.	Я больше ничего не знаю.
3. Let's see something else.	Давайте посмотрим что-нибудь еще.
4. Perhaps we'll go somewhere else.	Возможно, мы поедем куда-нибудь еще.
5. Please tell everybody (everyone) else.	Пожалуйста сообщите всем остальным.

ПРИМЕЧАНИЕ:

1. Местоимения, оканчивающиеся на - **body** и - **one** могут употребляться в притяжательном падеже:

I've found **somebody's** keys on the floor.	Я нашел чьи–то ключи на полу.

2. В сочетаниях типа **somebody else** в притяжательном падеже стоит слово **else**:

That is everybody **else's** opinion.

Это мнение всех остальных.

13.7. После *местоимений-производных* от **some, any, no, every** н е может стоять предлог **of**. Перед предлогом **of** в значении *из* употребляются соответственно местоимения **some, one, any, none, each**:

1. I'm sure **some of them** will be interested in our offer.

Я уверен, *что кто-нибудь из них* заинтересуется нашим предложением (*некоторые из них заинтересуются ...*).

2. **One of us** will stay to help.

Кто-нибудь из нас останется помочь.

3. Does **any of them** speak fluent English?

Кто-нибудь из них говорит по-английски бегло?

4. **None of us** knows it for sure.

Никто из нас не знает этого наверняка.

5. **Each of them** wants to take part in the discussion.

Каждый из них хочет принять участие в обсуждении.

EXERCISES

Прочитайте вслух и переведите на русский язык:

1. Someone wants to see you, Mr Bennett.
2. Is there anything interesting on the telly tonight?
3. There's something very important in today's newspaper.
4. We'd like to see something more up-to-date.
5. I can't suggest anything else, I'm afraid.
6. Have you got anything else to ask me while I'm here?
7. We haven't discussed our new ideas with anyone except you yet.
8. Nobody has ever had any trouble with this equipment.
9. Nobody has anything against (против) your suggestions.
10. I have nothing against it.
11. I can't see anything important here. I see nothing special in it.
12. I see nothing new in this design.
13. I'm sure everybody will support your idea.
14. I'll discuss it with everybody else as soon as I can.

15. If anybody rings me while I'm out, tell them I'll be back by three o'clock this afternoon.
16. I think we've met somewhere before, haven't we?
17. I've already looked for my telephone book everywhere. I can't find it anywhere!
18. Is there anything urgent to–day?
19. "Is there anything interesting in the catalogue?" "No, nothing special."
20. If that's everybody's opinion, I'm happy.
21. It isn't my key, I'm afraid, it's somebody else's.

2

— 139 —

Сделайте высказывания отрицательными:

1. There's something interesting on the educational programme this evening.
2. I know something about it.
3. We can find somebody who knows the subject better than John.
4. Something interrupted their conversation.
5. Somebody called you this morning.
6. He quarrelled with somebody.
7. I can ask somebody else.
8. Somebody else can answer that question.

3

Заполните пропуски словами, оканчивающимися на – *body*, – *thing*, – *where*.

1. "I rang up the embassy this morning, but ... answered the call." "Oh, I think you **dialled** the wrong number, Mr. Fennell, there's always ... to answer the calls at the embassy."
2. I wouldn't like to give ... any trouble, but we'll have to put off our meeting, I'm afraid. I can't do ... about it.
3. Has ... got any other questions to ask me?
4. Where can I find ... interesting to read?
5. ... understands me as well as you do.
6. I can't help you today, so ask ... else.
7. ... was congratulating him on his success and he looked happy.
8. Is ... ready for the talks?
9. They sell that book ..., so you can buy it easily.

_____

dial   [daɪəl]   набирать (номер)

Перефразируйте, как показано в образце:

Дано: **Nobody** knows it. (... of us)
Требуется: None of us knows it.

1. **Somebody** will help you to adjust the machine (... of us).
2. **Everybody** will get instructions how to operate the equipment (... of you).
3. **Nobody** will support this idea, I'm afraid (... of them).
4. Did **anybody** call to make an appointment for tomorrow (... of our counterparts)?
5. **Nobody** has asked us to put off the meeting (... of them).
6. Has **anybody** got any other questions to ask me (... of you)?

7. **Everybody** will be able to take part in the discussion (... of us).
8. Will **anybody** make arrangements for our next visit, or shall I do it (... of the secretaries)?
9. **Somebody**'ll have to translate, I'm afraid (... of you).

— 140 —

TOPIC FOR DISCUSSION AND NEW WORDS

What do you Believe in?

TV reporter. Today we're going to have a talk about something that will be of interest to everybody, I'm sure.
We're in a students' hostel, and these three girls are **sharing** a little flat here. Let me **introduce** them to you:

Julie, Jane, Susan.

TV man: Now, which of you girls will be the first to speak?
Jane: Well, let me begin, if I may.

TV man: Certainly!

Jane: Some time ago we all, I mean the three of us, felt that there was somebody else living in this flat besides us.

TV man Has any of you actually seen that "somebody"?

Julie: No, never, but we've heard something very **strange** several times.

TV man: Could you be a bit more exact, please? What was it?

Julie: Some funny signals, some **tapping, to be more exact.** Somebody was trying to **contact** us.

TV man: Oh, was he? And what did you do about it?

Susan: What did we do? We tried to find out who it was, naturally.

TV man: Oh, did you? Any luck?

Susan: Well, nothing to speak of, I'm afraid. We looked everywhere very carefully, but didn't see anything.

TV man: And still you were sure there was someone around.

Julie: Exactly. Something funny **happened** every day. One morning when there was nobody else in the flat besides me, I found the books on my shelf in a **terrible mess**. I didn't have enough time to put them in **order** before I went to college, but when I got back home, everything was in perfect order.

Jane: Yes, that's true. None of us could under— stand anything.

By the way, I can tell you something else. Would you like to listen?

TV man: I'd love to. Do tell us your story!

Jane: The other day I couldn't find my new **slippers** anywhere. I put on my old ones and went to the bathroom. When I got back, my new slippers were in their usual place next to my bed.

TV Man: Well, well ... Aren't you afraid to keep on living in this flat?

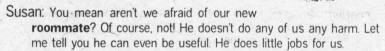

Susan: You mean aren't we afraid of our new **roommate**? Of course, not! He doesn't do any of us any harm. Let me tell you he can even be useful. He does little jobs for us.

TV man: Oh, does he? What kind of jobs?

Julie: Oh, all kinds of things. He lets us know when something's boiling in the kitchen and switches off the light and the telly when we forget to. You won't **believe** it, but he even makes us sandwiches sometimes.

TV man: Unbelievable! And still I think it was just somebody joking.

A voice. Do you?

Learn these words:

share *v*

We share everything with them.
He shares my opinion.
We shared a room in a hostel.

делить, разделять, пользоваться чем-л. совместно

Он разделяет мое мнение.
Мы жили в одной комна-
те в общежитии.

share *n*

доля, акция

introduce [ˌɪntrəˈdjuːs] *v*

зд. знакомить, представить
кому-л.

May I introduce Mr. Floyd **to** you?

strange *adj*

странный, незнакомый

tapping *n*

постукивание

to be more exact

точнее *(зд. вводная фраза)*

contact sb [kənˈtækt] *v*

связаться с кем-л.

Where can I contact the manager?

happen *v*

случаться, происходить

How did it happen?
It happened a long time ago …

What happened **to** him?

Как это случилось?
Это произошло много
лет назад.
Что с ним случилось?

terrible [ˈterɪbl] *adj*   ужасный, страшный

The weather's just terrible!

mess *n c*   *(разг.)* беспорядок

The room was **in** a terrible mess.

I must clear the mess in my flat.   *(разг.)* Я должен убрать
                                                              в квартире.

order *n*   зд. порядок

Ant. **disorder** [dɪsˈɔːdə]

All the files are in perfect order.

to put sth in order   привести что—л. в
                                                             порядок

Please put these papers in order, will you?

to be out of order   быть не в порядке

My car's out of order.

slippers *n pl*   комнатные туфли, тапочки

roommate *n c*   сосед (соседка) по комнате,
                                                              квартире

believe [bɪˈliːv] *v*   верить кому—л., чему—л.

Nobody believed him (his story)

to believe in sb (sth)   верить в кого—л.(что—л.)

He doesn't believe in anything!

Unbelievable! [ˌʌnbɪˈliːvəbl]   Невероятно! (воскл.)

EXERCISES.

Прочитайте вслух и переведите примеры на новые слова.

1. Everybody shares your opinion.
2. He shared everything with his roommates in the hostel.
3. We haven't got enough copies for everyone today, so you'll have to share.
4. Let me introduce you to your new colleagues.
5. Let me introduce you to each other.
6. Everything was strange to me at first.
7. I don't find anything strange here. Do you?

8. They were speaking in a strange language, and I couldn't understand anything.
9. None of them knew about it, most of them didn't, to be more exact.
10. I'll try to contact them all next week, towards the end of the week, to be more exact.
11. If you want to contact any of them, try to do so before lunch break.
12. "Has anything happened?" "Oh, nothing terrible!"
13. Can anyone help me to clear the mess?
14. Everything was in a terrible mess.
15. Everything is in perfect order.
16. There was a great disorder everywhere, nothing was in order!
17. How long will it take you to put everything in order?
18. None of us believed him.
19. Believe it or not, but it really happened.
20. I believe every word he says.
21. Not everybody believed that it was true.
22. Nobody believes in that method.
23. Everyone must pay his share.

2

Ответьте на вопросы по тексту. Обсудите интервью.

1. Do you believe all those things really happened?
2. Have you read anything of the kind in books or newspapers?
3. Do you think the TV man was right to arrange a televised interview?
4. Do you think many people were interested?
5. Do you believe somebody was really living in the flat besides the girls who shared it?

3

Переведите на английский язык.

1. Мне жаль, что я причиняю всем столько беспокойства, но нам придется снова отложить нашу встречу, потому что не все еще готово к обсуждению.
2. Правда, мы не сделали пока больших успехов, но мы кое-что сделали, и это лучше, чем ничего.
3. Боюсь, что Мисс Смит недостаточно бегло говорит по-русски, чтобы помочь нам на переговорах, я предлагаю попросить кого-нибудь еще.

4. В целом мне все очень нравится в этом каталоге, кроме некоторых моделей.

5. Пожалуйста, свяжитесь с ними по телефону и сообщите им о новой договоренности.

6. Возможно, не все разделяют мое мнение, но я абсолютно уверен в том, что мы можем поверить в эту идею, и она принесет нам большую пользу.

7. Разрешите мне представить вас друг другу. Это Алексей Петров – наш новый коллега. Я уже всем представил его, кроме вас.

8. Боюсь, никто из нас не читал книги, о которой вы говорите.

9. Мы никогда ни с кем этого не обсуждали, а вы?

10. Кто-нибудь из вас останется помочь с переводом?

11. Все еще верят в это.

12. Сначала никто из нас не поверил в эту идею.

13. Все в лаборатории было в идеальном порядке.

14. Нам не потребуется много времени, чтобы привести все в порядок.

15. Кто-нибудь из вас может связаться с управляющим сегодня?

16. Я не мог связаться с ними, потому что их телефон был поврежден.

17. Как это случилось?

18. Ничего страшного не произошло. Все будет в порядке очень скоро.

19. Я думаю, мы сможем связаться со всеми во-время, точнее не позднее следующей недели.

Unit 6

GRAMMAR

14. Глагольные безличные предложения; глаголы to rain, to snow

В английском языке существительным **rain** дождь и **snow** снег соответствуют глаголы **to rain** *дождить, идти* (о дожде) и **to snow** *снежить, идти* (о снеге). Подлежащим предложения с глаголами **to rain** и to **snow** может быть только безличное местоимение it, поэтому эти глаголы всегда стоят в третьем лице единственного числа.

1. It never **snows** here but it often **rains**. | Здесь никогда не бывает снега, но часто идут дожди.

2. Look! It's **raining**. | Посмотри, идет дождь.

3. It's **raining** hard. | Идет сильный дождь.

4. It's going **to rain** (it looks like rain.) | Собирается дождь (сейчас пойдет дождь).

5. I don't think it'**ll rain**. | Я думаю, дождя не будет.

EXERCISES

Прочитайте вслух и переведите.

1. It rains more and more often, it's getting colder and colder.
2. It doesn't often rain here at this time of year, it's usually dry and sunny.
3. " Does it ever snow in September?"
   "No, it never does, but it's often cold outside."
4. Everybody thinks it never snows in the summer, but it sometimes does, believe me!" " Oh, does it?"
5. " Isn't it going to rain?" "No, I don't think so".
6. It was snowing so hard when we left the house that we could hardly see the road.

7. "It looks like rain, doesn't it? " "Oh, yes, it does. It's going to rain any minute."

8. "It didn't snow much last winter, did it?" " Yes, it did, very much. We had a lot of snow last winter."

9. It's raining harder and harder, let's go back before it's too late, shall we? "

2

Прочитайте диалоги вслух и разыграйте их.

1

A. It's very cold outside today, isn't it?

B. Yes, but the **forecast** says it'll get warmer towards the weekend.

A. Let's **hope** for the best.

Learn these words:

forecast [´fɔːkɑːst] *n*   прогноз, предсказание,

weather forecast   прогноз погоды

economic [ˌekə´nɔmɪk] forecast   экономический прогноз

political [pə´lɪtɪkl] forecast   политический прогноз

2

A. What was the weather like in London when you were leaving?

B. Very **cloudy**, and it was raining all the time.

A. Oh, was it? I'm so happy it's **dry** and **sunny** here. They say it'll keep fine the whole week.

B. Let's hope for the best. But isn't it starting to rain ?

A. Oh, it's only a **shower**. It'll stop quite soon !

Learn these words :

cloudy [´klaudɪ] *adj*   облачный, пасмурый

cloud *n c*   облако

dry *adj*   сухой

sunny *adj*   солнечный

shower [ʃauə] *n*   зд. кратковременый дождь

Ant. **dry**   сухой

   to get wet   промокнуть

change [tʃeɪndʒ] *v*

                                    1. менять, изменять, переме-
                                      нить

   That has changed my plans.

                                      2. измениться, перемениться

   The situation has changed for the better.
   You haven't changed at all!

                                      3. разменять, поменять (о
                                      деньгах)

   Where can I change my money?

                                      4. пересесть (о транспорте)

   to change trains (buses, etc)
   to change from a train to a bus

icy *adj*   скользкий

dangerous [ˈdeɪndʒərəs] *adj*   опасный

   a dangerous situation
   a dangerous driver = a careless driver
   to drive dangerously = to drive carelessly

wheel [wiːl] *n c*   колесо, руль

   at the wheel   за рулем

speed *n u*   скорость

   speed limit [ˈlɪmɪt]   ограничение скорости
   to exceed [ɪkˈsiːd] the speed limit   превысить скорость

5

   Mr. Bennett has come to Moscow to discuss a contract. Pavel Antonov, his counterpart, is receiving him in his office. Before discussing some far more important things they talk about the weather:

Bennett The weather here's growing nearly as **changeable** as back home, isn't it?

3

A. What **nasty** weather we're having!

B. Yes, what an **awful** day! Just look out of the window, it's **pouring**!

A. Yes, and I've left my **umbrella** somewhere and can't remember where. How shall I get home in this **horrible** rain without an umbrella?

B. I'm terribly sorry I haven't got one to lend you, but I can **give you a lift home**, in you like.

A. Thanks awfully !

Learn these words :

nasty [´nɑ:stɪ] *adj*	отвратительный, мерзкий
awful [´ɔ:flɪ] *adj*	ужасный

Syn. **terrible,**
horrible [´hɔrɪbl]

awfully [´ɔ:flɪ] *adv*	ужасно, страшно (часто разг. усилит. наречие)

Syn. **terribly**

I'm awfully sorry (I'm terribly sorry).
It's awfully hot !

pour [pɔ:] *v*	зд. лить, литься (о дожде)
It's pouring!	Дождь льет как из ведра!
umbrella [ʌm´brɔlə] *n c*	зонт, зонтик
to give somebody a lift	подвезти кого–либо (на ма— шине, мотоцикле и т.п.)

4

A. What a nasty **wet** day! When will the weather change!

B. Turn on the telly. It's just the time for the **forecast!**

Weatherman: ... And now a few words about the weather tomorrow. The temperature will be a bit lower than today, so the roads may grow **icy** and **dangerous** to drive on. Please be careful at the **wheel**, don't forget the **speed limit!**

Learn these words:

wet *adj*	сырой, мокрый

Antonov: I couldn't agree more. We've never had such temperature **changes** before. And we used to have **frostier** winters, too.

B. This winter's very **mild**, isn't it?

A. Yes, it's extremely mild. There's hardly any snow in the country. I could only go skiing three times.

B. Isn't that a pity! Soon you'll start playing football in winter, like we do in England!

A. Not a bad idea! Why not have a game of football **for a change!**

Learn these words:

receive [rɪ´siːv] v — зд. принимать

changeable [´tʃeɪndʒəbl] adj — переменчивый, неустойчивый

change n c — перемена, изменение

   temperature changes — перепады температуры

   for a change — для разнообразия

frosty adj — морозный

frost n — мороз

mild [maɪld] adj — мягкий (зд. о погоде, климате)

like conj — как, подобно тому как

Прочитайте рассказ вслух и обсудите его.

The Weather
(after George Mikes [´dʒɔːdʒ ´mɪkɪʃ])

This is a very important topic in England. Perhaps, a long time ago, when you wanted to describe someone as unusually dull, you used to say: "He is the kind of person who always discusses the weather with you." Forget it. In England this is an extremely interesting topic and you must be good at discussing it.

EXAMPLES FOR CONVERSATION

   For Good Weather
    "Lovely day, isn't it?"
    "Yes, isn't it beautiful?"
    "The sun . . ."

"Isn't it marvellous?"

"Wonderful, isn't it?"

"It's so nice and hot ..."

"Personally, I think it's so nice when it's hot – isn't it?"

"I just love it – don't you?"

For Bad Weather

"Nasty day, isn't it?"

"Yes, isn't it awful?"

"The rain ... I hate rain ...!"

"I don't like it at all. Do you?"

"And in July! Rain in the morning, then a bit of sunshine, and then rain, rain, rain, all day long."

"I remember exactly the same kind of day in July 1936."

"Yes, I do, too."

"Or was it in 1928?"

"Yes, it was."

"Or in 1939?"

"Yes, that's right."

Now **note** the last few sentences of this conversation. There is a very important rule in it. You must never **contradict** anybody when discussing the weather. Even when it's **hailing** and snowing, and **hurricanes** are **uprooting** the trees from the side of the road, if anyone says to you: "Nice day, isn't it?" – answer at once: "Yes, isn't it lovely?"

Learn the conversations **above** by heart. If two are too difficult for you, learn **at least** one of them, and it will be useful for **any occasion**.

If you do not say anything **for the rest of your life,** just repeat this conversation, and people will still think you are a very clever man

with pleasant **manners.**

Learn these words:

topic [ˈtɔpɪk] *n c*   тема

It's an interesting topic of conversation.

describe [dɪ'skraɪb] *v*   1. дать описание, описать

Please describe the place **to** me more carefully.

                                              2. охарактеризовать, ото-
                                              зваться о чем—л. или ком—л.

The papers described his visit **as** useful.

sunshine *n u*   солнечный свет

There was a lot of sunshine on that day. (It was a very sunny day)

contradict [,kɔntrə'dɪkt] *v*   противоречить

      The two stories contradict   Эти два рассказа противо-
      each other.   речат друг другу.

hail *n v*   град, идти (о граде)

      It's hailing!

hurricane ['hʌrɪkən] *n c*   ураган

uproot [ʌp'ruːt]   вырвать с корнем

root *n*   корень

note   зд. обратите внимание на

above [ə'bʌv] *adv prep*   выше, свыше

      as stated above   как сказано свыше

      The temperature is ten degrees above zero ['zɪərəu]

Ant. **below** [bɪ'ləu]   ниже

at least   по крайней мере

occasion [ə'keɪʒn] *n c*   случай, событие

      for any occasion   на любой случай, для
                                              любого случая

      He wrote the music for the occasion.

rest *n*   остаток, остальная часть, ос-
                                             тальное

      the rest of the day (time, money, etc.)
      I left the rest at home.
      for the rest of your life   всю оставшуюся жизнь

manners *n pl*   манеры

5

Повторите, используя подсказанные слова.

Дано: It's so cloudy! • windy •
Требуется: It's so windy.

1. It's so **cloudy!**
   • frosty • sunny • dry and sunny • wet
2. What a **fine** day!
   • wonderful • sunny • windy • wet • awful • frosty •

— 153 —

3. I'm terribly sorry **I'm late!**
   • I can't come • have to go • haven't got enough time just now
   • can't give a definite answer •
4. The forecast says it's going to get **colder** soon.
   • warmer • much colder • a little warmer • colder towards the
   end of the week •
5. The papers described the visit as **useful**.
   • important • successful • ordinary • unsuccessful •
6. The commentator described the situation as **dangerous**.
   • horrible • terrible • changeable •

6

Подберите подходящие ответные реплики к высказываниям,
данным в колонке слева.

1. I'm terribly sorry to give
you so much trouble.

2. Will it rain tomorrow?   Thanks awfully!

3. I think the situation will   That's all right!
change for the better.

     No trouble at all!

4. I can give you a lift   Oh, no! I'm only doing 60
home.   miles.

5. I'm awfully sorry I couldn't let you know.

I hope so.

I hope not.

6. Aren't you exceeding the speed limit?

Well, yes and no ...

7. I've left my umbrella at home!

You can take mine.

8. Do you believe in political forecasts?

9. Will the weather change for the better?

7

Переведите на английский язык.

1. – Все еще идет дождь? – Да, но я надеюсь, он скоро пройдет.
2. – Вы думаете, похолодает? – Надеюсь, что нет. Я ненавижу холодную погоду!
3. – Вы слышали прогноз сегодня утром? – Да. Будет пасмурно, но дождя не будет.
4. – Продержится хорошая погода? – Надеюсь, что да.
5. – Я надеюсь, ситуация переменится к лучшему, по крайней мере, к концу месяца. – Ну что ж, будем надеяться на лучшее!
6. Если у тебя нет карты, опиши мне это место по крайней мере. Тогда мне будет легче его найти.
7. Газеты охарактеризовали недавние переговоры как очень полезные.
8. Он самый отчаянный водитель, которого я когда-либо видел.
9. Дорога скользкая, будьте осторожны за рулем, не превышайте скорости!
10. Я ужасно сожалею, что не мог подвезти вас вчера, моя машина была в неисправности.

Unit 7

GRAMMAR

15. <u>Особенности выражения будущего действия в</u> <u>придаточных предложениях времени и условия.</u>

15.1. В английских придаточных предложениях в р е м е - н и и у с л о в и я не только настоящее, но и будущее действие выражается н а с т о я щ и м временем:

1. We'll call you when we **get** to London.

Мы позвоним вам, когда **приедем** в Лондон.

2. He'll come to see us when he **isn't** so busy.

Он придет к нам в гости, когда не **будет** так занят.

3. We'll go to the country if the weather's fine.

Мы поедем за город, если **будет** хорошая погода.

4. If it **rains**, we'll stay in town.

Если пойдет дождь, мы **ос- танемся** в городе.

15.2. Помимо союза **when** *когда*, временные придаточные могут вводиться следующими союзами: **as soon as** *как только*, **after** *после того как*, **before** *перед тем как, прежде чем*, **while** *в то время как, пока*, **till (until)** *до тех пор пока не* . . . .

1. He'll give you a ring **as soon as** he **gets** home.

Он вам позвонит, как только **придет** домой.

2. I'll help you **after** I **finish** this translation.

Я вам помогу, после того как **закончу** этот перевод.

3. Look through all the documents very carefully **before** you **sign** them.

Просмотрите все докумен- ты очень внимательно, прежде чем вы их **подпи- шете.**

4. I'll go and make a call **while** you **are** busy.

Я пойду позвоню, пока вы **будете заняты.**

5. Go straight **till (until)** you **get** to the traffic lights.

Поезжайте прямо, пока не **доедете** до светофора.

ПРИМЕЧАНИЯ.

1. Союз **till** является более разговорным вариантом союза **until**. Обратите внимание на то, что эти союзы включают в себя отрицание (*ср. русский перевод*), поэтому сказуемое после них стоит в утвердительной форме.

2. Иногда после временнных союзов для обозначения **з а в е р ш е н н о с т и** действия употребляется не Present Simple a Present Perfect:

1. You'll change your opinion after you**'ve spoken** to him.	Вы измените свое мнение после того, как поговорите с ним.
2. I won't go home until I**'ve done** all my work.	Я не пойду домой до тех пор, пока не сделаю всей работы.
3. Don't let's make a final [faɪnl] decision before we**'ve listened** to everybody.	Давайте не принимать окончательного решения, прежде чем не выслушаем всех.

— 156 —

EXERCISES

Прочитайте вслух и преведите.

1. Please give him my heartiest congratulations when you see him.
2. If it keeps dry and sunny, we'll go to the country for the weekend.
3. If the weather doesn't change, we'll have to stay in town.
4. I'll be awfully sorry if you just waste your time.
5. We'll contact you when we have the information you are interested in.
6. We'll have another discussion as soon as we receive the final results.
7. Please let us know as soon as you get news from your counterparts.
8. We'll leave the house as soon as this horrible hurricane stops.
9. I'll sign the documents after I've looked through them once again.
10. We'll have to work hard till we've solved all our problems.
11. They won't change their decision until they get more reliable information.

2

Закончите мысль.

1. We'll be awfully sorry if the weather ... .
2. Everybody will be happy if the experiment ... .
3. We will buy these machines if they ... .
4. We'll contact the representative of the firm as soon as ...
5. Please don't leave the house before ... .
6. We won't leave the house until this terrible hurricane ... .
7. I'm sure you'll change your opinion after ... .
8. We'll be awfully sorry if he ... .

3

Переведите на английский язык.

1. Отдохните, когда (вы) устанете.
2. Я пойду перекушу, когда проголодаюсь.
3. У вас уйдет много времени, если вы поедете автобусом.
4. Если погода не переменится, мы поедем за город.
5. Позвоните мне, пожалуйста, перед тем, как (вы) выйдете из дому.
6. Мы очень огорчимся, если работа будет неудачной.
7. Все очень обрадуются, если его эксперимент будет удачным.
8. Боюсь, что мы не сможем поймать такси, если выйдем из дому в час пик.
9. Мы свяжемся с вами, как только получим все документы от фирмы.
10. Мы не сможем принять окончательного решения до тех пор, пока не выслушаем всех.

4

Проведите игру в классе, как показано в образце.

A. If the weather's fine ... .
B. If the weather's fine, we'll go to the country.
C. If we go to the country, we'll go for walk.
D. If we go for a walk ... etc.

GRAMMAR

16. Возвратные местоимения

16.1. Формы возвратных местоимений видны из следующей таблицы:

Личные местоимения	Возвратные местоимения
I	myself [maɪˈself]
you	yourself [jɔːˈself, jɔˈself]
he	himself [hɪmˈself]
she	herself [həˈself]
it	itself [ɪtˈself]
we	ourselves [auəˈselvz]
you	yourselves [jɔːˈselvz, jɔselvz]
they	themselves [ðəmˈselvz]
one	oneself [wʌnˈself]

16.2. Возвратные местоимения могут быть *усилительными.* В этой функции они соответствуют русскому место-имению **сам** (сама, само, сами)и имеют фразовое ударение.

1. I'll contact them **myself** (I **myself** will contact them).	Я **сам** свяжусь с ними (Я свяжусь с ними **сам).**
2. The manager **himself** gave all the instructions. (The manager gave all the instructions **himself**).	Директор **сам** дал все ука-зания. (Директор дал все указания **сам**).

В указанных примерах место усилительнго местоиме-ния не меняет смысла высказывания.

Если говорящий хочет особо усилить слово при помощи усилительного местоимения, оно ставится после этого слова и произносится с сильным ударением :

The president **himself** gave them the medals.	.*Сам президент* вручил им медали.

ПРИМЕЧАНИЕ: Предлог **by** перед усилительным местоимением подчеркивает, что действие было совершено с а м о -с т о я т е л ь н о , б е з п о с т о р о н н е й п о м о щ и :

Сравните:

I did it (all) **by** myself.	Я сделал это сам (мне никто не помогал).
I did it myself.	Я сделал это сам (это было сделано именно мною, а не кем-либо другим).

16.3. Все перечисленные местоимения могут придавать глаголу возвратное значение, т.е соответствующее русским возвратным глаголам на *-ся (-сь)*. В этой функции они н е имеют фразового ударения.

1. Let me **introduce myself**.	Разрешите *представиться*.
2. **Enjoy yourselves!**	Желаю вам хорошо *повеселиться!* (получить удовольствие и т.п.)
3. We **found ourselves** in a difficult situation.	Мы *оказались* в затруднительном положении
4. He **found himself** in an absolutely strange place.	Он *очутился* в совершенно незнакомом месте.
5. **Make yourselves** comfortable!	*Устраивайтесь* (располагайтесь) поудобнее!

ПРИМЕЧАНИЕ: Глаголы wash *умываться*, dress *одеваться*, shave *бриться*, и некоторые другие обычно употребляются без возвратного местоимения.

I **washed, shaved, dressed** and had breakfast.	Я умылся, побрился, оделся и позавтракал.

16.4. Английские возвратные местоимения могут соответствовать русскому возвратному местоимению **себя (себе, собой)**. В этом значении они также не имеют фразового ударения.

| 1. I want to buy myself a VCR. | Я хочу купить себе видео-магнитофон. |
| 2. He took too much medicine and only did himself harm. | Он принимал слишком много лекарств и только себе навредил. |

ПРИМЕЧАНИЕ: После глаголов feel *чувствовать себя* и behave *вести себя* возвратное местоимение не употребляется:

| 1. Today I **feel** well. | Сегодня я *чувствую себя* хорошо. |
| 2. He **behaves** like a child. | Он *ведет себя* как ребенок. |

Исключением является повелительное предложение, обращенное обычно к детям:

| Behave yourself! | Веди себя как следует! |

16.4. Возвратные местоимения могут употребляться после предлога:

| 1. He is hardly ever pleased with himself. | Он почти никогда не бывает доволен собой. |
| 2. Look after yourself! (= Take care of yourself!) | Берегите себя! |

ПРИМЕЧАНИЕ: Обратите внимание на случаи, в которых употребляется л и ч н о е, а не возвратное местоимение.

| 1. Have you taken a camera with **you**? | Вы взяли с собой фотоаппарат? |
| 2. Did he have any money on **him**? | У него были при себе деньги? |

EXERCISES

Прочитайте вслух и переведите на русский язык.

1. I hope you'll enjoy yourself.
2. Do come in and make yourselves comfortable!
3. We found ourselves on an awfully icy road.
4. I'll make coffee myself.
5. The President will receive the delegation himself.
6. Let me introduce myself. My name's Lawson.
7. They themselves decided to share the room, didn't they?
8. He promised to make all the arrangements himself.
9. I'm not going to change anything myself.

10. We are awfully sorry ourselves, but we weren't able to contact you in time and let you know.
11. I think she'll give you a lift herself.
12. He's fluent in several foreign languages and learned them all by himself!
13. He's behaved awfully towards his friends.
14. "How's your car behaving?" "Oh, quite well, thanks."
15. I couldn't keep my appointment with a colleague and I feel awful about it.
16. The problem itself is quite ordinary, but there's nobody to solve it.

2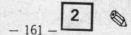

Переведите на английский язык:

1. Спасибо, но я могу все устроить сам.
2. Вы сами их поздравите, или мне сделать это?
3. Он сам вас подвезет до станции. 4. Она сама с нами согласилась.
5. Разве вы не сами отменили встречу?
6. Впредь мы будем внимательно читать все документы сами от начала до конца.
7. Разве вы не изменили программу сами?
8. Он сам принял нас в своем офисе.
9. Мы очутились в незнакомом месте.
10. Они оказались в затруднительном положении.
11. Они сами причинили себе массу хлопот.
12. К сожалению, я не смогу помочь вам, потому что я плохо себя чувствую.
13. Он чувствует себя совсем хорошо, спасибо.
14. Я не смог сообщить ему (let him know) и ужасно себя чувствую по этому поводу.
15. Новый телевизор не совсем хорошо себя ведет, боюсь, что мы не сможем наладить (fix) его сами.
16. Располагайтесь поудобнее!
17. Надеюсь вы хорошо повеселитесь на вечеринке.
18. Разрешите представиться. Моя фамилия Петров.

TOPICS FOR DISSCUSSSION AND NEW WORDS

Planning One's Daily Round

Have you ever thought that twenty–four hours isn't enough to do all you have to do? All of us have so many **duties** and **obligations!** In addition to the daily **routine** at offices, schools, hospitals, etc., we have always got some housework to do and shopping, we have to cook the meals, keep the house clean and **(last but not least)** see to the children. It's really **surprising** how much work some people **manage** to do, and quickly at that! But it often happens that we don't have enough time to do everything, and put it off till "some other time". What do you think is the **reason?** Why do some people manage and not others?

A lot depends on how you plan your daily **round.** If you plan your day carefully, you'll be able to do more, and it'll take you less time. If you ask someone to see you at a definite hour, **for instance,** the other person will also plan his time **accordingly.** If you know how long you can keep your visitor, you will try not to waste his time and have everything ready for the talk when he comes. Your visitor, in his turn, will not keep you longer than **necessary** and will leave as soon as you've discussed your problem. It doesn't mean that you will interrupt the talk before you finish the discussion. No, you'll go on discussing the **matter** until you settle every **point.** But the time limit you **set yourself** will help you not to waste time and to speak **to the point.**

Planning the day is **especially** necessary for people who want to make time for important things. Many **outstanding** people say that a daily **timetable** has helped them greatly to **achieve** what they have. There are some people, **however**, who will say that a strict timetable makes life dull and uninteresting. What do you think?

Learn these words:

round *n c*	раунд, тур, этап; *зд.* круг обязанностей
the first round of the talks	первый раунд переговоров
the second round of the contest	второй тур конкурса
duty *n c*	1. обязанность, долг

It was my duty to do it.	Сделать это было моим долгом.
	2. дежурство
Who's on duty today?	Кто сегодня дежурит?
obligation [ˌɔblɪˈgeɪʃn] *n c*	обязательство
to fulfil one's obligations under the contract	выполнять свои обязательства по контракту
routine [ruːˈtiːn] *n; adj*	рутина, рутинный, обычный, повседневный
one's daily routine	рутина, повседневные, обязанности
routine dutes (questions, etc.)	
last but not least	и, наконец ..., (досл. последний по порядку, но не по важности)
surprise [sɔˈpraɪz] *n*	сюрприз, неожиданность
What a pleasant surprise!	Какая приятная неожиданность!
surprising *adj*	удивительный, неожиданный
to be surprised	быть удивленным, удивиться
We were surprised to hear that ...	Мы с удивлением узнали, что ...
at that	к тому же
They've done the work very well and very quickly at that.	Они выполнили работу хорошо и к тому же быстро.
reason [ˈriːzn] *n c*	1. причина
Have you found out the reason (why) the experiment wasn't a success?	Вы выяснили причину, по которой эксперимент не удался?
They often change their plans **for** one reason or another (other), and sometimes **for** no reason at all.	Они часто меняют планы по той или иной причине, а иногда и вовсе без причины.
	2. причина, основание

There's every reason to believe that ... Есть все основания полагать, что ...

manage [ˈmænɪdʒ] *v*

1. руководить, управлять, за-
ведовать

Syn. **to run**

to manage a factory (an office, etc.)

2. справляться

I don't think he'll be able to manage
the work without an assistant.

Думаю, он не сможет
справиться с работою
без помощника.

3. удаться (кому–л.), суметь
сделать что–л., справиться

I'm sorry, I didn't manage to get
through to them.

К сожалению, мне не
удалось им дозвониться.

depend [dɪˈpend] *v*

зависеть

It depends on the weather.
It depends!

Это зависит от погоды.
Это зависит от обстоя-
тельств. (*Возможны
переводы*: посмотрим!
как когда, смотря как и
т.п.)

"Do you think they will agree?"

—Думаете, они согласят-
ся?

"It depends!" ("Well, it all depends!")

—Посмотрим! (Трудно
сказать, зависит от об-
стоятельств и т.п.)

"Will you come round?"
"It depends (on) how I feel."

— Вы приедете?
— Смотря, как буду себя
чувствовать.

for instance [fərˈɪnstəns]

например

Syn. **for example**

accordingly [əˈkɔːdɪŋlɪ] *adv*

соответственно

If you change your timetable, I'll
change mine accordingly.

Если вы измените свое
расписание, я соответст-
венно изменю свое.

necessary [ˈnesəsərɪ] *adj*

необходимый, нужный

Ant. **unnecessary**

ненужный

We've made all the necessary arragements.	Мы сделали все необходимые приготовления.
That's absolutely necessary!	Это совершенно необходимо!
Oh, that's absolutely unnecessary!	Это совершенно не нужно!
We find it necessary to solve the problem soon.	Мы считаем необходимым решить эту проблему быстро.

matter [´mætə] *n* — 1. дело, вопрос

That's a matter of opinion.	Это спорный вопрос.
It's a matter of life and death.	Это вопрос жизни и смерти.
That's (quite) another matter.	Это (совсем) другое дело.

2. дело, затруднение

What's the matter? (= What's happened?)	В чем дело? (Что случилось?)
What's the matter **with** the car?	Что с машиной?
There's something the matter with the engine (something's happened **to** the engine, something's wrong **with** the engine).	Что-то не в порядке с двигателем (Что-то случилось с двигателем).

3. (*обычно во мн.ч.*) вопросы, дела

business matters	деловые вопросы
money matters	денежные дела

matter *v* — иметь значение

What does it matter (**to** you)?	Какое это имеет значение (для вас)?
It doesn't matter.	Это не имеет значения.

point *n c* — 1. пункт, вопрос

There are two or three points in your proposal that we can't agree to.	В вашем предложении есть два-три пункта, с которыми мы не можем согласиться.

2. дело, смысл

The point (thing) is that ...	Дело в том, что ...
... that's the whole point!	... в том–то все и дело!
to speak (keep) to the point	говорить по существу

3. точка, позиция

my (his etc.) point of view	моя (его и т.д.) точка зрения
From his point of view ...	С его точки зрения ...

set *v* — зд. установить, поставить

to set a time limit — установить срок (регламент)

especially [ɪˈspeʃlɪ] *adv* — 1. в особенности, особенно — 166 —

I like it here, especially in spring.

2. особенно (*перед прилаг.*)

especially important (useful, reliable, etc.) — особенно, важный (полезный, надежный и т.д.)

outstanding [ˈautstændɪŋ] *adj* — выдающийся

an outstanding writer (actor, painter, scientist, etc.)

timetable [ˈtaɪmteɪbl] *n c* — расписание

achieve [əˈtʃiːv] *v* — достичь, добиться

to achieve success (good results, etc.)

achievement *n c* — достижение

It was a great achievement.

however [hauˈevə] *conj* — однако

Later, however, the weather changed.

strict *adj* — строгий

a strict rule (teacher, etc.)

EXERCISES

Прочитайте текст вслух. Предварительно отработайте произношение следующих словосочетаний.

at that   **is the reason**   **at our offices**

2

Найдите в тексте английские эквиваленты.

Двадцати четырех часов не хватает, чтобы сделать все, что надо • повседневная работа • и наконец • просто удивительно, сколько работы некоторым людям удается сделать, и к тому же быстро • откладываем это "на потом" • как вы думаете, в чем причина? • многое зависит от того, как вы планируете ...• другой человек спланирует свое время соответственно • вы постараетесь не тратить его время попусту и все приготовить • дольше, чем нужно • как только вы обсудите вопрос • регламент, который вы себе установите • говорить по существу • особенно необходимо.

3

Ответьте на вопросы по тексту.

1. Do you agree that twenty–four hours isn't enough to do we all have to do?
2. Is it true that everybody has a lot of duties and obligations?
3. What does it depend on?
4. Is the daily routine at offices, schools, hospitals, etc., always necessary, or do we sometimes have to do unnecessary work?
5. How much time do you (does your wife/husband) spend on the daily shopping?
6. How long does it take you to clean the flat and make the meals?
7. Can you say that you manage it all quickly?
8. Do you like putting things off till some other time?
9. Do you often have to do so? Why?
10. Is it true that some people manage better than others? What's the reason (What does it depend on)?
11. Do you find it necessary to plan your daily round? Give your reasons.
12. Are you good at planning your daily round, or do you find it difficult?
13. Do you manage to keep all the appointments you make?
14. Is it always easy to speak to the point? Do you always manage to speak to the point? What does it depend on?
15. Do you agree that planning the day is especially important for businessmen? Isn't it important for everybody?
16. Can you achieve anything really important if you can't plan your time?

17. Do you find that a strict timetable makes life dull? Give your reasons.

4 🔲

Прочитайте вслух и переведите примеры на новые слова.

1. I believe in planning my daily round. Do you?
2. The commentator described the first round of talks as very successful.
3. The doctor's out on his routine rounds.
4. The second round of experiments was less successful than the first, and nobody knew the reason.
5. I haven't done anything important, I only did my duty. — 168 —
6. It's my duty to settle it all myself.
7. I'll only be able to go on holiday after I've fulfilled all my obligations.
8. You'll achieve a lot more if you change your daily routine.
9. You'll make good progress in English if you don't only do your routine homework but also read a lot, try to speak English as often as you can, and (last but not least) listen to the radio.
10. Don't tell anybody. Let it be a surprise!
11. What a pleasant surprise!
12. His answer suprised everybody.
13. We were suprised to hear that the equipment was still at the factory.
14. It's really surprising how quickly they managed to do all their duties, and very well at that!
15. What's the reason?
16. For one reason or another they never fulfil their obligations.
17. They are always quarreling for no reason at all.
18. The real reason they don't manage it is quite different.
19. That's the reason why some people manage and not others.
20. If we put off our appointment till a later date, I'll change my plans accordingly.
21. If the situation on the market changes, we will change our prices accordingly.
22. Believe it or not, I managed it all by myself.
23. Everything depends on their decision.
24. What does it depend on?
25. It depends on how soon we settle the matter.
26. Not everything depends on us. That's the whole point!
27. The point is it doesn't depend on us.
28. A lot depends on your point of view.
29. What's the matter with the remote control unit?

31. If there's anything the matter with the engine, let us know. Don't do anything, before we come and look at it.

– 169 –

5

Повторите, используя подсказанные слова.

Дано: We're surprised to hear it.
• to hear that they've changed their plans•
Требуется: We're surprised to hear that they've changed their plans.

1. We're surprised **to hear it**.

• to see it • to see all these changes • to see that you've made some changes in the design • to hear that you've changed your opinion • to hear that their point of view is different • to hear that they haven't signed the contract yet •

2. There's every reason to believe that **they will fulfil all their obligations under the contract.**

• the situation will change • the situation will change in the near future • they'll make all the arrangements • they'll make all the necessary arrangements themselves • they'll settle the matter themselves • the second round of the talks will be more successful • we'll achieve a lot more if we don't change our decisions so often •

3. There are several reasons (why) **we can't fulfil our obligations.**

• they don't agree with us • they don't manage to do the work in time • I find that problem especially important • we can't achieve better results • so much depends on your decision • it's absolutely necessary • it's necessary to settle the matter by ourselves • he doesn't like to speak about money matters •

4. The point is **they don't even fulfil their routine duties.**

• I can't manage the job without an assistant • the time limit's too strict • we've got other obligations to fulfil • he contradicts himself • you can't always follow a strict routine • there's always something the matter with him • there's always something the matter with the engine •

6

Подберите подходящие ответы к высказываниям, данным в колонке слева. Продолжите мысль.

1. People who plan their daily round manage to do a lot more than those who don't.

Oh, there are several reasons, aren't there? First of all ...

2. We all have a lot of duties and obligations, don't we?

Well, yes and no. Talent alone isn't always enough for success, but ...

— 170 —

3. Why do some people manage to do all their duties and some don't?

Oh, it depends! I don't really think all of us are so terribly busy. Some ...

4. If we want to achieve something in life, we must follow this rule: Never put off till tomorrow what you can do today".

That isn't quite so, I'm afraid. My own opinion is ...

That is a good rule, of course, but ...

5. Planning the day and following a strict timetable is only necessary for outstanding people. Ordinary people can easily do without it, can't they?

I couldn't agree more ...

6. Success and achievement in life don't depend on one's talent. It's just a matter of luck, isn't it?

7

Заполните пропуски предлогами:

1. A lot depends ... how successfully we'll be able to discuss all the obligations of the Sellers and the Buyers ... the contract ... the first round ... the talks.

2. We have to let you know that the factory does not fulfil its obligations ... the contract ... one reason or another. The point is that if they do not begin to work better, we will not be able to finish our work ... time.
3. What's the matter ... that clock? It was ten minutes fast yesterday, and today it's five minutes slow!
4. "What do you think is the matter ... the machine?" "I'm afraid something has happened ... the engine."
5. Please try to speak ... the point, don't waste your time ... unnecessary things.
6. We can't agree ... your opinion ... several reasons.
7. Don't be afraid ... cold water. Nothing terrible will happen ... you. It'll only do you a lot ... good. I always begin swimming ... May. It doesn't matter ... me if the water is cold." "But I don't think everybody can do that, a lot depends ... your health".

9

Прочитайте диалоги вслух и разыграйте их, используя слова, данные в скобках.

1

A. When you don't quite agree with another person's **views**, the best thing is not to contradict him, but to listen carefully and try to understand.

B. Well, that's a matter of opinion. I personally think that it's much better to say what you really think. The sooner the better.

(• opinions • ideas • suggestions •)

2

A. There's always something the matter with the man. He can never **be it time** for some reason or other, and very often for no reason at all.

B. There's nothing we can do about it, I'm afraid. That's the trouble!

(• keep his appointments • fulfil his obligations •)

3

A. Let me congratulate you on your **great achievement**!

B. Thank you very much. I don't really think it's as great as all that.

A. Oh, yes, it is. It's really surprising how much your whole team has done!

B. Well, that's another matter. It really depended on the team much more than on myself.

A. Oh, but the ideas were all yours, weren't they?

(• success • outstanding results •)

9

Прочитайте сценарии и разыграйте их.

1. An outstanding writer gives an interview to TV people .

The writer gives an interview in his country cottage, where he is working at a new novel. He meets the TV people at the door, asks them to come in and make themselves comfortable, and offers them a cup of coffee; then they begin to talk. The writer was a doctor when he was young. He wrote his first books while he was still working at a health centre. Here are some of the questions the interviewer asks him: "How did you manage to find time for writing books? What kind of people did you meet during your daily rounds? Did you like your profession? What was the reason you gave up medicine and decided to become a professional writer? What is especially interesting in a writer's life? What does the success of a book depend on? What progress are you making with your new book? Do you plan your working hours? Do you find it necessary to follow a strict timetable?" The writer, naturally, gives full and interesting answers to all these questions.

2. Several students (A, B, C, D) are discussing their timetable at college .

The students have decided to discuss the matter, because many of them find it extremely difficult to fulfil all their duties.

A says there are too many lectures they have to attend (посещать). On Wednesdays, for instance, they have six! So it isn't surprising that they don't even have enough time to read.

B agrees with the first speaker and adds that there are also too many meetings, discussions and conferences most of which are just a waste of time.

C interrupts him by saying that discussions and conferences are absolutely necessary, but it's true there are too many, sometimes.

The whole trouble, however, is that the speakers do not always speak to the point and often forget about the time limit.

B says that's another matter. As to meetings, (что же касается собраний) even if everybody keeps to the point and does not exceed the time limit, they keep the students at college, so the fewer meeting there are the better for the students.

D says she couldn't agree more, because she is married and in addition to college she has to do a lot at home: cook, keep the flat clean, and, last but not least, look after her baby daughter.

All the students who take part in the discussion make suggestions. One of them, for instance, suggests that they should set a time limit for each of their discussions and conferences, especially for meetings. If everybody knows how long they will last, the students will be able to plan their time accordingly.

3. Mr Clark discusses the proogramme for his stay in Moscow with Alexander Ivanov, his business partner

Mr Clark, a British businessman, has come to Alexander Ivanov, his counterpart, to discuss the programme of his stay in Moscow where he has come to discuss several important business matters. Ivanov receives Mr Clark in his office. After saying hello to each other they sit down. They first talk about Mr Clark's journey to Moscow, the weather, etc. Then they get down to discussing Mr Clark's stay in Moscow. Ivanov suggests discussing the **itinerary** together. Mr Clark looks through the **draft** and asks some questions about it. The most important points of the programme are these:

Monday, 3rd April – a visit to the factory which is using the machines Mr Clark sold them a year ago.

Tuesday, 4th April – a meeting with the representatives of some other factories which are interested in buying Mr Clark's machines. A visit to the theatre in the evening.

Wednesday, 5th April – discussion of a new contract.

Thursday, 6th April – final discussions of the contract.

Friday, 7th April – signing the contract. Mr Clark suggests dinner at the restaurant in his hotel after signing the contract. They agree on each item of the programme. They both hope they will be able to do everything they have planned.

---

itinerary [aɪˈtɪnərərɪ] *n c*		программа визита, его маршрут
draft [drɑːft] *n c*		зд. проект (черновой вариант)
item [ˈaɪtəm] *n c*		здесь пункт

10

Переведите на английский язык.

1. По всеобщему мнению (по мнению всех), второй тур перего-воров был гораздо успешнее первого.

2. Если вы не выполните всех своих обязательств по контракту, нам придётся расторгнуть (cancel) его.

3. Если вы захотите отложить ваш визит, мы соответственно изменим наши планы.

4. Есть все основания полагать, что нам удастся выполнить все наши обязательства своевременно.

5. Мы пошлём вам факс, как только мы сделаем все необходимые приготовления для вашего визита.

6. Мы сумеем всё обсудить, если все будут говорить по существу.

7. – В чём дело? – Что–то случилось с машиной. Она остано-вилась безо всякой причины! Боюсь, что я не смогу справиться с этим сам. – Машина не может остановиться без причины. Разрешите взглянуть.

8. Неудивительно, что он так много успевает сделать, и к тому же очень хорошо! Он очень тщательно планирует свой рабочий день.

9. – От чего это зависит? – От качества, я думаю.

10. – Ты поедешь с нами завтра? – Как получится.

11. – Вы очень заняты по вторникам? – Как когда.

Unit 8

CRAMMAR

17. <u>Три типа условных предложений.</u>

17.1. Вы уже знаете первый тип условных предложений, которые употребляются, когда говорящий считает свое предположение вполне реальным, осуществимым.

Предположения, относящиеся к настоящему времени:

1. If you're tired, have a rest.	Если вы устали, отдохните.
2. We agree to make some changes if you find it necessary.	— Мы согласны сделать некоторые изменения, если вы находите это необходимым.

Предположения, относящиеся к будущему времени.

1. The discussion **won't take** long if everybody speaks to the point.	Обсуждение *не займет* много времени, если все *будут* говорить по существу.
2. If it **doesn't rain**, we'll go to the country.	Если *не будет* дождя, мы *поедем* за город.

17.2. Условные предложения второго типа выражают предположения, которые говорящий также относит к настоящему или будущему, но считает менее вероятными.

1. I'd change my plans if it **depended** on me alone (I would change my plans...).	Я бы изменил свои планы, если бы это зависело только от меня.
2. You'd **feel** much better if you **gave up** smoking. (You **would** feel much better ...).	Вы бы чувствовали себя гораздо лучше, если бы бросили курить.

3. I can let you know tomorrow. **Would** that **suit** you?	Я могу сообщить вам завтра. Вас бы это устроило?
4. We **wouldn't suggest** it if we didn't find it necessary.	Мы бы этого не предлагали, если бы не считали это необходимым.

Как видно из примеров, в условных предложениях второго типа в главном предложении употребляется вспомогательный глагол **would** [wud], который в утвердительном предложении не имеет ударения и поэтому произносится в редуцированной форме **I'd**, **you'd**, и т.д., а в придаточном употребляется форма, совпадающая с Past Simple.

17.3. Глагол **be** в условном придаточном предложении (т.е. после **if**) имеет форму **were** для всех лиц:

1. I'd drive faster, if the road **weren't** so bad.	Я бы ехал быстрее, если бы дорога не была такой плохой.
2. If I **were** you, I wouldn't waste so much time on it.	(Если бы я был) на вашем месте, я бы не тратил на это столько времени.

ПРИМЕЧАНИЕ: В разговорном английском языке встречается употребление **was**, однако форма **were** в данном случае считается более правильной.

17.4. В условных предложениях помимо **would** могут употребляться **could** и **might** с соответствующим изменением смысла высказывания:

1. We **could** stay in the country longer if the weather weren't so changeable.	Мы могли бы побыть за городом подольше, если бы погода не была такой неустойчивой.
2. If we caught a taxi now, we **might** get there in time.	Если бы мы сейчас поймали такси, мы, может быть, доехали бы туда вовремя (такая возможность не совсем исключается).
3. I'd be very happy if you **could** come and stay with us.	Я был бы очень счастлив, если бы вы могли приехать и пожить у нас.

ПРИМЕЧАНИЕ: В первом лице единственного и множественного числа наряду с **would** может иногда употребляться и **should** [ʃud]

I **shouldn't** be surprised if nobody supported this suggestion (=I **wouldn't** be surprised ...)	Я бы не удивился, если бы никто не поддержал это предложение.

EXERCISES

— 177 — Прочитайте вслух и переведите.

a. 1. You'd make better progress if you worked harder.
2. I'd do it all myself if I had more time.
3. I'm sure everybody would speak to the point if we set them a stricter time limit.
4. I'd be very happy if we arranged it all ourselves without giving any trouble to other people.
5. You wouldn't have so much trouble with your car if you didn't let other people use it so often.
6. If he agreed to speak at the conference, we'd all be very happy.
7. It would be very convenient for me if we could put off our appointment till next Thursday.

b. 1. They'd agree to pay more for the equipment if it were more up–to–date.
2. We'd buy more of these sets if your prices weren't so high.
3. If I were you, I wouldn't do it.
4. If I were him, I'd think twice before giving a definite answer.
5. The road's so icy. I'd be especially careful at the wheel if I were you.
6. I wouldn't be surprised if they didn't agree with us.
7. I shouldn't be surprised if he were late again.

3

Соедините два высказывания в одно, как показано в образце.

Дано: You don't look after your car, and that's the reason it gives you so much trouble.

Требуется: If you looked after your car, it wouldn't give you so much trouble.

1. He eats too much, that's why he's fat.
2. I can't help you to settle the matter, because it doesn't depend on me alone.
3. The weather's so awful! We won't go to the country for the weekend.
4. My car's out of order. I can't give you a lift.
5. Not everybody's here, so we can't get down to business yet.
6. They don't speak to the point. We waste too much time.
7. I don't believe his story — I don't know all the facts.
8. I'm ill, I'll have to put off our appointment.

3

Прочитайте тексты вслух. Скажите, что произошло бы с — 178 — этими людьми, если бы они вели другой образ жизни.

What would Happen if they Changed their Way of Living?

1

This girl never eats as much as she'd like to, but she doesn't **mind** it, because she wants to be in good **shape.** She spends more than an hour a day doing **aerobic exercises.** In addition to that she takes long walks, and never goes to bed later than twelve o'clock. She doesn't smoke. She must keep in shape because of her job. She's a successful fashion **model.** Her job's both interesting and well-paid, and she doesn't want to lose it. There's another reason, too. She's going to try her luck in an international beauty contest. So she's learning to speak English and play the piano.

What would happen if she ate as much as she wanted, if she didn't take enough exercise, and (last but not least) if she went to bed late and smoked? Could she take part in a beauty contest if she didn't speak a foreign language or play a musical instrument? What do you think?

Learn these words:

mind [maɪnd] *v* — *зд.* возражать, иметь что—л, против

I don't mind if we put it off (= I don't mind putting it off). — Я не возражаю, если мы это отложим.

Do you mind if I open the window? (= my opening the window) — Вы не возражаете, если я открою окно?

Would you mind opening the window! — Будьте любезны, открой— те окно (*досл.* вы не воз— ражаете открыть окно?).

shape *n* — форма

Syn. **form**

to be in (good) shape — быть в хорошей форме
to keep in shape — держаться в форме

aerobics [eə'rəubɪks] — аэробика

aerobic exercises

model — *зд.* модель, манекенщица

Syn. **a fashion model**

exercise *n u* — движение, физическая на— грузка

to take a lot of (enough, too little, etc.) exercise — много (достаточно, мало и т.д.) двигаться

2

This man's got a family and a job, but he may lose both in the near future. The thing is he doesn't know how to plan his daily routine, so he never has enough time to do his work well. He always puts things off for another time. That's the reason he hardly ever keeps appointments and is often late to work. So it's perfectly natural that his colleagues don't find him reliable and **prefer** to **deal with** somebody else, not him. His wife and he often quarrel. Nobody's pleased with him, and he isn't pleased with

Прочитайте вслух и переведите.

1. I don't mind if we cancel the meeting on Friday.
2. They don't mind if we deal with it next time.
3. Do you mind if we make a few changes in our plan?
4. Do you mind if we keep the window open?
5. Do you mind if I smoke?
6. Do you mind having a smoke?
7. Would you mind repeating the last sentence?
8. Would you mind my calling back at five?
9. Would you mind calling back at five?

5

Повторите, употребляя подсказанные слова.

1. I don't mind if we **discuss it again.**

   • put it off till next week • sign the contract tomorrow morning
   • ask somebody else • deal with the problem next time • don't
   deal with it today •

2. Do you mind if I **smoke**?

   • turn on the telly • turn the sound down a little • switch to
   another channel • use your telephone • leave a message with
   you •

3. Would you mind **opening the window?**

   • closing the door • turning on the light • turning off the radio •
   repeating the last word •

4. I'd prefer to **wait.**

   • deal with these questions at once • deal with another company
   • deal with somebody else • sign it tomorrow •

5. I prefer **discussing it now**.

   • settling it right away • receiving a definite answer • dealing
   with a more reliable partner • dealing with it next time •

6. He's **pleasant** to deal with.

himself either, but he can't do anything about it. That's the whole trouble.

What would happen if he began to plan his daily routine? Would it be easier for him to keep appointments and do things in time? Would other people be more pleased with him? Would he be more pleased with himself?

Learn these words:

prefer [prɪ´fɜ:] v   предпочитать

Which would you prefer, tea or coffee?

I prefer walking to driving.   Я предпочитаю ходить пешком, а не ездить на машине

Would you prefer to come next week?   Вы предпочли бы прийти на следующей неделе?

deal with (dealt, dealt) [di:l, delt] v   1. иметь дело с ...

He's very pleasant to deal with.   С ним очень приятно иметь дело.

2. вести дела, торговать, сотрудничать

We have never dealt with that firm.   Мы никогда не вели дел с этой фирмой.

3. заниматься (уделять внимание, разбираться)

I'll deal with it myself.   Я займусь этим сам.
We've got several problems to deal with.   У нас есть несколько проблем, которыми надо заняться.

4. быть о чем–л. (о книге, статье и т.д.)

What does the article deal with?   О чем эта статья (что говорится в этой статье)

deal in   торговать чем–л.

They deal in office equipment.   Они торгуют оборудованием, для учреждений (офисов).

• unpleasant • difficult • very easy • very nice •

7. They deal in **electronic equipment.**

• office equipment • office furniture • personal computers • clocks and watches

8. What does **the book** deal with?

• the article • his paper • the story •

6

Придумайте продолжение.

— 182 —

1. I'd be very sorry if you ...
2. I shouldn't be surprised if ...
3. I wouldn't give you so much trouble if the matter ...
4. If you gave up smoking, you ...
5. If I were you, I ...
6. It wouldn't do him any harm if he ...
7. You'd make better progress in your English if you ...
8. They might agree to our suggestions if we ...
9. It would do you a lot of good if ...
10. Do you mind if I ...
11. If I were rich, I ...

7

Продолжите цепочку высказываний, как показано в образце.

First student: If we didn't have any lectures today ...

Second student: If we didn't have any lectures today, we'd go to a café.

Third student: If we went to a cafe, we'd order a nice meal.

Fourth student: If we ordered a nice meal, we'd enjoy it ... etc.

8

Переведите на английский язык:

1. Всем было бы очень удобно, если бы мы перенесли нашу встречу на следующий понедельник.
2. Я бы предложил ничего не менять.
3. Мы не причиняли бы вам столько беспокойства, если бы дело не было таким важным.

4. Если бы это зависело от нас, мы бы начали работу немедленно (сразу).

5. Он бы справлялся с этим, если бы у него был помощник.

6. Я бы предпочел не откладывать это на следующую неделю.

7. На вашем месте я бы бросил курить.

8. На его месте я бы имел дело с более надежными партнерами.

9. Я бы занялся этой проблемой сам, если бы у меня было достаточно времени.

GRAMMAR
(continued)

17.5. Условные предложения т р е т ь е г о типа относят-ся к п р о ш л о м у и выражают предположения по поводу того, что у ж е н е с о с т о я -л о с ь .

1. If I'**d known** he was ill, I'd have **visited him**. (If I **had known** ... I **would** have visited ...)	Если бы я знал, что он был болен, я бы его навестил.
2. If I'**d had** enough money then, I'd **have** bought the picture. (If **I had had** ... I **would have bought** ...)	Если бы у меня было тогда достаточно денег, я бы ку-пил эту картину.
3. We **wouldn't have wasted** so much time yesterday if everybody **had come** in time.	Мы бы не потратили вчера столько времени напрасно, если бы все пришли во-время.

Как видно из примеров, в главном предложении употребляется **would** + *перфектный инфинитив* (**would have done**) в придаточном (после союза **if**) - **had** + *третья форма смыслового глагола* (**had done**). В утвердительном предложении и **would** и **had** могут иметь одинаковую редуцированную форму **'d**:

I'**d** have phoned you if I'**d** known. (I **would** ... I **had** ...)

ПРИМЕЧАНИЕ: В быстрой разговорной речи **would have** может быть произнесено [΄wudəv]. **Wouldn't have** может быть произнесено [΄wudntəv].

17.6. Вместо **would** могут употребляться **could** и **might** с соответ-ствующим изменением смысла.

1. If all the documents had been in order we **could have signed** the contract yesterday.	Если бы все документы были в порядке, мы могли бы подписать контракт вчера.
2. If he'd seen the doctor at once, he **might have done** without an operation.	Если бы он обратился к врачу сразу, он мог бы обойтись без операции (возможно, обошелся бы).

ПРИМЕЧАНИЕ: Иногда встречается и смешанный тип условных предложений - комбинация второго и третьего типов.

If I were you, I wouldn't have given up music.	На вашем месте я бы не бросил музыку.

EXERCISES

Прочитайте вслух и переведите.

1. Nothing would've happened if you'd followed the instructions.
2. I wouldn't have cancelled the appointment if I hadn't fallen ill.
3. We'd have managed to do more if we'd begun earlier.
4. We'd have contacted them long ago if someone had told us that it was necessary.
5. I'd have arranged everything myself if you'd asked me in good time.
6. We'd have stayed there longer if the weather hadn't changed.
7. Wouldn't you have agreed if you were me?
8. If I were you, I wouldn't have believed it.
9. Believe me, if I'd had at least five free minutes to talk to you yesterday, I'd have done so.

2

Повторите, используя подсказанные слова:

1. We'd have contacted them if **you'd told us.**

• you'd let us know• we'd received your fax • it had been necessary • it had been urgent • the matter had been urgent •

2. Nothing would have happened if **you'd followed the instructions.**

• we'd dealt with it ourselves • you'd agreed with us • they'd described it more carefully • we'd arranged it in good time • they

hadn't changed the project • I hadn't exceeded the speed limit •
they hadn't cancelled the appointment•

3. We wouldn't have wasted so much time if **they'd explained
it all more carefully.**

 • you'd described the method more exactly • we'd begun earlier •
they'd let us know in good time • we hadn't changed anything •

Прочитайте рассказ вслух и продолжите его, как показано
в упражнении 4.

– 185 – Don't Hurry at the Wheel!

   This policeman has stopped a
dangerous driver, who exceeded the
speed limit. The driver has to pay a fine.
He was at a party yesterday, so it was
difficult for him to get up in time this
morning, and he left the house later than
usual. He was in a **hurry** to get to work
and drove too fast. When he **noticed**
the policeman, it was too late ...

Learn the new words:

hurry [ˈhʌrɪ] *n*	спешка
to be in a hurry	(торопиться, спешить, быть в состоянии спеш-ки)
He was in a hurry to leave.	Он торопился уйти.
There's no hurry.	Ничего спешного (никакой спешки).
hurry *v*	спешить, торопиться (может употр. в повелительных предложениях)
Don't hurry!	Не спешите!
Hurry up!	Поторапливайтесь!
Hurry them up!	Поторопите их!
notice [ˈnəutɪs] *v*	заметить (увидеть)
He was hurrying somewhere and didn't notice me.	Он куда-то торопился и не заметил меня.

We would have noticed the mistake if there hadn't been such a terrible hurry.	Мы бы заметили ошибку, если бы не было такой ужасной спешки.

 4

Придумайте свой рассказ о том, чего бы не произошло, если бы ...

If he hadn't been at a party yesterday he would have woken up in time.

If he had woken up in time he would ...

If ...

 5

Прочитайте рассказы и перескажите их.

1

Ladies and Gentlemen.

A lady, who was travelling by train, took a seat in a **compartment** where a man was smoking one cigarette after another. "If you were a gentleman ," she said to him after some time, "you'd have stopped smoking when a lady **entered** the compartment." "If you were a lady," he answered, "you wouldn't have entered a smoking compartment." "If you were my husband," the lady exclaimed, "I'd give you **poison!**" "If I were your husband, I'd take it," was the **reply.**

Learn these words:

compartment [kəm`pɑːtmənt] *n c*	купе
a smoking compartment	купе для курящих
enter *v*	входить в
exclaim [ɪks´kleɪm] *v*	воскликнуть
poison [pɔɪzn] *n u*	яд
reply [rɪ´plaɪ] *n c*	ответ

Unit 9

GRAMMAR

18. <u>Пассивный (страдательный) залог</u> - **The Passive Voice.**

18.1. Английский глагол имеет два залога - уже знакомый вам *активный* (действительный) the Active Voice и *пассивный* (страдательный) the Passive Voice, который употребляется, когда объект действия более важен для говорящего, чем исполнитель (субъект) этого действия:

Активный залог	Пассивный залог
1. We **keep** all the documents in perfect order.	1. All the documents **are kept** in perfect order.
Мы *содержим* все документы в образцовом порядке.	Все документы *содержатся* в образцовом порядке.
2. The manager **arranged** everything in good time.	2. Everything **was arranged** in good time.
Менеджер все *организовал* своевременно.	Все было организовано своевременно.
3. They'll **solve** the problem in the near future.	3. The problem **will be solved** in the near future.
Они решат проблему в ближайшем будущем.	Эта проблема будет решена в ближайшем будущем.
4. The secretary's just **sent** the mail **off** (has just sent).	4. The mail's just **been sent off** (has just been sent off).
Секретарь только что *отправил* почту.	Почта только что *отправлена*.
5. Some TV reporters **are filming** the match.	5. The match **is being filmed** for television.
Телерепортеры *снимают* матч.	Матч *снимают* для телевидения.

2

He Was Lucky

A. I've just **borrowed** 50 pounds from Mr. Harris.
B. Oh, have you? But Mr. Harris doesn't know you, does he?
A. Of course he doesn't. If he'd known me, he wouldn't have lent me a penny!

Learn this word:

borrow   [ˈbɔrəu] v   одалживать, занимать, брать
                                          взаймы

– 188 –

Ant. to lend.

 6

Переведите на английский язык.

1. Ничего бы не произошло, если бы вы были внимательнее.
2. Я бы остался на фильм вчера, если бы у меня было больше времени.
3. Мы бы не потратили напрасно столько времени, если бы мы знали все правила.
4. Если бы вы сообщили всем заблаговременно, вчера пришло бы больше народу.
5. Мы не пропустили (miss) бы начала, если бы кто-нибудь нас подвез.
6. Я бы позвонил всем сам, если бы я знал все номера телефонов.
7. Вы бы не имели столько неприятностей с этим оборудованием, если бы вы более тщательно следовали инструкциям.
8. Если бы он нам не помог, мы бы не справились с работой сами.
9. Вчерашнее интервью могло бы быть более удачным, если бы репортер не прерывал людей так часто.
10. Если бы мы остались вчера дома, мы бы не пропустили эту интересную программу.

6. When we came to the factory, the workers **were** still **installing** the new equipment.

Когда мы приехали на завод, рабочие все еще *устанавливали* оборудование.

6. When we came to the factory, the new equipment **was** still **being installed.**

Когда мы приехали на завод, новое оборудование все еще *устанавливалось*.

Как видно из примеров, пассивный залог образуется из вспомогательного глагола **be** *и третьей формы смыслового глагола* (Participle Two). Изменяется только вспомогательный глагол **be**, форма смыслового глагола остается неизменной.

В речи нормального темпа вспомогательные глаголы в утвердительных предложениях произносятся в редуцированных формах:

The question was asked several times |wɔzˊɑːskt |.
The plan's been changed |ˊplænzbɪn |.
The match has been put off |ˊmætʃɔzbɪn |.

18.2. Принцип образования вопросительной, отрицательной, вопросно-отрицательной формы и присоединенных вопросов виден из следующих примеров:

1. How often **are** these problems **discussed?**
2. **Was** the house **built** very long ago?
3. **Was** it still **being built** when you came to live here?
4. **Has** the matter **been settled** yet?
5. **Haven't** the bills **been paid** yet?
6. That film **hasn't been shown** on TV.
7. That film's never **been shown** on TV, has it?

ПРИМЕЧАНИЕ: В высказываниях с пассивным сказуемым и с п о л н и т е л ь действия чаще всего н е указывается, но если говорящий считает нужным его указать, он употребляет перед соответствующим словом предлог by:

America was discovered **by Columbus** in 1492.
[kəˊlʌmbəs]

Америка была открыта Колумбом в 1492 году.

Если ту же мысль выразить в активном залоге, слово, обозначающее исполнителя, станет подлежащим:

Columbus discovered America in 1492.

Колумб открыл Америку в 1492 году.

Предлог **with** стоит перед словом, обозначающим *инструмент* или *материал, вещество;* предлог **of** стоит перед словом, обозначающим *материал:*

1. It was made **with** simple tools.	Это было сделано простыми инструментами.
2. The ground was covered **with** snow.	Земля была покрыта снегом.
3. The table is made **of** expensive wood.	Стол сделан из дорогого дерева.

18.3. Времена пассивного залога употребляются в тех же случаях, что и соответствующие времена активного залога.

Следует обратить внимание на то, что у некоторых глаголов, например, **build, pack, settle, break, send off,** Present Simple Passive по значению почти не отличается от Present Perfect Passive:

1. The goods **are packed.** The goods **have been packed.**	Товар упакован.
2. The matter's **settled** (is settled). The matter's **been settled** (has been settled).	Дело урегулировано.

Однако у других глаголов, в меньшей степени показывающих завершенность, результат действия, разница между этими формами может быть существенной, поэтому в сомнительных случаях предпочтение следует отдавать форме Present *Perfect* Passive особенно, если в предложении имеются такие наречия, как **just, already, yet:**

1. The problem's already **been settled** (has already been settled).	Проблема уже решена.
2. The mail's just **been sent off** (has just been sent off).	Почта только что отправлена.
3. No decisions **have been taken** yet.	Еще не принято никаких решений.

18.4. Пассивный залог имеет свои формы инфинитива,

которые употребляются по тем же правилам, что и инфинитив активного залога:

1. The discussion had **to be interrupted.**	Обсуждение пришлось прервать.
2. The work must **be done** as soon as possible.	Работа должна быть сделана как можно скорее.
3. The plan can't **be changed**, I'm afraid.	Боюсь, что план не может быть изменен.

EXERCISES

1

Прочитайте вслух и переведите.

1. The mail's usually brought at 9 p.m.
2. Are the orders always fulfilled in time?
3. It's a pity the lecture wasn't taped.
4. All the machines have been tested, and the results have been written down and filed.
5. The telly hasn't been switched off, I'm afraid.
6. The appointment's been called off, hasn't it?
7. Who's been appointed head of the delegation?
8. If we use the old methods, a lot of time may be wasted, and very little will be achieved.
9. When can the new equipment be installed?
10. The experiment will be described in several journals.
11. A conference on those problems is being held now.
12. The lists are still being typed.
13. The machine was being tested when we came to the factory.
14. Something important was being discussed, so I sat down to listen.
15. These machines are going to be tested again.

2

Перефразируйте, употребляя пассив (исполнителя действия можно не указывать, если в этом нет необходимости)

Дано: We test each piece of equipment very carefully.

Требуется: Each piece of equipment is tested very carefully.

1. The policeman fined the driver for exceeding the speed limit.
2. I'm sure we'll settle the matter very easily.

3. They started the company a hundred years ago.
4. Have you changed anything?
5. How soon will they repeat that TV programme?
6. We haven't solved the problem yet.
7. Have you prepared all the documents?
8. We haven't found the reason yet.
9. Have they tested all the machines?
10. We won't repeat that mistake in future.
11. A discussion will follow the lecture.
12. They are interviewing the delegates.
13. What are they building over there?
14. We were taping the lesson when you phoned.

3

Какие вопросы нужно было задать, чтобы получить эти ответы?

1. This monument was put up **three hundred years ago.**
2. **Only one** of his books has been translated into Russian.
3. The meeting was put off, **because the day wasn't convenient for most of the people.**
4. **Some pop singers** were being interviewed when I switched on the telly.
5. These contests are held **every four years.**
6. Your order will be fulfilled **in five days' time.**

TOPICS FOR DISCUSSION AND NEW WORDS

What are the Reasons?

Many great cities of the world were **built** hundreds of years ago. During their long **history** some of them were **destroyed** several times for one reason or another, and then **rebuilt.**

London, for instance, was **burnt down** in the Great **Fire** of 1666.

When Napoleon's army entered Moscow in 1812, the city was nearly empty and in **flames.** Most of the houses were soon destroyed by the fire, and many were badly **damaged.**

A lot of beautiful cities were left **in ruins** after the World Wars.

Serious damage is done to cities and villages by **floods**, hurricanes and **earthquakes** and still more by wars and industrial **pollution.**

Learn these words:

build (built, built) [bɪld, bɪlt] *v*	строить, построить
rebuild *v*	строить заново, восстанавливать
history [ˈhɪstərɪ] *n*	1. история (исторические события)

the history of Great Britain
modern history

	2. история (учебный премет)
He read history at Oxford.	Он изучал историю в Оксфорде.

Сравните:

history	история (исторические события)
story	история (рассказ, сюжет, статья в журнале, газете и т.п.)
Nobody believed that story.	Никто не верил этой истории.
The next story in the programme …	Следующий сюжет в программе …

destroy [dɪˈstrɔɪ] *v*	разрушать, уничтожать
Syn **ruin** [ˈruːɪn] *v*	
ruins *n pl*	зд. руины, развалины
burn *(burnt, burnt) v*	зд. гореть, сжигать
to be burnt down	быть сожженным, сгореть дотла
fire *n*	огонь, пожар
flame *n c*	пламя

— 193 —

serious [ˈsɪərɪəs] *adj*	серьезный
damage [ˈdæmɪdʒ] *v*	повреждать, портить, нано-сить урон
You're damaging your health.	Вы портите свое здо-ровье.
The goods were damaged in transit [ˈtrænzɪt].	Товар был поврежден в пути
damage *n*	урон, ущерб, повреждение, порча
to do sb/sth a lot of (great) damage	причинить сильное по-вреждение, нанести большой урон

— 194 —

flood [flʌd]	*n c*	наводнение
earthquake [ˈɔːθkweɪk]	*n c*	землетрясение
pollution [pəˈluːʃn]	*n u*	загрязнение (окружающей среды)

EXERCISES

 1

Прочитайте вслух и переведите примеры на новые слова.

1. modern history, natural history, Russian history.
   He's interested in the history of literature.
   History repeats itself.
2. It's an old story.
   It's a true story.
   That's quite another story.
3. The bridge was destroyed by a bomb [bɔm].
   All his papers were destroyed in the fire.
   All his hopes have been destroyed!
4. The carpet's ruined!
   The flowers have been ruined by the rain.
   He's ruining his health by drinking.
   The city was ruined by the bombs.
   The country was ruined by the war.
5. Several villages were badly damaged by the flood.
   All the goods were badly damaged.
   Was the car badly damaged?
7. A lot of damage was done by the earthquake.

How serious was the damage?
8. It's a serious matter.
If she were more serious about her work, she wouldn't make so many mistakes.
He's seriously ill.
The house was seriously damaged by the flood.
The papers were seriously damaged in the flames.

2

Перефразируйте, употребляя пассив. Сделайте выделенное слово подлежащим.

1. They will build **a stadium** here in the near future.
2. The earthquake ruined **several big cities.**
3. Storms and floods have done **a lot of damage** to the village.
4. The fire has done **a lot of damage.**
5. The flood has seriously damaged **the city library.**
6. Industrial pollution is ruining **our city!**

3

Ответьте на вопросы.

1. How well do you know the history of the city you live in?
2. What are the reasons why cities and villages were destroyed in the past?
3. Do you remember in which year the Great Fire of London was?
4. Why was Moscow burnt down in 1812?
5. Earthquakes and floods can do a lot of damage, can't they? Can they be forecast?
6. Does industrial pollution do more harm than earthquakes, storms or floods?

TOPICS FOR DISCUSSION AND NEW WORDS
(continued)

At a World Fair

The **exhibition grounds** are full of life. **Pavilions** are being **set up**, and boxes, and **cases** of exhibits are being **unpacked** ...

In a few weeks the place will be **crowded** when a lot of visitors come to the new world fair.

Now it is a few weeks later, and the picture is quite different. All the preparations have been made, the exhibits are beautifully arranged on the stands, and the attendants are ready to receive the first visitors.

The fair's **in full swing** ...

It's hard to say which of the **sections** is the most popular.

Industry, **agriculture**, science, **art**, education, medicine – every **sphere** of life is **represented** here.

The fair naturally **attracts** a lot of businessmen. Offers are made, and very often contracts are signed.

Learn these words:

fair *n c* ярмарка

   a World fair

exhibition grounds *n pl* зд. территория выставки   — 196 —

pavilion [pə´vɪljən] *n c* павильон

set up *v* 1. установить, поставить

   to set up a pavilion (a tent, etc)

                              2. воздвигнуть (поставить)

   to set up a monument

                              3. учредить, организовать, основать, создать компанию (совместное предприятие и т.д.)

   to set up (start) a company (a joint venture [´ventʃə], etc.)

case [keɪs] *n c* зд. ящик

pack *v* паковать, упаковывать

unpack *v* распаковывать

crowd [kraud] *n* толпа

crowd *v* толпиться, переполнять

crowded *adj* переполненный, насыщенный

   to be crowded with people (cars, etc.)

   We've got a crowded programme. У нас насыщенная программа.

later позже, потом, позднее, впоследствии

Сравните:

a few days **later**	через несколько дней (только о прошлом)
in a few days	через несколько дней (как правило, о будущем)

---

preparation [ˌprepəˈreɪʃn] *n u*	подготовка
without preparation	без подготовки
preparations *n pl*	приготовления
preparations for a journey (a congress, etc.)	
in full swing	в полном разгаре
section *n c*	секция, отдел, раздел
agriculture [ˈægrɪkʌltʃə] *n u*	сельское хозяйство
art *n*	искусство
modern art	современное искусство
a work of art	произведение искусства
sphere [sfɪə] *n c*	сфера
represent [ˌreprɪˈzent] *v*	представлять, являться представителем
Who will your company be represented by?	
Who will represent your company?	
attract [əˈtrækt] *v*	привлекать, притягивать
to attract everybody's interest	привлекать всеобщий интерес
attractive [əˈtræktɪv] *adj*	привлекательный
an attractive woman (idea, offer, etc.)	

EXERCISES

1

Прочитайте вслух и переведите примеры на новые слова.

1. industry and agriculture; fairs and exhibitions; science and art.
2. an attractive face; their attractive offer.
3. Nothing can be done well without preparation.
4. A lot of work is being done in preparation for the agricultural fair.
5. A team of TV reporters came to film the last–minute preparations for the exhibition.
6. This company was set up a few years ago.
7. We find the idea of setting up a joint venture very attractive.
8. The preparations for setting up a joint venture are in full swing.
9. Various art schools are represented in this museum.
10. Our order could be larger if your prices were more attractive to us.

— 198 —

2

Перефразируйте, употребляя пассив, сделайте выделенное слов подлежащим.

1. The workers have already set up **all the tents.**
2. They set up **their joint venture** a long time ago, didn't they?
3. Have you packed **all the catalogues** yet?
4. Some exhibits in the educational section attract **a lot of visitors.**
5. When the press arrived at the exhibition grounds, the managers were making **last–minute preparations** before the opening ceremony [ˈserɪmənɪ].
6. Who will represent **your company** at the next conference?
7. Are they still discussing **the offer?**
8. They will discuss **various problems in industry and agriculture.**
9. The flood did **a lot of damage to the country's agriculture**.
10. The best athletes will represent **the club** at the Games.
11. We are still discussing **your proposal.**
12. They were signing **the contract** when the press arrived.

3

Ответьте на вопросы.

1. Have any interesting exhibitions or fairs been held recently?

2. Have you been to any of them? If so, say a few words about it.
3. Why are international exhibitions held? Have you ever worked at one?
4 What kind of exhibitions and fairs attract most visitors?
5. What do you know about joint ventures?

4

Переведите на английский язык.

1. Интервью было показано по телевидению на прошлой неделе.
2. Мы уверены, что проблема будет решена в ближайшем будущем.
3. Фирма будет представлена несколькими специалистами.
4. Подождите немного. Сейчас подписываются последние документы.
5. Когда будет обсуждаться этот вопрос?
6. Когда мы пришли, обсуждался очень важный вопрос.
7. Когда я приехал на выставку, экспонаты все еще расставляли на стендах.
8. Почему отменили матч?
9. Почему отложили встречу?
10. Все урегулировано, не правда ли?
11. Обо всем договорились, не правда ли?

TOPICS FOR DISCUSSION AND NEW WORDS (continued)

On the Isle of Kizhi

Guide: This church is an excellent example of Russian **wooden architecture**. It was built at the **turn** of the seventeenth **century** and is made of **wood.** It was built with an **axe** alone, no other **tools** were used by the craftsman, and the wooden parts were joined without any **nails.**

Tourists: Fantastic!
Unbelievable!
Incredible!

Tourist A: It's the most beautiful wooden church I've ever seen! Who was it designed by?.

Guide: It was designed and built by one and the same man. There's a **legend** about him. Would you like to hear it?

Tourists: Yes, yes, of course!

Guide: Well, the legend says that after finishing his work he looked at the church and thought: "I'll never be able to build anything better than this, even if it takes me a **lifetime**!" "So he threw his **axe** into the **lake** and left the **island for good!"**

Learn these words:

isle [aɪl] *n c*	остров *(поэт. и в географ. названиях)*
the British Isles	Британские острова
island [ˈaɪlənd] *n c*	остров
on an island	
church [tʃɔːtʃ] *n c*	церковь
wooden [ˈwudn] *adj*	деревянный
wood [wud] *n c u*	1. *(исчисл.)* небольшой лес
forest [ˈfɔrɪst] *n c*	большой лес, лесной массив
A wood's smaller than a forest.	
We went for a walk in the wood(s).	
	2. *(неисч.)* дерево (строительный материал)
These boxes are made of wood.	
architecture [ˈɑːkɪtekʃɔ] *n u*	архитектура
architect *n c*	архитектор
century [ˈsentʃɔrɪ] *n c*	век, столетие
at the turn of the century	на рубеже веков ; в начале (или в конце) века,
axe [æks] *n c*	топор
tool *n c*	инструмент
craftsman [ˈkrɑːftsmən] *n c*	мастер, умелец
join *v*	зд.соединять
nail *n c*	1. зд. гвоздь.

design *v*

зд. проектировать, создать проект

legend [ˈledʒənd] *n c*

легенда

lifetime

(вся) жизнь

the work of a lifetime

труд всей жизни

throw, (threw, thrown)
[θrəu͵θru:͵θrəun] *v*

бросать

Don't throw these papers away, keep them.

— 201 — **lake** *n c*

озеро *(в геогр. назв. не имеет артикля)*

Lake Baikal

for good

навсегда, насовсем

Syn. **for ever**

EXERCISES

Прочитайте и переведите примеры на новые слова.

1. modern architecture; classical architecture; green architecture; English architecture of the eighteenth century; an outstanding architect.
2. an old church; some beautiful churches; a little village church.
3. The furniture's made of expensive wood. What kind of wood is it made of? It would be even more expensive if it were made of better wood. The wooden parts are all hand–made.
4. May I join you? I'll join you later. We'd be happy if you joined us on Sunday. He would have gone to college if he hadn't joined the army. Will you join me for lunch?
5. The island and the town are joined by a bridge. All the parts of this model are joined together with little steel nails.
6. Who was that building designed by?
   The building was designed as a big shop, but it's used for exhibitions.

2

Заполните пропуски предлогами.

1. Who was the monument designed ...?
2. What kind ... wood is this church built ...?
3. The splendid green architecture ... this place has been described ... many travellers.
4. All the equipment ... the lab is made ... steel and plastic.
5. What shall I fix the shelves ...?
6. All the dishes ... the table were cooked ... the hostess.
7. The last match was won ... the Sheffield team, wasn't it?
8. I saw it ... my own eyes and heard it ... my own ears.
9. Could you give me something to write ...?

— 202 —

3

Ответьте на вопросы.

1. Have you ever been to Kizhi? If so, when?
2. Where else can you see examples of Russian wooden architecture?
3. Do you like sightseeing?
4. Which do you find more interesting – to go sightiseeing with a guide or all by yourself?
5. Do you usually read anything about the place before you go sightseeing?
6. Do you take photos, or make slides or films when sightseeig?
7. Could you show us some photos, slides or films you have made and tell us about the places you've been to?

4

Какие вопросы нужно задать, чтобы получить эти ответы.

1. This hospital was designed by **Kazakov**.
2. All these little wooden houses were built with **very simple tools**.
3. All that damage has been done by **the flood**.
4. The city's being designed by **several well – known architects**.
5. It would take **a lifetime** to build such a house with only simple tools!
6. All these churches were built by **Russian craftsmen**.
7. The church is built of **wood**.

5

Повторите, используя подсказанные слова.

1. It would take you a lifetime if you **worked alone.**
   • didn't use the right tools • weren't prepared to work very hard •
2. The work would have taken us a much longer time if we hadn't **prepared for it carefully**
   • asked experts to join us • set up a join venture • drawn up a careful plan • found the right team of specialists •
3. I'd join **you** if I had time.
   • them • their team • my friends •
4. Will you join me for **lunch**?
   dinner • lunch at one o'clock • dinner this evening •

6

Переведите на английский язык.

1. Этот дом – образец английской архитектуры восемнадцатого века. Он был построен одним из самых известных (well–known) архитекторов того времени.
2. Все деревянные части этих игрушек сделаны очень простыми инструментами.
3. История этого острова полна легенд, которые были собраны и записаны известным писателем прошлого века. Это был труд всей его жизни.
4. Я бы с удовольствием присоединился к вам, если бы не был так занят.
5. – Вы пообедаете со мной? – Спасибо, с удовольствием.

GRAMMAR
(continued)

18.6. Пассивный залог (продолжение)

Из значения пассивного залога (объект действия важнее исполнителя) следует, что он существует только у глаголов, способных иметь после себя дополнения, то есть объекты действия. Эти дополнения становятся подлежащими пассивной конструкции.

Подлежащим становится прямое дополнение (*кого, что?*)

Активный залог	Пассивный залог
1. He arranged **everything** in good time.	1. **Everything** was arranged in good time. Все было организовано своевременно.

Подлежащим становится косвенное дополнение (кому, кого?)

Активный залог	Пассивный залог
1. The teacher allowed [ə´laud] **Jim** to miss classes on Friday.	1. **Jim** was allowed to miss classes on Friday. Джиму разрешили пропустить занятия в пятницу.
2. We asked **him** to take part in the discussion.	2. He was asked to take part in the discussion. Его попросили принять участие в прениях.
3. The hostess introduced **me** to all the guests.	3. **I** was introduced to all the guests. Меня представили всем гостям.
4. Someone wants **you** on the phone.	4. **You** are wanted on the phone. Вас просят к телефону.

Подлежащим становится предложное дополнение (о ком, о чем, для кого, для чего? и т.д.)

Активный залог	Пассивный залог
1. Everybody listened to **the speakers** very carefully.	1. **The speakers** were listened to very carefully. Выступающих внимательно слушали.
2. Both children and adults were looking for **the lost dog** everywhere.	2. **The lost dog** was being looked for everywhere. Пропавшую собаку искали везде.

Как видно из примеров, если подлежащим пассивной конструкции становится предложное дополнение, предлог остается на своем месте после глагола и произносится без ударения, но достаточно отчетливо.

ПРИМЕЧАНИЯ:

1. Многие глаголы могут иметь два дополнения - прямое *(что?)* и косвенное *(кому?)*. К таким глаголам относятся, например, give, **send**, **show**, **lend**, **pay**, **offer**.

В пассивном залоге с этими глаголами возможны два варианта:

They gave *the boy* a *lot of presents* on his birthday.

{
1. **The boy was given** a lot of presents on his birthday.

2. **A lot of presents were given** to the boy on his birthday
}

Предпочтение чаще отдается первому варианту, когда подлежащим пассивного предложения является лицо, а не предмет.

2. Есть и такие глаголы, которые в пассивном залоге употребляются только с подлежащим - предметом, а не лицом. К таким глаголам относятся, например, **explain** и **describe**.

Активный залог	Пассивный залог
1. They explained **everything** to me very carefully.	1. **Everything** was explained to me very carefully.
2. The commentator described **the situation** to the viewers as very dangerous.	2. **The situation** was described as very dangerous.

EXERCISES

Прочитайте вслух и переведите

a. 1. I was asked to fill in the form in both Russian and English.
2. We weren't told to give the English translation. If we'd been told to, we'd certainly have done so.
3. The tourists are asked to be in the hotel lobby at exactly ten.
4. The children were allowed to stay up as long as the adults.
5. The singer was given so many flowers that she could hardly

hold them.
6. Our counterparts have just been shown round the factory.
7. All the important things have been explained to them.
8. He's been appointed ambassador to an African country.
9. Excuse me, you are wanted on the phone.
10. He's never been taught to play the piano, has he?

b. 1. Two more typists have just been sent for.
2. His recent publication's much talked about.
3. All the children are looked after by trained nurses.
4. If everything hadn't been agreed on in good time, we'd have found ourselves in a very difficult situation.

2

Перефразируйте, употребив пассив. Сделайте выделенное слово подлежащим.

Дано: Требуется:

Nobody asked **me** to call   I wasn't asked to call back.
back.

1. A friend has invited **me** to a birthday party.
2. Did they ask **you** many questions?
3. Their counterparts don't allow **them** to change anything in the design.
4. They appointed **him** president of the new firm.
5. We've already sent for **the doctor.**
6. We'll agree on **the changes** at the next meeting.
7. People talked about **his recent work** at the conference.
8. We have already dealt with **the price problem.**

3

Какие вопросы нужно было задать, чтобы получить эти ответы?

1. **Jane** was asked to file those papers, not me!
2. **Joan's** wanted on the phone, not John!
3. I was only offered that job **a few days ago**.
4. This monument was designed by **a very well−known architect.**
5. The date'll be agreed on **next week**.
6. I was taught the piano **at a music school.**
7. **Three** specialists are going to be interviewed for the job.

4 🔲

Прочитайте и переведите, обращая особое внимание на форму инфинитива.

1. Everything can be arranged in good time.
2. Our obligations under the contract can only be fulfilled if we are given answers to all the questions on this list.
3. If the weather doesn't change for the better, the match may be cancelled.
4. If the fire brigade hadn't arrived so quickly, the house might have been destroyed by the fire.
5. If I don't get well by Friday, our appointment will have to be put off.
6. All spheres of life are going to be represented at the exhibition.
7. Is anything else going to be done in the near future?
8. This equipment has to be looked after like a baby!
9. All these things will have to be agreed on.

5

Повторите, употребляя подсказанные слова.

1. These exhibits must be **packed very carefully**.

   • packed in wooden boxes • sent by air • looked at again • examined carefully • arranged on those stands •

2. The matter can be **discussed at once**.

   • discussed again • settled very easily • settled in a different way • dealt with right away •

3. The appointment may be **cancelled**.

   • called off • put off till some other time • fixed for another date•

4. These papers have to be **read very carefully**.

   • looked through again • looked at once more• signed and filed•

5. This idea's going to be **discussed**.

   • talked about • developed • understood by everybody • supported •

TOPICS FOR DISCUSSION AND NEW WORDS

1

An Interview for a Job

These three girls have just been interviewed for a job, but only one will be **chosen** by the interviewers.

During the interview they were asked a lot of questions, and then they were told to type out some business letters. They were also asked to send some messages by telex and telefax, and use a computer.

Here are some notes the interviewers made while the **applicants** were answering their questions:

Sheila Simpson. Age 26. **Married.** Two children. Had two years' **experience** of work as a secretary with Byrd & Co. **Ltd.** Gave up the job when her second child was born. Doesn't mind if me make **inquiries** about her at her **former** place of work. Is fluent in French and German.

Alice Campbell. Age 28. **Divorced.** No children. Has a job as shop assistant in a **department store**, but isn't satisfied with it for two reasons:

a) finds it unpleasant to deal with some of the **customers;**

b) lives a long way from the store.

Lucy Davies. Age 19. **Unmarried.** No working experience. Was taught to type and operate a computer at school. An excellent figure and a lovely face! Could be a fashion model, but prefers a **secretarial** job as a start for her business **career.** Doesn't mind answering personal questions.

Which of them would you give the job to?

Learn these words:

choose (chose, chosen)

[tʃuːz, tʃəuz, ´tʃəuzn] *v* выбирать

to choose an apple (a friend, a book, etc.)

If I were him, I'd have chosen a more interesting subject for a paper.

applicant [´æplɪkənt] *n c* кандидат, претендент

Syn. **candidate** [´kændɪdət]

— 209 —

application [ˌæplɪ´keɪʃn] *n c* зд. заявление

The manager received seven applications for the job.

to make an application **to** ... написать заявление в ...
for ... по поводу, о ...
He made an application to the firm Он написал (подал) за-
for the position of manager. явление
на фирму о приеме на
должность менеджера.

experience [ɪks´pɪərɪəns] *n u* 1. опыт (жизненный, профессиональный и т.п.)

He hasn't had enough experience У него нет (не было) до-
for this position. статочного опыта для
этой должности.

working (teaching, производственный (пре-
etc.) experience подавательский и т.п.)
опыт

experience in/of опыт в этой работе
this sort of work

experience *n c* 2. случай, приключение, пе-
режитое

It was a pleasant (unpleasant, unusual, etc.) experience.

experienced [ɪks´pɪərɪənst] *adj* опытный

Ant. **inexperienced** неопытный

an experienced teacher (doctor, nurse, etc.)

Ltd (limited) лимитед (сокращение после
названия акционерного об-
щества с ограниченной от-
ветственностью)

Benson & Co. Ltd (Benson and Company Limited)

inquiry (enquiry) [ɪnˈkwaɪərɪ] *n c*   справка, вопрос, запрос

an inquiry office	справочное бюро
to make inquiries (about...)	наводить справки о ...
to make an enquiry for ...	сделать запрос на ... (заявить о намерении ку– пить товар)

former [ˈfɔːmə] *adj*   бывший, прежний

My former chief (teacher, student, etc.)

divorce [dɪˈvɔːs] *v n*   развестись; развод

department store   универсальный магазин
  [dɪˈpɑːtmənt stɔː]

customer [ˈkʌstəmə] *n c*   покупатель, клиент

figure [ˈfɪgə] *n*   фигура, цифра

secretarial [ˌsekreˈteərɪəl] *adj*   секретарский

career [kəˈrɪə] *n c*   профессия, занятие, карьера

personal [ˈpɜːsənl] *adj*   личный, персональный, зд.
  личного характера

EXERCISES

Закончите предложение, употребив слова, данные в скобках.

Дано: If the girls couldn't type, use a telex, a telefax and a
computer they (not to be invited for an interview).

Требуется: If the girls couldn't type, use a telex, a telefax and a
computer they wouldn't have been invited
for an interview.

1. If business messages were only sent by telex, the girls (not to
be asked to type out business letters).
2. The girls wouldn't have been asked how they could work with
a computer if computers (not to become an ordinary piece of
office equipment).
3. If Sheila hadn't had another baby, she (not to give up her
former job).
4. If Lucy didn't want to go into business, she (not to make an

application for a job with the firm).

5. If Lucy preferred a home to a career, she (to try to find herself someone to marry).
6. If the interviewers aren't pleased with the results of the interview, none of the girls (to be chosen for the job).
7. If none of the girls is chosen for the job, other candidates (to be interviewed).

Перефразируйте, употребив пассив. Сделайте выделенное слово подлежащим.

Дано: They are going to interview **some other candidates.**

Требуется: Some other candidates are going to be interviewed.

1. They are going to interview **three girls** for a job.
2. They will only choose **one of them** to work with their firm.
3. They told **the girls** to type the letters both quickly and carefully.
4. They have actually taken a **decision**, but they haven't told **the girls** about it.
5. They will ask **the girls** to find out the decision the next day by telephone.
6. We have already made **some inquiries**.
7. They would prefer **a more experienced worker.**
8. The manager asked **the customer** to explain why she wanted her money back.

Ответьте на вопросы

1. Do you think an interview for a job is a good way to choose the right worker?
2. Is it always necessary to make inquiries about the applicant?
3. Have you ever interviewed anyone for a job?
4. Would you always prefer an experienced worker to a beginner?
5. Do many experienced workers like to share their experience with their inexperienced colleagues?
6. Could an inexperienced worker be easier to deal with than an experienced one? What does it depend on?
7. Have you ever been interviewed for a job?
8. What questions were you asked?

Learn these words:

auction [ˈɔːkʃn] *n c*   аукцион

     to sell (buy) sth at an auction

private [ˈpraɪvɪt] *adj*   частный

     private property   частная собственность
     [ˈprɔpəti]

enormous [ɪˈnɔːməs] *adj*   огромный

     The play was an enormous success.

enormously [ɪˈnɔːməsli] *adv*   чрезвычайно, невероятно

3 —
     The town has changed enormously during recent years.

sum *n c*   сумма

owner [ˈəunə] *n c*   владелец

from now on   отныне

invitation [ˌɪnvɪˈteɪʃn] *n c*   приглашение

invite [ɪnˈvaɪt] *v*   приглашать

work *n c*   зд. произведение

a work of art   произведение искусства

collector [kəˈlektə] *n c*   коллекционер

disaster [dɪˈzɑːstə] *n c*   катастрофа, бедствие

     a political (economic) disaster
     It was a disaster!
     The flood was a terrible disaster.

gallery [ˈgæləri] *n c*   галерея

     a picture gallery
     the Tretyakov Gallery

afford [əˈfɔːd] *v*   разрешить себе, позволить
                                      себе (после *can* или *be able*
                                        to)

     I can't afford a more expensive car yet.
     You can afford a short holiday, can't you?

Внимание! После глагола **afford** употребляется **инфинитив**.
I can't afford *to spend* so much time on telephone conversations!

4

Разыграйте следующие эпизоды:

1. Интервью с кандидатами, претендующими на должж фирме.
2. Обсуждение результатов интервью теми, кто его про

Действующие лица:

менеджеры, их помощники, секретарь, претенденты на ность.

Выражения и вопросы, которые вы можете исп вать:

Who's next?

Do come in! Won't you sit down? Make yourself comfort

Do you mind if we ask you a few questions (give you test, ask you to write a fax, etc.)?

What sort of school (college) did you go to? How well did at school (college)? How long did you work in various job your present one? Why do you want to change it?

What sort of work would you prefer to do?

TOPICS FOR DISCUSSION AND NEW WOF (continued)

At an Art Auction.

This is an art **auction** in Great Britain. A picture from a **private** collection has just been sold for an **enormous sum** , and its new **owner** is being congratulated. The picture will be sent to his home in the United States, and **from now on** it will only be seen by those who will have a personal **invitation** from him. It may never be exhibited in museums or picture galleries.

A lot of works of art are bought at auctions by private col This is a **disaster** for museums and picture galleries, whic **afford** to pay such **enormously** high prices. That may be the why many works of art will be lost to the public for good the owner decides to exhibit them.

unless [ʌn´les] *conj*　　　　если только не …

Syn. **if not**

He won't come unless he's invited personally.

Он не приедет, если только его не пригласят персонально.

EXERCISES

1

Прочитайте и переведите примеры на новые слова.

1 an art auction; a furniture auction; a book auction; a public auction; to hold an auction; to be sold by auction.

2. private property; public property; collective property; national [´næʃnəl] property.

3. an enormous success; an enormous difference; enormous progress; an enormous sum; (an) enormous interest; an enormous collection; an enormous disaster.

4. This auction's usually held once a year.
When was the auction held?
Was the picture bought at an auction?
Their property may be sold by auction.

5. If I could afford a more expensive car, I'd buy one.
I'd go on holiday if I could afford to.
I can't afford to be idle.
Now they can afford to buy a larger house.
If they could afford to have a larger family, they'd have another child.
I'm afraid I can't afford it yet.

2

Повторите предложения, используя подсказанные слова.

1. We can't afford to **waste so much time.**

• wait so long • buy such expensive things • have such a long holiday• spend so much money • buy things at auctions•

2. We won't sign the contract unless **you make all the necessary changes.**

• they change the design • they agree to our proposals • we have a better idea of the situation • the economic situation changes for the better •

3. It would have been a disaster if they hadn't **agreed to help.**

• invited experienced specialists • had enough experience • hadn't dealt with the problem at once •

3

Ответьте на вопросы по тексту.

1. The new owner of the picture is enormously rich, isn't he?
2. Will the picture be exhibited in museums or picture galleries?
3. What's the reason why many works of art are sold by auction and bought by private collectiors?
4. Do you agree that it's a disaster for museums and picture galleries?
5. Is a picture that goes to a private collection always lost to the public for good?
6. Why can't museums and picture galleries afford to buy works of art at auctions?
7. Have you ever been to an auction?
8. Have you watched one on the telly?
9. How often do you go to picture galleries and art exhibitions?
10. How often are art exhibitions held in your city?
11. Can you afford the time to go to many exhibitions?

Unit 10

GRAMMAR

19. Прошедшее время группы **Perfect (Past Perfect)**

19.1. Past Perfect образуется из прошедшего времени вспомогательного глагола **have** и третьей формы **(Participle 2)** смыслового глагола.

Утвердительная форма:	I **had known** (I'd known [aɪd ´nəʊn])
Вопросительная форма:	**Had** you **known?** [´hædju´nəʊn]
Отрицательная форма:	We **hadn't known**

— 216 —

19.2. Past Perfect употребляется, когда речь идет о действии, которое уже совершилось (или еще не совершилось) до другого прошедшего действия:

1. We arrived five minutes late. The train **had gone!**	Мы прибыли с опозданием на пять минут. Поезд *ушел!*
2. The room was in awful disorder. Someone **had been** in it!	Комната была в страшном беспорядке! Кто—то в ней *побывал!*
3. We couldn't answer your fax at once. We **hadn't taken a final decision** by that time yet.	Мы не смогли ответить на ваш факс сразу. К тому времени мы еще *не приняли окончательного решения.*
4. I didn't join you for lunch, because I'**d had a snack** in a café and wasn't hungry.	Я не пошел с вами обедать, потому что *успел перекусить* в кафе и не хотел есть.
5. I remembered (that) I **hadn't turned off** the telly.	Я вспомнил, что *не выключил* телевизор.

6. He thought (that) he **had seen** the man before.	Он подумал, что *видел* этого человека раньше.
7. He said (that) they **had discussed** everything.	Он сказал, что они все *об-судили*.
8. They told us (that) they **had managed** to solve the problem.	Они сказали нам, что им *удалось решить* эту проблему.

19.3. Эта временная форма всегда выражает идею *предшествования* другому *прошлому* действию, например, когда рассказ о последовательных событиях в прошлом содержит экскурсы в еще более отдаленное прошлое:

His paper was listened to with great interest and he was asked a lot of questions.	Его доклад был выслушан с огромным интересом, и ему задали много вопросов.
He **had come** from a small town, and nobody **had heard** of him before.	Он *приехал* из небольшого города, и никто о нем раньше *не слышал*.

ПРИМЕЧАНИЯ.

1. В сложноподчиненных предложениях времени с союзами **before** и **after** употребление Past Perfect зависит от того, есть ли необходимость *подчеркивать* предшествование одного действия другому. Если такой необходимости нет, употребляется простое прошедшее время, так как слова **before** и **after** сами показывают последовательность действий.

1. I turned off the light before I left the room.	Я потушил свет, прежде чем вышел из комнаты.
2. After the host (had) introduced the guests to each other, they all went to the dining room and sat down to table.	После того как хозяин представил гостей друг другу, все прошли в столовую и сели к столу.

2. **Past Perfect** *может не употребляться*, когда время совершения действия выражено *точной датой*:

1. We found out that they (had) started a joint venture in 1989.	Мы выяснили, что они основали совместное предприятие в 1989 г.

2. He said he was born in 1960.

Он сказал, что родился в 1960 г.

19.4. **Past Perfect** употребляется и в страдательном залоге (**Past Perfect Passive**):

When the fire brigade *arrived*, a large part of the building **had been destroyed** by the fire.

Когда *прибыла* пожарная команда, большая часть здания *была* уже *уничтожена* огнем.

EXERCISES

Прочитайте вслух и объясните, почему употреблено то или иное время.

1. When we arrived at the theatre, the play had already begun.

2. When we arrived at the theatre, the play hadn't begun yet.

3. When we arrived at the theatre, the play was beginning.

4. It was five to ten in the morning. The exhibition had not opened yet, but all the preparations for the opening ceremony had been made, and a lot of people who had come to watch it were standing outside and waiting.

5. Many reporters wanted to talk to the winner, but he was too tired to talk. He had run a long **race** and wanted to rest. He was very **happy, because** it was his first real **victory**. He had never taken part in such an outstanding event before.

race [reɪs] *n*

любое соревнование на скорость: бег, скачки и т.д.

victory ['vɪktərɪ]

победа

2

Раскройте скобки, употребив необходимую глагольную форму.

When we (join) a group of tourists, who (stand) in front of an old church and (listen) to the guide, she already (tell) them most of the story. When she (finish) speaking, I (go up) to her and (ask) her a few questions. She (be) kind enough to answer them, and

I (find out) that the church (be designed and built) at the turn of the 15th century by an unknown architect.

3

— 219 —

Прочитайте начало детективных рассказов и придумайте свои версии окончания.

1. When John was driving home, he had an unpleasant feeling that something had happened while he was away. He parked the car and went to open the front door. He turned the key, the door opened, and he found himself in the hall. When he went into the sitting room, he saw that someone had been there, because the room was in a terrible mess. Then he remembered that he hadn't **locked** the front door. He turned to go and lock the door and saw a man standing in the hall. John thought he had seen the face before. "What are you doing here?" he asked. "I. . .I have lost my way," the **stranger** answered. . .

Learn these words:

lock *v*   запереть

stranger ['streɪndʒə] *n c*   незнакомец.

2. When the detectives arrived, the auction was in full swing. A picture by a famous painter had just been sold. The new owner had paid an enormous sum for it. He did not know that the picture had been **stolen** from an art gallery in a small European state. The **auctioneer** did not know that either, but the detectives did. . .

Learn these words:

steal (stole, stolen) *v*   украсть

auctioneer [‚ɔːkʃə'nɪə] *n c*   аукционер

 4

Переведите на английский язык.

1. Когда я приехал повидаться с ним в гостинице, он уже дал интервью журналистам и отдыхал.
2. Когда я приехал к нему в гостиницу, мы связались с нашими партнерами по телефону и назначили с ними встречу.
3. Когда прибыл ваш факс, мы еще не получили определенного ответа от наших партнеров.

4. Когда я вошел в конференц-зал, свое сообщение делал какой-то молодой архитектор. Его внимательно слушали. Я нашел место и тоже начал слушать. Мне очень понравились его идеи. Он проделал большую работу в своем городе, чтобы сделать его более современным, более удобным для людей и более красивым.

5. Когда мы присоединились к туристам, которые слушали своего гида, он рассказывал им легенду об истории этого места. Я никогда раньше не слышал этой легенды и нашел ее настолько интересной, что решил ее записать.

6. Я не был уверен, что выключил газ и решил вернуться домой.

7. Мы узнали, что наши партнеры еще не приняли окончательного решения.

8. Они сказали нам, что все необходимые приготовления уже сделаны.

GRAMMAR

20. <u>Понятие о простых формах причастий.</u>

Participle One (writing, translating)

Participle Two (written, translated)

20.1. Эти причастия уже встречались нам в составе глагольных форм.

Причастие первое - во временах группы **Continuous** (*I'm writing; I was writing*)

Причастие второе - во временах группы **Perfect** и в пассивном залоге:(*I've written. It was written. It has been translated*.)

20.2. Причастия употребляются и самостоятельно в функциях, сходных с функциями русских причастий и деепричастий. В положении *перед* существительным они являются определениями и отвечают на вопрос *какой?*

1. The **leading** athletes	*Ведущие* спортсмены
2. His **ruined** hopes	Его *рухнувшие* надежды
3. The **damaged** goods	*Поврежденный* товар
4. The **cancelled** appointment	*Отмененная* встреча
5. Her **smiling** face	Ее *улыбающееся* лицо

20.3. В положении *после* существительного причастие обычно сопровождается пояснительными словами, образуя причастный оборот:

1. The athlete *leading in the first event* is a representative of a college team.	Спортсмен, *ведущий в первом виде соревнований*, является представителем вузовской команды.
2. People *smoking so much* can't be healthy.	Люди, *курящие так много*, не могут быть здоровыми.
3. The match *cancelled last week* will be held next Sunday.	*Отмененный на прошлой* неделе матч состоится в следующее воскресенье.
4. The policeman went up to the man *standing next to the car*.	Полицейский подошел к человеку, *стоявшему рядом с машиной*.

Как видно из примеров, английский определительный причастный оборот всегда стоит после определяемого существительного (в русском языке он может стоять и до и после определяемого существительного).

20.4. Так же, как и в русском языке, причастные обороты не характерны для разговорной речи, но они весьма употребительны в художественной литературе (в описаниях), научной и общественно-политической литературе и деловых документах.

Как и в русском языке, определительный причастный оборот является стилистическим способом сократить определительное придаточное предложение.

1. There were trees on both sides of the road leading to the church.	По обеим сторонам дороги, ведущей к церкви, росли деревья.
(There were trees on both sides of the road which led to the church).	(По обеим сторонам дороги, которая вела к церкви ...)
2. We enclose a list of goods damaged in transit.	Прилагаем список товаров, поврежденных в пути.
(... which were damaged in transit)	(... которые были повреждены в пути)

20.5. Причастный оборот с причастием первым может также сокращать и *обстоятельственные* придаточные предложения, например, придаточное предложение *време-ни*:

1. *While looking through the documents*, he found several errors [`erɔz] in them.	Просматривая документы, он нашел в них несколько серьезных ошибок.
(While he was looking through the documents . . .)	(Когда он просматривал документы. . .)
2. *When crossing the road* in England, look first to the right, not to the left.	Переходя дорогу в Англии, сначала посмотрите направо, а не налево.
(When you cross the road . . .)	(Когда будете переходить дорогу. . .)

Как видно из примеров, в функции обстоятельства Participle One соответствует русскому *деепричастию*.

Перед Participle One часто употребляются союзы while *в то время как* и when *когда*, которые на русский язык в деепричастных оборотах не переводятся.

20.6. Причастный оборот в функции обстоятельства *причины* является стилистическим способом сократить придаточное предложение *причины*:

1. *Knowing the town very well* he was an excellent guide (As he knew the town. . .)	*Хорошо зная город*, он был прекрасным экскурсоводом.
2. *Not knowing the working instructions* we couldn't use the equipment.	*Не зная инструкций по эксплуатации*, мы не смогли пользоваться этим оборудованием.
(As we didn't know. . .)	(Так как мы не знали. . .)
3. Being very busy he couldn't attend the conference.	Будучи очень занятым, он не смог присутствовать на конференции
(As he was very busy. . .)	(Так как он был очень занят . . .)

ПРИМЕЧАНИЕ: Причастный оборот с глаголом **be** (**being ill, being tired**) не может быть обстоятельством времени. Русскому предложению: *Находясь в Кижах, мы посмотрели образцы* *деревянной архитектуры* — соответствует: *When we were in Kizhi...*, или — *When in Kizhi, we...* . Однако причастный оборот с **be** может выражать причину:

Being ill he couldn't come	*Будучи больным,* он не смог прийти.
(As he was ill...)	(Так как он был болен...)

EXERCISES

— 223 — **Прочитайте и переведите образцы книжно-письменной и официальной речи.**

1. We would like to contact someone in your institute interested in our programme and sharing our ideas.
2. All the workers operating this equipment must read the instructions very carefully and follow them.
3. The city has houses representing various architectural styles.
4. The houses damaged by the flood will be rebuilt.
5. Congratulating the film director on his success, the speaker said that his film was a great achievement of the whole team.
6. While introducing her guests to each other, the hostess says a few kind words to each of them.
7. When planning your daily routine, don't forget to leave time for outdoor exercise.
8. Not knowing our partners' point of view, we decided not to give a definite answer.
9. Being very strict, he never allowed his students to miss classes.

Перефразируйте, употребляя придаточные или самостоятельные предложения вместо причастных оборотов.

1. It was a film about some researchers making interesting experiments in a sphere of science unknown to most of the viewers.
2. While reading the letter, he smoked one cigarette after another.
3. When driving in this road, do not exceed 60 miles per hour.
4. Feeling very tired, he cancelled all his appointments.
5. Being very careful, he never drives dangerously.

TOPICS FOR DISCUSSION AND NEW WORDS

A FEW FACTS FROM THE HISTORY OF BIG CITIES

London, the capital of Great Britain, is one of the oldest cities in Europe.

When Julius Ceasar crossed the English Channel and **invaded** Britain as far as the Thames in the middle of the first century **BC** , people had already **settled** there and were living on both sides of the **river**.

Like many other very old cities, London was never planned. It **grew** around two centres — a **fort** the **Romans** built on one **bank** of the Thames, and an **abbey**, **founded** later on the other bank. As time went by, the place round the Roman fort developed into the City of London, the country's business centre, the abbey is now known as Westminster Abbey.

By the middle of the first century **AD** London had already been in **existence** for about a hundred years. Roads leading to other towns had changed into streets, market grounds became squares. London was growing . . .

— 224 —

At about the same time, in the year 1147, in a part of the world Londoners had never heard of, a town was founded by a **prince** on a **site** which he chose for its beauty and convenient **location** in the middle of a **magnificent** forest, on the bank of a river called the Moskva. The river gave its name to the city which later became the **capital** of the Russian **state**. When the first trade contacts were established between England and Russia, the English **pronounced** the name of the Russian capital their own way *Muscovy*. From this comes the modern **Muscovite**, a person living in Moscow.

If we **compare** the maps of Moscow and London, we can see a **similarity** between them.

Like London, Moscow was never planned. It grew up around its centre, which had been **surrounded** by a wooden wall by the first **residents**. The wooden wall was later **replaced** by a **brick** one, and **palaces**, **cathedrals** and churches were built **inside** it, **forming** what is now known as the Kremlin.

Now again, new houses were built around this centre, forming enormous **rings**, and the roads to other towns **gradually** changed into streets running across them.

(to be continued)

Имена собственные, географические названия и общепринятые сокращения.

Julius Caesar   Юлий Цезарь
    [´dʒuːljəs ´siːzə]
the English Channel   Ламанш

Запомните: названия рек употребляются с **определенным артиклем.**

the Thames [temz]	Темза

BC [bɪˊsiː](Before Christ) [kraɪst]	до Рождества Христова; до нашей эры.
in 45 BC	
AD [eɪˊdiː] (Anno Domini *Lat*) [ˊænəuˊdɔmɪnaɪ]	после Рождества Христова; . . .нашей эры
in 57 AD	
the Romans [ˊrəumənz]	римляне *(ист.)*
When in Rome do as the Romans do.	Когда живешь в Риме, поступай как римляне (пословица)
Rome was not built in a day.	Рим не был построен за день (пословица)
Westminster Abbey [ˊwestmɪnstərˊæbɪ]	Вестминстерское аббатство
Muscovite [ˊmʌskəvaɪt]	москвич

Learn these words:

invade [ɪnˊveɪd] *v*	вторгаться в. . ., напасть на . . .
Napoleon invaded Russia in 1812.	
river [ˊrɪvə] *n c*	река
settle *v*	зд. поселиться
fort *n c*	форт, укрепленное военное поселение
grow (grew, grown) *v*	расти
found (founded, founded) *v*	основать
bank *n c*	зд. берег реки

Для вашего сведения:

shore [ʃɔː] *n c*	берег моря или большого озера (полоса земли вдоль берега)

to walk along the shore

coast [kəust] *n c*	берег моря или океана (район, часть которого выходит к морю или океану)

the North Pacific coast
on the south coast of France

seaside *n u*	море—приморское место отдыха

We're going to the seaside for our holiday.

beach *n c*	пляж
embankment [im'bæŋkmənt] *n c*	набережная реки

The Thames embankment

seafront ['siːfrʌnt] *n c*	набережная моря или океана

existence [ig'zistəns] *n u*	существование

Do you believe in the existence of life on other planets?

exist [ig'zist] *v*	существовать

The Roman Empire existed for several centuries.	Римская империя просуществовала несколько веков.

prince [prins] *n c*	князь, принц
site *n c*	зд. место, площадка
location [ləu'keiʃn] *n c*	расположение, местоположение

a suitable location for the new factory.

magnificent [mæg'nifisnt] *adj*	великолепный
state *n c*	государство; штат

establish [ɪ´stæblɪʃ] *v*   основать, учредить, установить

  Syn. set up

  to establish a business (a company, etc.)

  to establish business (diplomatic, cultural) relations

pronounce [prə´nauns] *v*   произносить

capital [´kæpɪtl] *n c*   1. столица

                                 2. капитал

compare [kəm´pɛə] *v*   сравнивать

  The two designs can't be compared.

  Let me compare my translation with yours.

similarity [sɪmɪ´lærɪtɪ] *n*   подобие, сходство

similar [´sɪmɪlə] *adj*   подобный, сходный, похожий, аналогичный

  We have similar views on many things.

  Model A is similar **in** quality **to** model B.

  We can offer you other models of similar quality.

surround [sə´raund] *v*   окружить, обнести

  To be surrounded by   быть окруженным кем–л,
  (with) sb sth.   чем–л.

  The journalists surrounded him.

  The palace was   Дворец был окружен вы–
  surrounded by (with) a   сокой стеной.
  high wall.

resident [´rezɪdənt] *n c*   постоянный житель

replace [rɪ´pleɪs] *v*   заменить

  George Harris has   Джордж Харрис сменил
  replaced Bob Simpson as   Боба Симпсона на посту
  Director General.   Генерального директора.

  The broken part must be   Сломанная деталь долж–
  replaced by (with) a new   на быть заменена новой.
  one.

brick *n adj*   кирпич, кирпичный

  The house is made of brick.

  It's a brick house.

palace [pælɪs] *n c*	дворец
cathedral [kə´θiːdrəl] *n c*	собор
inside [´ɪnsaɪd] *prep*	внутри
[ɪn´saɪd] *adv*	
Ant. outside [´autsaɪd] *prep*	снаружи
[aut´saɪd] *adv*	
form *v*	образовывать, образовать, формировать
ring *n c*	кольцо

EXERCISES

1

Прочитайте текст. Предварительно отработайте произношение следующих слов.

[ɪ]	[æ]	
inside	land	gradual
similar	abbey	similarity
exist	magnificent	establish
existence		
[ɔ]	[ɔː]	
swampy	shore	
forest	forming	

2

Подберите в тексте английские эквиваленты.

В середине первого века до нашей эры • подобно многим другим очень старым городам • с течением времени • деловой центр страны • то, что сейчас известно, как... • к середине первого века нашей эры • превратились в улицы • примерно в то же самое время • выбрал это место за его красоту и удобное расположение • когда были установлены первые торговые связи • произносили название по-своему • отсюда — современное "Москвич" • как и Лондон.

3

Ответьте на вопросы по тексту.

1. When did Julius Caesar invade the British Isles?
2. Were any people already living there at that time?
3. Did the Romans find any human settlements on the Thames?
4. Was London built according to an architectural plan?
5. Did it grow around only one centre like most cities?
6. Do you think the Thames played an important part in its development?
7. Which city is older, London or Moscow?
8. How long had London been in existence when Moscow was founded?
9. Who was Moscow founded by?
10. How can you describe the place chosen for the construction of Moscow?
11. When were the first trade and diplomatic contacts established between Russia and England?
12. What kind of similarity between London and Moscow can we see if we look at the maps of both cities?
13. Why was the centre of Moscow surrounded with a wooden wall by the first residents?
14. Which of you know the reason (why) the wooden wall was replaced by a brick one?
15. What was built inside the wall and outside?

4

Прочитайте и переведите примеры на новые слова.

1. Trade and cultural contacts already existed between Russia and England at the time of Ivan [aivn] the Terrible.
2. I have similar ideas on the subject, but I wouldn't say mine are exactly the same as yours.
3. We can offer you another model of similar quality.
4. I'm happy to say that the college founded a few years ago has grown into an important research centre.
5. If it hadn't been for the city's residents, the magnificent forests surrounding it on all sides wouldn't be in existence now.
6. The hotel serves meals to residents only.
7. They live in a small town on the south coast of Italy.
8. There were gradual changes for the better.
9. Our views were changing gradually.

10. The old equipment was gradually replaced by the most up-to-date.
11. I'll have to replace those tyres. They are badly damaged.
12. The stock exchange was established in the last century.
13. I wouldn't believe it if it weren't an established fact.
14. I suggest exchanging opinions on the subject.
15. I suggest that you compare your results with theirs.
16. "How does your new model compare with the old one? Are they very different?" "No, I'd say they are very similar, but the new one is more up-to-date."
17. These two pictures can't be compared. One is clearly so much better than the other. There's no comparison between them!
18. The contract would have been cancelled if they hadn't fulfilled all their financial obligations.

5

Прочитайте диалоги вслух и инсценируйте их.

1

A. According to the map, the museum isn't very far from here.

B. Let me have a look. Well, it's most definitely somewhere down this road, but it may be a long walk. Look! There's a policeman, let's ask him.

A. Excuse me officer, can you tell us the way to the Museum of Modern Art?

P. Certainly. Walk down this road to the third traffic light, cross the road, turn right, walk a bit, and take the first turning on the left and you'll see the museum. It's **opposite** the City Bank, you can't miss it.

B. Thank you very much. I've written it all down. Is it a very long walk? Wouldn't it be a better idea to take the bus?

P. Well, I don't think so. It isn't very far, and you'll enjoy the walk.

A. Thanks again.

P. Not at all.

opposite [´ɔpəzıt]   зд. напротив

2

A. Excuse me, how do I get to Albert Road?

B. Albert Road? Let me see . . . Take the 24 bus. The stop's over there across the road. The 24 will take you as far as the new City Library. Get off there, and change to the 15 bus, it'll take you to Albert Road.

A. Thank you ever so.

B. That's all right.

Разыграйте следующие эпизоды

1. К вам на улице подошел иностранец и попытался задать вам вопрос, пользуясь русско—английским разговорником. Узнав, что вы говорите по—английски, он обрадовался и попросил объяснить ему как пройти или проехать к одной из достопримечательностей вашего города. Дайте подробные объяснения. Для игры используйте карту вашего города.

2. Вы находитесь в англоязычной стране. Спросите прохожего, как пройти или проехать в гостиницу, (музей, банк, на стадион и т.п.). Для игры используйте этот рисунок.

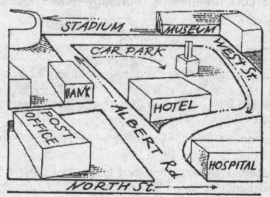

TOPICS FOR DISCUSSION AND NEW WORDS
(continued)

A FEW FACTS FROM THE HISTORY OF BIG CITIES

2

Unlike old cities, such as London or Moscow, that grew by themselves, without any **preliminary** architectural plans, cities built later were planned by architects before **construction** started.

The best example of a Russian city built **according to** a plan is, without any **doubt, St. Petersburg,** founded by **Peter the Great**. Peter wanted to found a new capital for his new Russia, and for this **purpose** chose a piece of **territory** on the Baltic Sea that had been **taken over** by Russia after a war with Sweden. It was **swampy** land on which it was extremely difficult to build anything, but a convenient place for a port that could give Russia an **outlet** to the seas and other countries. The city was built in **record** time, but it required enormous **effort**, and cost a large **number of human** lives. The city is famous for its wonderful planning, and its magnificent palaces, monuments, cathedrals, and other places of interest.

Most towns and cities in North America were built according to a plan. One such town was founded by the Dutch on territory bought from **Indians**. It is known that part of the territory, called the **Manhattan Island**, was exchanged for **beads** and other **ornaments**, all in all **worth** twenty–four dollars at that time. The Dutch called their new town **New Amsterdam**, but when the territory was taken over by the British in 1664, they renamed it New York **in honor** of the **Duke** of York. Now New York, where millions of people are **engaged** in industry, banking and **finance**, is **considered** the financial and business capital of the United States.

Имена собственные и географические названия

Indians	индейцы
Manhattan Island	
[mæn´hætən´ailənd]	Остров Манхэттен
New Amsterdam	Новый Амстердам
[´njuːæ´mstə´dæm]	
New York [´njuː´jɔːk]	Нью–Йорк

Learn these words:

unlike [ʌn´laik] *prep* в отличие от...

   Ant. like подобно, как и...
   Unlike his brother, he's a very serious person.

preliminary [prɪ´lɪmɪnərɪ] *adj* предварительный

   a preliminary discussion (agreement, arrangement, etc.)

construction [kən´strʌkʃn] *n* строительство

   The new underground (...все еще строится)
   line is still under
   construction.
   The construction of the palace took several years.

according to [ə´kɔːdɪŋtə] *prep* согласно (чему–л.)

   according to the timetable по расписанию

according to him	по его словам
according to the radio.	по сообщению радио

doubt [daut] *n* — сомнение

There's no doubt about it.
There's no doubt that the plan is correct.

He is, without any doubt, the best specialist in this field.	Он, безусловно, лучший специалист в этой области.

purpose [´pɔːpəs] *n* — цель

What's the purpose of your visit?

territory [´terɪtəry] *n* — территория

take over *v*

1. занять, отвоевать

2. сменить, принять чьи-л. обязанности, пост, должность, дела и т. п.

When Mr Green grew old, his elder son took over.	Когда г-н Грин состарился, его дела принял старший сын.

land *n c*

1. земля, суша

There's more water than land on the Earth.
swampy [swɔmpɪ]
 land

болотистая местность (земля)

land *v*

2. приземлиться, пристать к берегу, высадиться

The plane landed on time.
When did people first land on the Moon?

port *n* — порт

outlet [´autlet] *n c* — зд. выход

an outlet (market) for goods

рынок сбыта

record *adj* — рекордный

record output (crop etc.)

рекордный выпуск (урожай, и т.п.)

require [rɪˈkwaɪə] v   1. требовать, потребовать

   Syn. take

   The reconstruction of the   Строительство завода по-
   factory will require a lot   требует массу денег.
   of money.

                                 2. требоваться

   Syn. need

   We require ten more   Нам требуется еще де-
   computers.   сять компьютеров.

   This country has got all it   Страна располагает всем
   requires to build a   необходимым чтобы по-   — 234 —
   healthy economy.   строить здоровую эконо-
                                   мику.

requirement
   [rɪˈkwaɪəmənt] *n c*   требование (к качеству или ко-
                                   личеству)

   to meet the requirements   удовлетворять требова-
                                   ниям

   I hope this model will   Надеюсь, что эта модель
   meet all your   удовлетворит всем вашим
   requirements.   требованиям.

effort [ˈefət] *n*   усилие, усилия

   to make an (every) effort   приложить (все) усилия,
   to do sth.   чтобы сделать что-л.
   We'll make every effort to fulfil your order soon
   (= We'll do our best. . .).

cost [kɔst] *n*   стоимость

   the cost of production   стоимость производства
   production costs   издержки производства
   the cost of living   стоимость жизни
   at the cost of. . .   ценою. . .

cost (cost, cost) *v*   стоить

   The project may cost too much.
   It cost him a lot of time   Это стоило ему. . .
   and effort.

number *n*	зд. число, количество *(с исч. сущ.)*

Сравните:

a number of books (students, etc.)	ряд книг (студентов и т.п.)
the number of books (students, etc.)	число (количество) книг (студентов и т.п.)

human [´hju:mən] *adj*	человеческий
a human being	человек (человеческое существо)
a human factor	человеческий фактор
human rights	права человека
exchange [ɪks´tʃeɪndʒ] *v*	1. обменивать, обменять
to exchange dollars *for* pounds	
	2. обмениваться, обменяться
to exchange greetings	обмениваться приветствиями
(delegations, students, etc.)	(делегациями, студентами и т. д.)
exchange *n c*	обмен
in exchange *for*...	в обмен на...
(foreign) exchange *n u*	валюта
Syn. **currency** [´kʌrənsɪ]	
the rate of exchange	валютный курс
exchange *n c*	биржа
a stock exchange	фондовая биржа
a commodity exchange	товарная биржа
a labour exchange	биржа труда
bead [bi:d] *n c*	бусина
ornament [´ɔ:nəmənt] *n c*	украшение

— 235 —

worth [wɜ:θ] *adj*

1. стоящий, имеющий сто-
имость;

2. заслуживающий чего-л.

to be worth

The game is worth the
candle.

стоить, заслуживать

Игра стоит свеч.

A bird in the hand is
worth two in the bush.

Одна птица в руке стоит
двух в кустах *(послови-
ца)*

Ср. русское: лучше синица в руках, чем журавль в небе.

The matter isn't worth
wasting time on.

На это дело не стоит
тратить времени.

honour [ˈɔnə] *n c*

честь

in honour of . . .

в честь кого-л.

duke *n c*

герцог

engage [inˈgeidʒ] *v*

1. нанять, нанимать

to engage a guide (secretary, etc.)

2. занять, занимать, быть за-
нятым

This seat is engaged (taken)

to be engaged (in)

заниматься чем-либо

finance [ˈfainæns] *n*

финансы

the Minister of Finance

министр финансов

the Finance Manager

финансовый директор

finance *v*

финансировать

The project was financed by several companies.

financial [faiˈnænʃl] *adj*

финансовый

the financial year

финансовый год

financial obligations

финансовые обязатель-
ства

consider [kənˈsidə] *v*

считать (иметь мнение)

I consider it a great
honour to be here with
you today.

Я считаю большой чес-
тью быть сегодня здесь с
вами.

| He is considered (to be) the best specialist in this field. | Он считается лучшим специалистом в этой области. |

EXERCISES

1

Прочитайте текст. Предварительно отработайте произношение следующих слов.

| territory | require | purpose |
| preliminary | requirements | St.Petersburg |

2

Подберите в тексте английские эквиваленты.

В отличие от старых городов таких, как Лондон и Москва •без предварительного плана • по плану • несомненно • с этой целью • выход к морям • в рекордный срок • это потребовало огромных усилий • славится замечательной планировкой, великолепными дворцами и другими достопримечательностями • большинство городов в Северной Америке • известно, что часть этой территории • всего стоимостью в 24 доллара • заняты в промышленности • считается финансовой столицей.

3

Ответьте на вопросы.

1. Why did Peter the Great want a new capital for Russia?
2. Why did the construction of St.Petersburg require enormous effort and cost a large number of human lives?
3. Was it worth doing?
4. What can you say about the location of St.Petersburg?
5. What is St.Peterburg famous for?
6. Have you ever been there?
7. What had been the name of New York before it was taken over by the Dutch?
8. In whose honour was it renamed?
9. Why is New York considered the financial capital of the United States?
10. What is the capital of the United States?

4 🔲

Прочитайте и переведите примеры на новые слова.

1. Unlike many other big cities, it isn't very noisy.
2. Unlike many other people, he prefers to travel by train.
3. This is only a preliminary plan.
4. A preliminary agreement has already been signed.
5. The building is still under construction.
6. The gallery is under reconstruction.
7. We operate the equipment according to the instructions.
8. According to a preliminary arrangement, there will be another discussion before the contract is signed.
9. According to the latest reports, the situation hasn't changed.
10. There's no doubt that all the financial obligations will be fulfilled.
11. That piece of land is, without any doubt, the best site for the construction of a health centre.
12. What a magnificent location!
13. Most people learn foreign languages for practical purposes.
14. This piece of equipment can be used for various purposes.
15. It's perfectly natural that they are looking for new outlets for their goods.
16. He took over the firm from his father.
17. The firm has been taken over by an international corporation.
18. How many machines do you require?
19. The reconstruction will require a lot of money and a great effort, too.
20. We'll require a large number of experienced specialists.
21. A number of important changes have been made in the preliminary project.
22. Please let us know the exact number by telex.
23. Diplomatic relations between the two countries were established a long time ago.
24. We would like to establish good business relations with your company.
25. The company was established at the turn of the century.
26. How do you pronounce it?
27. If you compare the two projects, you will see a similarity between them.
28. We'll make every effort to minimize the production costs.
29. This project is, without any doubt, worth the money it cost.
30. Is the article worth reading?
31. I'm sorry this seat's engaged.

32. I tried to get through to him several times, but the number was engaged.

33. A new stock exchange has been established.

34. The construction of the hospital will be financed by the state.

35. It's considered an established fact.

36. He's considered an outstanding actor.

37. After the concert reporters surrounded him.

38. The site is surrounded by a thick forest.

Прочитайте диалог. Придумайте свой вариант начала и разыграйте весь эпизод.

Part of a Business Talk.

A.   According to the catalogue, this model can be used for several purposes. Does that mean that you want a higher price?

B.   Well, the price will largely depend on the number of machines you're going to order.

A.   We need twenty now, but we may require many more in the near future.

B.   I think we could agree on $.1,000 **per unit**. Would that suit you?

A.   Yes, I think so.

B.   Believe me, it is, without any doubt, the best equipment you can get at this price.

B.   Oh, yes. It meets all our requirements. There's another problem I'd like to settle today. The point is we want to have the machines very soon, not later than April.

A.   Well, that wouldn't be easy, but we'll make every effort to do it for you. Anything else?

B.   No, that's all, I think. The rest can be left to our assistants. Do you mind?

A.   Not at all. Oh, it's half past one already! Will you join me for lunch?

B.   Oh, thanks, with pleasure.

Learn these words :

per [pə(r)] *prep*   предлог латинского проис-
                                          хождения, означающий *с еди-*
                                          ницы. Сущ. после него не
                                          употр. с артиклем.

per hour   в час

per day	в день
per head	на душу

unit [juːnɪt] *n c*   *зд.* единица оборудования

$1,000 per unit (a thousand dollars per unit)

Прочитайте диалоги вслух. Запомните выражения, которые могут вам понадобиться, если вам придется знакомить кого-либо с достопримечательностями вашего города.

1

A. How long are you going to stay here after the congress, Mr. Fennell?

B. A week or so, I think. Is it possible to see anything of Moscow in a week?

A. Well, yes, but of course not much.

B. What do you think I should see first?

A. Well, if you are interested in **historical** places, you **should** go to the Kremlin first. It would be a good idea to go to Ostankino or Kuskovo, too.

B. That would be fine, but I'd like to leave some time for art galleries, too.

A. We could go to the Tretyakov Gallery tomorrow, there's a marvellous collection of Russian artists there, and the day after tomorrow we could see the Museum of Fine Arts.

B: Wonderful! I feel most **grateful** to you. When do I see you tomorrow, then?

A. Tomorrow's Saturday. What about ten in the morning?

B. Right. See you!

A. Till tomorrow!

Learn these word:

should *v mod*	модальный глагол, выражаю-щий совет, рекомендацию; возможные переводы: следу-ет, следовало бы, надо бы (подробно см. стр 315)
You should spend more time out–of–doors.	Вам надо (следует) боль-ше бывать на свежем воздухе.

You shouldn't waste your time on it!

historical [hı´stɔrıkl] *adj*	1. исторический, не вымышленный
	2. на историческую тему (о книге, фильме и т.п.)
a historical event (person, fact, etc.)	историческое событие (лицо, факт и т.п.), т.е. не вымышленное
a historical novel (film, play, etc.)	исторический роман (фильм, пьеса и т.п.) т.е. на историческую тему
historic [hı´stɔrıkl] *adj*	исторический, повлиявший на ход истории
a historic event (place, battle, discovery, etc.)	историческое событие (место, сражение, открытие и т.п.) т.е. отмеченное в истории
grateful [´greıtfl] *adj*	благодарный

We would be grateful to you if you could send us your latest catalogues.

2

Victor Lavrov is taking Bill Landon, his American counterpart round Moscow. They are driving to Ostankino.

B. I can **recognize** this monument. It's a **statue** of Pushkin, isn't it?

V. Quite right. It's my favourite Moscow monument.

B. And that building on the left . . . What a fine piece of architecture!

V. It used to be called "The English Club" before the Revolution. I'm sorry I don't remember the architect's name . It's such a pity I'm not a professional guide!

B. That's all right! I don't much like sightseeing with professional guides. You're doing well enough for me.

V. Oh, thanks, then I'll go on. Soon you'll see the clock on the **Puppet** Theatre. At exactly twelve all the doors in the clock opren, and figures of animals come out and dance. It's worth seeing. A lot of people come to watch.

B. I'd like to see one of their plays if I manage to leave some time for theatres. Our programme's going to be very crowded, isn't it?

V. Oh, not as crowded as all that! We can go on Saturday evening.

Learn these words.

recognize [ˈrekəɡnaɪz] *v*

1. узнать (опознать)

He had changed so much that I didn't recognize him at once.

Он так изменился, что я его не сразу узнал.

2. признать (воздать должное)

His talent wasn't recognized.

Его талант не был признан.

statue [ˈstætjuː] *n c*

статуя

a statue of . . .

puppet [ˈpʌpɪt] *n c*

кукла, марионетка

a puppet theatre

кукольный театр

7

Разыграйте следующие эпизоды.

1. Вы встречаете в аэропорту гостя (делового партнёра) из англоязычной страны и везете его в гостиницу. По дороге рассказываете ему о тех местах, которые вы проезжаете. Ответьте на его вопросы.

2. Ваш гость хочет посмотреть достопримечательности вашего города. Он здесь находится впервые. Ответьте на его вопросы. Покажите ему город. Пригласите его в театр, музей, и т.п.

Unit 11

GRAMMAR

21. <u>Согласование времен в сложно-подчиненных предложениях (Sequence of Tenses).</u>

21.1. Это правило касается в основном сложно-подчиненных предложений с дополнительным придаточным. Вы уже знаете такие предложения и умеете их употреблять, если главное предложение стоит в *настоящем* времени, *будущем* времени или *повелительном наклонении*:

1. I think the time's convenient for everybody.	Я думаю, что это время удобно для всех.
2. I'm not sure that everybody liked our suggestion.	Я не уверен, что всем понравилось наше предложение.
3. Please explain to them that they'll be able to join us in a few days.	Пожалуйста, объясните им, что они смогут присоединиться к нам через несколько дней.

В этих случаях употребление времен в придаточном предложении не регулируется каким-либо особым правилом - времена употребляются по смыслу подобно тому, как это происходит и в соответствующих русских предложениях.

21.2. Однако если а н г л и й с к о е главное предложение стоит в *прошедшем* времени, употребление времен в дополнительном придаточном подчиняется правилу с о г л а с о в а н и я (последовательности) времен. Суть этого правила заключается в том, что после главного предложения в *прошедшем* времени, в придаточном дополнительном н е употребляются *настоящие* времена и *простое будущее*.

1. I **thought** you **spoke** Russian.	Я думал, что вы говорите по—русски.

21.5. Действие придаточного предложения, б у д у щ е е по отношению к действию глагола-сказуемого главного предложения в прошедшем времени выражается особой временной формой — будущим в прошедшем (Future in the Past):

1. We **agreed** that the goods **would be packed** in wooden boxes.	Мы **договорились**, что товар **будет упакован** в деревянных ящиках.
2. The director **hoped** (that) the film **would be** a success.	Режиссер **надеялся**, что фильм **будет иметь** успех.
3. I **wasn't sure** I'd **get through** to them at once.	Я **не был уверен**, что сразу им **дозвонюсь**.

21.6. Согласование времен распространяется и на *временное* или *условное* предложение, следующее за дополнительным придаточным.

1. He **said** (that) he **would phone** us as soon as he **got** to London.	Он **сказал**, что **позвонит** нам как только **приедет** в Лондон.
2. She **said** she **would visit** us if she **had** enough time.	Она **сказала**, что **навестит** нас, если у нее **будет** время.

EXERCISES

Переведите на русский язык, обращая особое внимание на согласование времен в английских примерах.

a. 1. I thought you spoke Russian.
2. I knew he was a historical person.
3. I thought the seafront was a long way from the hotel.
4. He said the embankment was worth seeing.
5. I wasn't sure the book was worth reading.
6. The speaker said it was a historic discovery.
7. Did you say it was a historical novel?
8. He asked where he could exchange dollars for the local currency.
9. He said the matter was hardly worth troubling about.
10. The buyers found that the goods met all their requirements.
11. They wrote that they required ten more machines.

2. He **said** he **was** very busy and **couldn't** stay for the lecture.

Он сказал, что он очень занят и не может остаться на лекцию.

3. I **was sure** (that) you **knew** everything.

Я был уверен, что вы все знаете.

4. She **thought** we **were waiting** for her.

Она думала, что мы ее ждем.

Эта разница объясняется тем, что в русском языке действие придаточного предложения сопоставляется с фактическим настоящим моментом, а в английском точкой отсчета является дейстие г л а в н о г о предложения, поэтому временная форма глагола-сказуемого п р и д а т о ч н о г о предложения зависит от того, является ли выраженное им действие *одновременным*, *предшествующим* или *будущим* по отношению к действию глагола-сказуемого г л а в н о г о предложения.

21.3. Действие придаточного предложения, о д н о в р е - м е н н о е действию главного предложения с глаголом-сказуемым в прошедшем времени, может выражаться простым или продолженным прошедшим временем (Past Simple или Past Continuous).

1. We **wrote** to our partners that we **liked** their new ideas.

Мы написали нашим партнерам, что нам нра- вятся их новые идеи.

2. I **wasn't sure** that he **knew** my address.

Я не **был** уверен, что он **знает** мой адрес.

3. We **didn't know** (that) they **were** still **having** talks.

Мы **не знали,** что у них все еще **идут** переговоры.

21.4. Действие придаточного предложения, п р е д ш е - с т в у ю щ е е действию главного предложения, выражается прошедшим временем группы Perfect (Past Perfect).

1. I **thought** (that) they **hadn't received** our letter yet.

Я **подумал,** что они еще **не получили** нашего письма.

2. We **didn't know** that you **had** already **discussed** the problem.

Мы **не знали,** что вы уже **обсудили** эту проблему.

12. He said the purpose of his visit was to talk about cultural exchanges for the next few years.

b. 1. I didn't know Mr Carter had taken over as finance manager.
   2. He told us they'd had a very useful exchange of opinions.
   3. It was really surprising how the rate of exchange had gone up.

c. 1. Everybody knew that the project would require a great effort.
   2. They wrote that a new stock exchange would be established in the near future.
   3. They said the reconstruction would require more time and money if a few changes weren't made in the project.
   4. They wrote they would send another fax after they spoke to the representative of the sellers.
   5. He was sure the matter would be settled after we had another discussion.
   6. They told us they would let us know their decision as soon as their finance director came back from his holiday.
   7. They said they wouldn't be able to give a definite answer till they received a telex from their partner.

— 246 —

2 ✎

Поставьте сказуемое главного предложения в прошедшее время и сделайте соответствующие изменения в придаточном предложении.

1.

Дано: I think I know it.
Требуется: I thought I knew it.

1. They **say** the hotel's a mile from the shore.
2. They **write** they are going to the south coast of Spain for their holiday.
3. He **says** he doesn't even know such problems exist.
4. The newspapers **write** that he is, without any doubt, the best actor of the year.
5. I **think** the game's worth the candle.
6. **Do** you **know** when they are going to discuss the preliminary project?
7. He **knows** we have similar views on the problem.
8. **Do** they **say** it is an established fact?

Дано: She says she heard it on the radio.
Требуется: She said she had heard it on the radio.

1. He **knows** she didn't say that.
2. I **think** he recognized me.
3. She **says** she didn't see it.
4. It's really surprising that the factory was built in record time.
5. We **are** surprised to hear that your question wasn't answered at once.
6. He **says** he didn't recognize her.

3.

Дано: I hope you have settled it.
Требуется: I hoped you had settled it.

1. She **thinks** she has lost the key.
2. He **says** he has never thought of that.
3. We **are** surprised to see that nothing has been changed.
4. He **says** the defective parts have been replaced.
5. They **write** that preliminary contacts have already been established.

4.

Дано: I'm sure everything will be all right.
Требуется: I was sure everything would be all right.

1. The experts **find** the construction will cost an enormous sum.
2. Everybody **understands** the new project will require a great effort.
3. He **says** we'll have a short rest when we get to the river.
4. They **write** that they will be able to give us an idea of the cost of the project when they receive all the necessary documents.
5. The air hostess **says** we will only be allowed to get up from our seats after the plane lands.

Переведите на английский язык.

1. Я думаю, это хорошая идея.

2. Я подумал, что это хорошая идея.

3. Мы знаем, что эти культурные связи все еще существуют.

4. Мы знали, что эти культурные связи все еще существуют.

5. Они пишут, что поселились на берегу моря.

6. Они написали, что поселились на берегу моря.

7. Мы знаем, что этот форт все еще существует.

8. Мы знали, что этот форт все еще существует.

9. Он говорит,что строительство потребует много денег?

10. Он сказал,что строительство потребует много денег?

11. Он говорит, что это только предварительное решение.

12. Он сказал, что это только предварительное решение.

13. Он пишет, что у них уже были предварительные обсуждения.

14. Он сказал, что у них уже были предварительные обсуждения

15. Они пишут,что сравнили результаты и обсудят их в ближайшем будущем.

16. Они написали, что сравнили результаты и обсудят их в бли—жайшем будущем.

17. Он говорит, что заменит сломанную деталь (part) новой.

18. Он сказал, что заменит сломанную деталь новой.

19. Он надеется, что установит новый мировой рекорд.

20. Он надеялся, что установит новый мировой рекорд.

21. Он был уверен, что они купят эту модель, если цена не будет очень высокой.

22. Он сказал, что мы поговорим об этом, когда он вернется из отпуска.

GRAMMAR

22. Прямая и косвенная речь.

22.1. В английском языке, так же как и в русском, есть д в а способа передачи чужой речи. Один из них вам уже хорошо знаком - это простое п о в т о р е - н и е чужого высказывания с сохранением его грамматических, лексических и интонационных осо-бенностей - так называемая **прямая речь:**

1. The commentator says: "It's a new record."

2. The old lady asked, "Is this my seat?"

3. The doctor asked, "How do you feel today?"

4. He lecturer said to the students: "Look at this map!"

5. "I'm busy," he said.

6. "Please make yourselves comfortable," she said to us.

7. "Can you call back?" she asked.

8. "Where is it?" he asked me.

Другой способ передачи чужой речи - п е р е с к а з чужой мысли в косвенной речи, при котором происходят грамматические изменения, по смыслу заменяются некоторые слова и соответствующим образом меняется интонация.

22.2. Утвердительное предложение в косвенной речи.

Прямая речь	Косвенная речь
1. She says, "I'm happy."	She says (that) she's happy.
2. He said, "I don't agree with you."	He said (that) he didn't agree with me.
3. "I don't know anything about it," he said to me.	He told me (that) he didn't know anything about it.
4. "I've never been there," he said to us.	He told us (that) he had never been there.

Как видно из примеров, утвердительное предложение в косвенной речи становится дополнительным придаточным, которое после главного предложения в прошедшем времени подчиняется правилу согласования времен.

Если в косвенной речи указывается лицо, к которому обращено высказывание, глагол say заменяется глаголом tell.

ПРИМЕЧАНИЯ:

1. После глагола, вводящего прямую речь, перед кавычками может стоять либо запятая, либо двоеточие (чаще запятая).

2. Правило согласования времен может в косвенной речи не соблюдаться, если высказывание представляет собой общеизвестную истину.

Прямая речь	Косвенная речь
1. The teacher said to the children, "Twice two is four."	The teacher told the children (that) twice two is four.
2. The doctor said to him: "Smoking is bad for even stronger people than you."	The doctor told him (that) smoking is bad (или was bad) for even stronger people than him.

В современной английской речи такое несоблюдение согласования времен допускается и в тех случаях, когда говорящий передаёт в косвенной речи то, что он сам считает безусловной истиной в настоящий момент. Это особенно характерно для радио и телевизионных репортажей и газетных сообщений о текущих событиях.

Прямая речь	Косвенная речь
The President said: "The political climate has changed for the better."	The President said (that) the political climate has changed (*или* had changed) for the better.

Поскольку с о б л ю д е н и е согласования времён ни в одном из этих случаев н е я в л я е т с я — 250 — о ш и б к о й, изучающему английский язык целесообразно его п р и д е р ж и в а т ь с я.

22.3. Модальные глаголы **must** и **should** остаются в косвенной речи б е з и з м е н е н и я независимо от того, в каком времени стоит сказуемое главного предложения. Глагол **can** после главного предложения в п р о ш е д ш е м времени превращается в **could**, а **may** в **might**:

Прямая речь	Косвенная речь
1. He said, "I **must** go and make some calls."	He **said** he **must** go and make some calls.
2. She said to me: "You **should** spend more time out-of-doors."	She **told** me I **should** spend more time out-of-doors.
3. He said, "I **can** easily contact them myself."	He **said** he **could** easily contact them himself.
4. She said, "It **may** be true."	She said it might be true.

22.4. Сослагательное наклонение остаётся в косвенной речи б е з и з м е н е н и я:

Прямая речь	Косвеннная речь
She said: "I would have come if I had known."	She said she would have come if she had known.

22.5. Как было сказано выше (п.21.1.), при передаче чужого высказывания в косвенной речи иногда приходится менять некоторые слова, как того требует смысл. Аналогичные замены происходят и в русском языке.

Их необходимость или отсутствие таковой зависит от того, какой промежуток времени был между высказыванием и его передачей в косвенной речи, т.е. какой момент является точкой отсчета.

Прямая речь	Косвенная речь
1. When I met him **last week**, he said: "I'll call on you **tomorrow** (*завтра*)."	When I met him **last week**, he said he would call on me the **following (next) day** (*на следующий день*).
2. When we were having a holiday at the seaside, my wife liked the place so much that she said, "Oh, I would like to live **here** (*здесь*)!"	When we were having a holiday at the seaside, my wife liked the place so much that she said she would like to live **there** (*там*).
3. He called me **a few days ago** and said, "I've had an important message **today** (*сегодня*)."	He called me a few days ago and said he'd had an important message **that day** (*в тот день*).
4. Miss Bennett called **last week** and said to me: "All the documents were sent off **two days ago** (*два дня тому назад*)."	Miss Bennett called last week and told me (that) all the documents had been sent off **two days before** (*за два дня до этого*).

Такая замена слов не нужна, когда смысл того не требует:

Прямая речь	Косвенная речь
1. I've just seen her and she said: "I'll deal with it **tomorrow**."	I've just seen her and she said she'd deal with it **tomorrow**.
2. I spoke to the manager a minute ago, and he said: "All the bills were paid **yesterday**."	I spoke to the manager a minute ago and he told me (that) all the bills were paid **yesterday**.

EXERCISES

1

Прочитайте вслух образцы прямой и косвенной речи. Следите за интонацией.

1. She says, "I'll join you in a minute!"
   She says she'll join us in a minute.
2. He said, "The match has been cancelled."
   He said the match had been cancelled.
3. He said, "I'm absolutely sure!"
   He said he was absolutely sure.
4. He said, "We have a crowded programme for next week."
   He said we had a crowded programme for next week.
5. She said, "I can't afford to buy it."
   She said she couldn't afford to buy it.
6. The manager said, "I must deal with it at once."
   The manager said he must deal with it at once.
7. He said: "My colleagues may be interested in contacting you."
   He said his colleagues might be interested in contacting us.

2

Передайте высказывания в косвенной речи. Прочитайте их вслух, следя за интонацией.

1. The expert said, "There's a similarity between the two projects."
2. The manager said to his colleagues, "We must look for new outlets for our goods."
3. He said, "The purpose of my visit here is to exchage opinions with you."
4. The air hostess says, "The plane is landing."
5. He said to us, "The machine meets the highest requirements, without any doubt."
6. Mr Bennett said to us, "The project will be financed by several companies."
7. The manager said to the interviewers, "The construction has been completed in record time."
8. The finance manager said, "I can only give you preliminary figures."
9. He said, "The old equipment must be replaced even if it requires a lot of money."
10. He said, "You should introduce these changes gradually, not all at once."

11. The Director General said to the architects, "The project may cost more than it's worth."

12. The interviewer said, "It's been a useful exchange of ideas."

Проведите игру, как показано в образце. Участники: **A., B., C., D.,** и т.д.

Образец:

A. I love detective stories.

B. (to C.) Excuse me, what did A. say? I couldn't catch it.

C. She said she loved detective stories. I hate them.

D. (to E) Excuse me, what did C. say? I didn't hear the end.

E. He said he hated detective stories. I prefer historical novels.

A. Excuse me ... and so on.

Переведите на английский язык.

1. Выступая на пресс-конференции, он сказал, что целью его визита является обмен мнениями с ведущими специалистами в этой области (сфере).

2. Он сказал своим коллегам, что постепенные изменения в работе компании абсолютно необходимы.

3. Президент сказал, что в результате его визита были установлены новые контакты между обеими странами.

4. Он объяснил, что эксперимент может потребовать больших усилий.

5. Эксперт сказал инженерам, что часть оборудования должна быть заменена.

6. Представители фирмы заявили (сказали), что они согласились бы финансировать проект, если бы (они) нашли, что это стоит сделать.

7. Он сказал, что все необходимые контакты были установлены в рекордный срок.

8. Я подумал, что (я) должен поздравить их с (их) успехом.

9. Продавец сказал мне, что любые товары (goods), купленные в этом магазине, могут быть заменены, если они не подойдут покупателю по той или иной причине.

GRAMMAR
(continued)

22.6. <u>Специальные вопросы в косвенной речи.</u>

Прямая речь	**Косвеннная речь**
1. She **asks** me, "Where is it?"	She **asks** me where it **is**.
2. She **asked** me, "Where is it?"	She **asked** me where **it was**.
3. He asked her: "When does the train arrive?"	He asked her when the train arrived.
4. He asked her, "Why are you leaving so soon?"	He asked her why she was leaving so soon.
5. We asked them, "How did it happen?"	We asked them how it had happened.
6. "What's the matter?" the policeman asked.	The policeman asked what the matter was.
7. "Who does it depend on?" she asked.	She asked who it depended on.
8. He asked us, "Which of you can explain it?"	He asked which of us could explain it."
9. "How soon shall I call back?" he asked.	He asked how soon he should call back.

Как видно из примеров, при передаче специального вопроса в косвенной речи в о п р о с и т е л ь- н о е слово превращается в с о ю з н о е, а сам вопрос становиться дополнительным придаточным предложением с п р я м ы м порядком слов.

ПРИМЕЧАНИЕ: Модальный глагол shall по правилу согласования времен превращается в should.

EXERCISES

1

Прочитайте вслух примеры из правила 21.6, следите за интонацией.

2

Передайте высказывания в косвенной речи. Прочитайте их вслух, следя за интонацией.

1. "How much time is left?" he asked.
2. She asked, "How far's the bus stop?"
3. "How long will it take you to make preliminary arrangements?" we asked him.
4. We asked her, "How well does your colleague speak Russian?"
5. He asked: "Why can't a definite answer be given soon?"
6. He asked us: "Which of you would like to join me?"
7. He asked me, "How do you like it here?"
8. She asked the secretary, "How soon will Mr Hill be back from lunch?"
9. "What are you looking for?" he asked the boy.

3

Проведите игру, как показано в образце.

Образец:

A. Where do you live?
B. In Green Street.
C. (to D.) Excuse me, what did A. ask, and what did B. answer?
D. A asked where B. lived, and B. answered he lived in Green Street (Then D. asks a special question of his own to go on with the game, and so on.)

4

Переведите на английский язык.

1. Он спрашивает, от кого зависит решение.
2. Она спросила, почему отменили встречу.

3. Я не знал, сколько времени уйдет на то, чтобы сравнить результаты.

4. Он спросил, сколько машин нам потребуется.

5. Не могли бы вы объяснить мне, почему мы должны дать определеннный ответ так скоро.

6. Корреспондент спрашивает, сколько народу собирается при−нять участие в дискуссии.

7. Я не понимаю, каким образом (как) что−либо может быть построено так скоро.

8. Они спрашивают, когда была основана компания.

9. Они хотели знать, как скоро мы сможем связаться с нашими контрагентами.

10. Они спросили, когда мы собираемся заняться этим вопросом. — 256 —

GRAMMAR
(continued)

22.7. Общие вопросы в косвенной речи.

Общие вопросы превращаются в косвенной речи в дополнительные придаточные предложения, которые вводятся безударными союзами **if** или **whether** [´weðə], соответствующими по своему значению русской час−тице **ли:**

Прямая речь	Косвенная речь
1. The manager asked: "Does the time suit everybody?"	The manager asked **if** the time suited everybody.
2. "So do you agree with me?" he asked us.	He asked **whether** we agreed with him.
3. I asked the secretary, "Can I call back tomorrow?"	I asked the secretary **if** I could call back the next day.
4. "Oh, is the game worth the candle?" he asked.	He asked **whether** the game was worth the candle.
5. "Have you heard the news?" she asked me.	She asked **if** I'd heard the news.
6. "Well, is there anything else to do?" he asked.	He asked **if** there was any−thing else to do.
7. "Shall I repeat it?" he asked.	He asked **if** he should repeat it.

Обратите внимание на то, что в косвенной речи не передаются такие слова, как *oh, so, well* и т.п.

ПРИМЕЧАНИЕ: Союз **whether** предпочитается союзу **if** в сочетании **whether ... or** not:

I don't know **whether** they'll join us **or not**.	Я не знаю, присоединятся ли они к нам, или нет.

22.8. Союз **if – ли,** вводящий косвенный общий вопрос (д о п о л н и т е л ь н о е придаточное предложение), не следует путать с его омонимом **if – если,** вводящим у с л о в н о е придаточное, в котором не употребляется простое будущее время и будущее в прошедшем:

Дополнительное придаточное	Условное придаточное
(возможно будущее время)	(будущее время не употребляется)
1. He asks **if we'll stay** to see the film.	I'll call you **if we stay** to see the film.
(... останемся ли ...)	(... если останемся)
2. He asked if we would take part in the discussion.	He said they would take part in the discussion if they had time.
(...примем ли мы участие ...)	(...примут участие, если у них будет время)

22.9. Согласно той же логике, что и в русском языке, о т в е т на общий вопрос в к о с в е н н о й речи н е может содержать слов Yes и No:

Прямая речь	Косвенная речь
1. The policeman asked, "Is the damage very serious?" "Yes, it is", they answered.	The policeman asked if the damage was very serious, and they answered that **it was**.
2. I asked him, "Will you come on time?" "Yes, I will," he answered.	I asked him if he would come on time, and he said **he would**.
3. The reporter asked the scientist, "Are you pleased with the results?" "Yes, very!" he answered.	The reporter asked the scientist if he was pleased with the results, and he answered he **was very pleased**.

EXERCISES

1

Прочитайте вслух примеры из правила 21.7., следите за интонацией.

2

Передайте высказывания в косвенной речи. Прочитайте их вслух, следя за интонацией.

1. He asked, "Is it true?"
2. He asked me, "Is it very frosty outside?"
3. "Is it true (that) the match has been cancelled?" he asked her.
4. She asked me, "Do you agree with me?"
5. She asked me: "Are you hungry?"
6. They asked us, "Is it absolutely necessary to change our preliminary arrangements?"
7. She asked him, "Oh, how could you afford to buy such an expensive thing?"
8. He asked, "Would you like to have another look at the text?"
9. She asked the doctor, "Shall I follow a strict diet?"
10. He asked us: "Must we really make serious changes in the programme?"

3

Проведите игру, как показано в образце.

Образец:

A. (to B.) Do you find the rule we're learning very difficult?
B. No, not really.
C. (to D.) Excuse me, what did A. ask, and what did B. answer?
D. A. asked B. if he found the rule we're learning very difficult, and B. answered he didn't think so.

> (Then D. asks a general question of his own to go on with the game, and so on.)

4

Переведите на английский язык.

1. Туристы спросили гида, был ли этот город построен по плану.
2. Мы спросили продавца, надежна ли эта модель.

3. Я не знал, много ли времени займет предварительное обсуждение проблемы.

4. Я спросил его, может ли он подвезти меня до дома.

5. Управляющий спросил, все ли согласны с тем, что многое в работе компании требует серьезных изменений.

6. Я спросил, находят ли мои коллеги предложение наших контрагентов достаточно привлекательным.

7. Их спросили, могут ли они заплатить такую огромную сумму за эту картину.

8. Их спросили, смогут ли они сами заменить дефектные части (defective parts).

9. Я спросил моих коллег, можем ли мы приступить к делу.

GRAMMAR
(continued)

22.10. Высказывания, введенные глаголом **wonder**.

Иногда говорящий начинает свое высказывание со слов **I wonder**, превращая его тем самым п о ф о р м е в к о с в е н н ы й вопрос.

1. **I wonder** if she knows we are here.	Интересно, знает ли она, что мы здесь.
2. **I wonder** what really happened.	Интересно, что же произошло на самом деле.
3. **I wonder** how long we'll have to wait.	Интересно, сколько времени нам придется ждать.

ПРИМЕЧАНИЯ:

1) Обратите внимание на то, что такой вопрос задается о т п е р в о г о лица, при чем глагол **wonder** стоит в н а с т о я щ е м времени. Если глагол **wonder** стоит в п р о ш е д ш е м времени, это значит, что вопрос н е был произнесен в с л у х, о нем только п о д у м а л и:

I **wondered** why he was contradicting himself.	Я подумал, почему он противоречит сам себе.

2) Высказывание, введенное глаголом **wonder**, может представлять собой в е ж л и в у ю п р о с ь- б у или п р и г л а ш е н и е. В этом случае глагол **wonder** может употреблятся не только в настоящем времени, но и в прошедшем продолженном (Past Continuous).

1. I **wonder** if you could explain it to me again.	Не могли бы вы объяснить это мне еще раз? (просьба).
2. I **was wondering** if you would like to join us for lunch on Saturday.	Я подумал, не хотели бы вы пообедать с нами в субботу (приглашение).
3. I **was wondering** whether you could take part in the discussion of the preliminary project.	Я подумал, не могли бы вы принять участие в обсуждении предварительного проекта (просьба).

EXERCISES

Прочитайте вслух, следя за интонацией.

1. I wonder if the time suits everybody.
2. I wonder if all the documents have been filed.
3. I wonder if it's really necessary to make any changes.
4. I wonder how it happened.
5. I wonder how soon we'll get their answer.
6. I wonder why we're wasting so much time.
7. I wonder if you can tell me the way to the city centre.
8. I wonder if you could stay and have a look at those papers.
9. I was wondering if you would like to have a snack before we got down to business.
10. I was wondering if you would like to go to the country for the weekend.

2

Перефразируйте высказывания, начав их со слов *I wonder*.

Дано: Could you tell me the time?
Требуется: I wonder if you could tell me the time.

1. Could you tell me the way to the British Museum?
2. Could I put off the appointment till some time next week?
3. Could you let me have a look at those pictures?
4. How did it happen?
5. Is it convenient to call them so late?
6. Are those changes really necessary?

7. Does the time suit everybody?

GRAMMAR
(continued)

22.11. Вопросы, содержащие вводную фразу **do you think.**

Общий вопрос.

1. Do you think the problem is very difficult?	Как вы думаете, это очень сложная проблема?
2. Do you think it'll take much time?	Как вы думаете, это займет много времени?
3. Do you think it's worth seeing?	Как вы думаете, это стоит посмотреть?

Как видно из примеров, такой вопрос начинается с **Do you think**, после чего идет п р я м о й порядок слов.

Специальный вопрос.

1. When do you think we can get down to business?	Как вы думаете, когда мы сможем приступить к делу
2. Why do you think we haven't had a definite answer yet?	Как вы думаете, почему мы до сих пор не получили определенного ответа?
3. Who do you think it depends on?	Как вы думаете, от кого это зависит?
4. Which of them do you think knows the problem better?	Как вы думаете, кто их них знает эту проблему лучше?
5. How long do you think it'll take to study the matter?	Как вы думаете, сколько времени пойдет на то, чтобы изучить этот вопрос?
6. Where do you think we could get the information we are interested in?	Как вы думаете, где мы могли бы получить интересующие нас сведения?

Как видно из примеров, в вопросах такого типа вводная фраза **do you think** следует за вопросительным словом, далее порядок слов п р я м о й.

EXERCISES

— 262 —

1

Прочитайте вслух примеры из правила **21.11.**

2

Перефразируйте вопросы, начав их со слов **Do you think**

1.

Дано: Is that machine very difficult to operate?
Требуется: Do you think that machine's very difficult to operate?

1. Does our success depend on all those changes?
2. Is the time convenient for everybody?
3. Is the exhibition worth seeing?
4. Will many people be interested?
5. Is the new model more reliable?
6. Did they quarrel for no reason at all?
7. Did he tell you the truth?
8. Is the new method worth introducing?
9. Was the lecture a success?
10. Will this be a successful venture?

2.

Дано: When does the lecture begin?
Требуется: When do you think the lecture begins?

1. How long will they be in conference?
2. Who can I talk to about it?
3. Which of them is a better specialist?
4. Who will support the idea?
5. Why wasn't the experiment successful?
6. Why isn't the new model as reliable as the old one?
7. How soon can we start work on it?

Переведите на английский язык.

1. Как вы думаете, мы сможем встретиться в ближайшие несколько дней?
2. Как вы думаете, многим людям понравится эта идея?
3. Как вы думаете, мы сумеем сделать все необходимые приготовления своевременно?
4. Как вы думаете, кто заинтересуется этой идеей?
5. Как вы думаете, почему последний эксперимент не был таким же удачным, как другие два?
6. Как вы думаете, когда они дадут более определенный ответ?
7. Как вы думаете, сколько ему лет?
8. Как вы думаете, когда они выполнят все свои обязательства по контракту?
9. Как вы думаете, эти изменения действительно необходимы?

GRAMMAR
(continued)

22.12. Просьбы и приказания в косвенной речи

При передаче просьб и приказаний в косвенной речи повелительное наклонение превращается в инфинитив. Такие типы высказываний вам хорошо известны.

Прямая речь

1. The manager said to his secretary: "Please get all the documents ready."

2. He said to me: "Please don't forget to make all the necessary calls."

Косвенная речь

The manager asked the secretary to get all the documents ready.

He asked me not to forget to make all the necessary calls.

EXERCISE

Передайте просьбы в косвенной речи.

1. "Please switch it on," he said to me.
2. "Please explain it again," she said to him.
3. He asked the stand attendant, "Please show me how to operate it."

– 263 –

4. She said to the children, "Don't make so much noise!"
5. "Please be especially careful with this piece of equipment," he said to me.
6. "Please don't forget to switch the set off," he said to his assistant.
7. "Please put this stand in the foreground of the picture," the manager said to the reporter.
8. The manager said to his secretary, "Please call off all the appointments for tomorrow."

GRAMMAR
(continued)

22.13. <u>Другие виды высказываний в косвенной речи.</u> – 264 –

В английском языке, так же как и в русском, в косвенной речи могут передаваться не только утверждения, вопросы, просьбы и приказания, но и другие типы высказываний, например, предложения, предупреждения, советы, разрешения и т.д. В зависимости от цели высказывания, оно может в косвенной речи вводиться такими глаголами как **advise** [əd´vaɪz] *советовать*, **recommend** [ˌrekɔ´mend] *рекомендовать*, **remind** [rɪ´maɪnd] *напоминать*, **suggest, propose** *предлагать*, **warn** [wɔːn] *предупреждать (об опасности или возможной неприятности)* и другими глаголами, подходящими по смыслу.

Прямая речь	Косвенная речь
1. "You should take a holiday and have a good rest," the doctor said to him.	The doctor **advised** him to take a holiday and have a good rest.
	The doctor **recommended** that he (should) take a holiday . . .)
	The doctor recommended him **to take** a holiday . . .
2. "Don't forget to call Mr. Harris," he said to his secretary.	He **reminded** his secretary to call Mr. Harris.
3. "Please don't forget that we're going to the theatre," she said to her husband.	She **reminded** her husband that they were going to the theatre.

4. "Don't leave your car unlocked," he said to me.	He **warned** me **not to** leave my car unlocked.
5. "You can use my car while I'm away," he said to me.	He **allowed** me to use his car while he was away.
6."Let's have a walk after lunch," he said to me.	He **suggested** having a walk after lunch.
7. "Let me give you a lift," he said to her.	He **offered** her a lift.
8. "The talks were extremely useful," the prime minister said.	The Prime Minister **described** the talks **as** useful.

Как видно из примеров, при передаче чужого высказывания говорящий пользуется не только основными правилами, но и другими, довольно разнообразными способами. Кроме того, хороший рассказчик перемежает косвенную речь с прямой, стараясь избежать монотонности речи, сделать рассказ интересным для слушающих. Прямая речь эмоциональнее косвенной, поэтому она всегда присутствует в юмористических рассказах, анекдотах и т.п. При изложении чужой речи в письменных, особенно деловых документах предпочитают пользоваться средствами косвенной речи. Аналогичные предпочтения существуют и в русском языке.

EXERCISES

Прочитайте вслух и переведите.

1. He advised me to give up smoking.
2. She recommended that we should send our little daughter to a ballet school.
3. He advised me to give up teaching and go into business.
4. The secretary reminded him to contact Mr Pierce as soon as possible.
5. The manager reminded the secretary to let everybody know that the company meeting had been put off.
6. She reminded her husband that they had been invited to their friend's birthday party.

7. The hostess invited us in, and asked us to make ourselves comfortable.
8. The doctor warned him not to overuse that medicine.
9. The policeman warned the driver not to exceed the speed limit again.
10. His boss allowed him to take a short holiday.
11. She allowed her little son to watch the telly till ten.

TOPICS FOR DISCUSSION AND NEW WORDS

Sports and games

1

The Russian **national** hockey team has just taken part in an international **championship** held in Canada. They won two matches, lost two and **drew** one. (They **beat** their **opponents** three two and two **nil**, and drew four all).

At the press conference that followed the games the captain and the **coach** gave an interview.

Question: Which of your **players** do you think did best this time?

Answer: All of them played **equally** well; it's difficult to **single out** any **particular** one.

Q. You've got several new men in the team. Are you pleased with their **performance**?

A. I think our young players did **fairly** well, but we must certainly put in a lot of hard work before the winter **Olympics**.

Q. What can you say about your Canadian **opponents?**

A. I think they played first class hockey, **particularly** Bobby Smith, who **scored** several beautiful **goals**, and Dick Clayton, the **goalkeeper**. I was **impressed**.

Q. What do you think of the arrangements for the games? Was the whole thing well done?

A. It was very good indeed, and we'd like to thank our hosts for their warm **reception** and **hospitality**. They did their best to make us feel at home.

The next day several press reports **appeared** in the newspapers. Here are two of them. One of the papers wrote:.

The coach and the captain of the Russian ice hockey team say they can't single out any of their players, because all of them played equally well. They also **admit** that they will have to work hard if they want to win the Olympics. They find that the home team gave a good performance, particularly Bobby Smith and Dick Clayton.

A sports commentator from another newspaper **published** this report:

I asked the Russian coach if he could single out any of his players, and he said they had all played equally well. I also wanted to know whether they were pleased with the performance of their younger men. Mr. Sedov, the coach, said they had done fairly well, but they must put in a lot of hard work before the Olympics. Then Mr. Sedov **went on to say** that the hosts had played first class hockey, and he was impressed. He also said that the Russians had been quite **happy about** the arrangements for the games.

Learn these words:

national [´næʃnəl] *adj* — национальный, государственный

a national dress (holiday, etc)
national economy *народное хозяйство*
the national team — сборная команда

nation [´neɪʃn] *n c* — нация, народ

the United Nations Organization (the UN) — Организация Объединенных Наций (ООН)

nationality [ˌnæʃə´nælɪtɪ] *n c* — гражданство

championship [´tʃæmpɪənʃɪp] *n c* — чемпионат

draw (drew, drawn) [drɔː, druː, drɔːn] *v* — зд. сыграть вничью

They drew four all. — Они сыграли вничью со счетом 4:4.

beat (beat, beaten) [biːt, biːtn] *v* — бить, побить; *зд.* победить

They beat the other team three two.
Never beat children!

opponent [ə´pəunənt] *n c* — оппонент; противник, соперник (в споре, спорте)

nil [nɪl] *n* — ноль (в спорте)

The result of the game was three nil.

captain [´kæptɪn] *n c* — капитан (судна, команды и т.п.) *после глагола-связки*

He's (the) captain of the national team.

coach [kəutʃ] *n c*	зд. тренер
coach *v*	тренировать

He coaches (trains) them for the summer games.

player *n c*	зд. игрок (спорт.)
equal [´iːkwəl] a*dj*	равный
on equal terms	на равных условиях

equally [´iːkwəlı] *adv*	одинаково
equally well	одинаково хорошо
equally good	одинаково хороший
single out *v*	выделить, отметить
particular [pə´tıkjulə] *adj*	особый, данный, особенный
in this particular case	в данном случае
for no particular reason	без особой причины
Nothing particular happened.	Ничего особенного не произошло.
particularly [pə´tıkjuləlı] *adv*	особенно, в особенности

Syn. **especially**

He was particularly interested in the history of the city.
The work was particularly important.

performance [pə´fɔːməns]*n*	1. исполнение, работа
Are you satisfied [´sætısfaıd] with the performance of the machine?	Вы удовлетворены работой машины?
The team put up a good performance.	Команда показала хорошую игру.
	2. исполнение (*муз. театр.*)
I liked his performance.	Мне понравилось его исполнение.
The band will give two more performances.	Оркестр выступит еще два раза.
fairly [´fɛəlı] *adv*	довольно (умеренно)

Syn. **quite**

This is a fairly easy book.
I want a fairly large car (not small, but not very large).

Olympics [ə´lɪmpɪks] *n*	Олимпийские игры

Syn. **the Olympic Games**

score *v*	*(спорт.)* забить гол; выиграть очко, балл

to score a goal
to score 5 points

score *n*	*(спорт.)* счет

The score was 1 to 3

goal [gəul] *n c*	1. цель

He achieved his goal.

2. гол

to win (lose) by three goals

goalkeeper	вратарь
impress [ɪm´pres] *v*	произвести впечатление на …

Nobody was impressed by his speech.	Его речь ни на кого не произвела впечатления.

His speech impressed nobody.

reception [rɪ´sepʃn] *n*	1. прием

We were given a very friendly reception.

to hold a reception	дать (устроить) прием

2. прием (видимость или слышимость)

The reception isn't very good today.	Сегодня не очень хорошая слышимость (видимость)

hospitality [ˌhɔspɪ´tælɪtɪ] *n*	гостеприимство

She is known for her hospitality.

hospitable [´hɔspɪtəbl]	гостеприимный

Ant. **inhospitable**

do one's best   делать все возможное

Syn. **to do all one can,**

    to do everything possible

I'll do my best to help you.

make *v*   зд. заставить

What makes you think so?   Что заставляет вас так
                                    думать?

I wonder what made them give up the idea.

appear [ə´pɪə]   появляться   — 270 —

Ant. **disappear** [ˌdɪsə´pɪə]   исчезать

He always appears unexpectedly.

admit [əd´mɪt] *v*   1. признать, допустить

He didn't admit that he was wrong.

It's generally admitted that ...   Общепризнано, что ...

                               2. принять (в учебное заве-
                               дение и т.п.)

He has been admitted to the   Он был принят в универ-
university [ˌjuːnɪ´vəːsɪtɪ] n   ситет

publish [´pʌblɪʃ] *v*   публиковать, опубликовать

EXERCISES

Прочитайте текст вслух, предварительно отработав
произношение следующих слов:

national	opponent	particular
nation	performance	particularly
nationality	reception	hospitable
		hospitality

2

Подберите в тексте английские эквиваленты.

они выиграли два матча, проиграли два и один свели вничью • они победили своих противников со счетом 3:2 и 2:0 • сыграли вничью 4:4 • на пресс-конференции, которая последовала за играми • сыграл лучше всех • на этот раз • одинаково хорошо • трудно выделить кого-либо в отдельности • вы довольны тем, как они выступили? • довольно хорошо • хорошенько поработать • показали первоклассный хоккей • забил несколько красивых голов • на меня произвело впечатление • что вы думаете об организации игр • они сделали все возможное, чтобы мы чувствовали себя как дома • затем он сказал •

3

Ответьте на вопросы.

1. Has Russia a strong national hockey team now?
2. Where are international hockey championships usually held?
3. How often are they held?
4. Do you think the Russian team did very well in this particular match?
5. Why do you think so? Why didn't the coach single out any particular player?
6. Do you think he was very pleased with the performance of his team in this match?
7. I wonder what the result of a match depends on (the coach, the captain, the player, the weather, etc.)?
8. What did the coach mean by saying that the young players did fairly well?
9. What did he say about their opponents?
10. Why were the Russians particularly impressed by Bobby Smith and Dick Clayton?
11. Were the Canadians hospitable hosts?
12. How was the interview described in the newspapers?
13. Do the reporters use any direct questions and answers in their articles about the interview?
14. Do you find indirect speech more natural in a newspaper report?

4 🎞

Прочитайте вслух и переведите примеры на новые слова.

1. a national flag; a national holiday; a national park; the national hockey team; the national economy; international cooperation; international contacts; international exchanges.
2. Which of you know how many member–countries there are in the United Nations Organization?
3. Where will the next chess championship be held?
4. The Goodwill Games held in Seattle [sı'ætl] in the summer of 1990 attracted athletes from many countries.
5. He always beats me at tennis! They beat their opponents three nil. Her heart beat fast as she ran.
6. The commentator said the teams had drawn three all.
7. I wonder who'll take over as captain of the team.
8. A team's success often depends on the coach.
9. They want to find a new man to coach the players.
10. We want to speak on equal terms.
11. I wonder if the two firms are equally reliable.
12. He plays the guitar and the banjo equally well.
13. If you aren't happy about the performance of the machine, we'll replace it.
14. Our football team's performance has been excellent this year.
15. They'll give two more performances before leaving Britain.
16. His performance as Othello was terrible.
17. I can speak Spanish fairly well, but I find it difficult to understand people if they speak too fast.
18. What was the score?
19. Who scored the first goal?
20. Do you think they will achieve their goal?
21. Everybody was very impressed by the pianist's performance. I wasn't particularly impressed, were you?
22. He said the film hadn't impressed him at all.
23. We were impressed by the friendly reception they gave us.
24. I wonder why radio reception is so poor today.
25. They're the most hospitable people I've ever met.
26. I was impressed by (with) their hospitality and kindness.
27. We write to thank you for your warm reception and hospitality.
28. We are grateful for your hospitality.
29. He said he'd do his best to solve the problem as soon as possible.
30. I wonder what makes you think so.

31. I wonder what made him disappear from the party without saying good–bye to anybody.
32. When do you think your new book will appear?
33. He has appeared in every large concert hall in Europe.
34. I admit the result wasn't very impressive, but believe me, the team was doing its best to win the match with a better score.
35. It won't be easy, I admit, but we must do our best to solve the problem.
36. The story has been published in several magazines.

5

Прочитайте диалоги вслух и разыграйте их. Опишите каждую ситуацию, пользуясь средствами косвенной речи.

1

On the Phone

Mike: Are you watching the hockey, John?

John: Of course I am. How can I miss a game when my favourite team's playing?

M. I was just wondering if you could tell me the score. Something went wrong with my telly a few minutes ago. There's no reception on this particular channel.

J. Three to two. Clayton has just scored a marvellous goal!

M. Oh, good! An exciting game, isn't it?

J. Oh, yes! Come over and let's watch it together.

M. Thanks a lot! I'll be at your place in ten minutes.

2

At the Airport

Ivanov : I'm sorry the time has come for us to say good–bye to each other. Are you happy about the results of your visit here?

Bennett Absolutely. Now I'm sure we are going to have a good market here. I'll do my best to make my colleagues **realize** that the game is worth the candle!

I. It is, without any doubt!

B. I'm afraid we haven't got much time left now. I want to thank you all for your hospitality and warm reception.

I. **The pleasure was all ours.** We hope to see you soon again. I hope you have a pleasant flight!

B.   Thank you. I'll send you a fax as soon as I've talked to my people at home.

3

At an Exhibition of Agricultural Equipment

Smith: How did you like the Finnish tractors?

Petrov: Well, they aren't bad, but I wasn't particularly impressed. They're most definitely not the last word in agricultural machinebuilding.

S.   No, they aren't, but they're small, cheap and not difficult to operate.

P.   I've seen similar machines in the Dutch pavilion. They're all computerized.

S.   But that makes them more difficult for an ordinary farmer to use, doesn't it?

P.   Well, I admit they require more skill from the operator, but the new **generation** of farmers has enough education to understand the instructions, of course, if they're clear and simple.

Learn these words:

realize [´rɪəlaɪz] v   1. осознать, понять

Syn. **understand**

   Does he realize the difficulty?

   He realized (that) he was wrong.

                                            2. реализовать, осуществить

   It won't be easy to realize your plan.

pleasure [´pleʒə] n   удовольствие

   The pleasure was all ours.   *(досл.)* Все удовольст-
                                            вие было нашим. (Ответ
                                            на благодарность).

   A. I'm so grateful to you.

   B. The pleasure's mine. (=My pleasure!)

skill n   мастерство, умение, квалифи-
                                            кация, навык.

   Her skill as a teacher (nurse, coach, etc.)

| a skilled worker | квалифицированный ра— |
| | бочий |

generation [ˌdʒenəˈreɪʃn]   поколение

TOPICS FOR DISCUSSION AND NEW WORDS (continued)

Discussing Sports and Games

Three British and two Russian journalists are talking about sports and games in a programme for Russian television. Here is part of their conversation.

Donaldson: By the way, which are the most popular games in **this country?**

Nikolayev: If you mean games that are popular with both fans and players, it's ice–hockey and football.

Pierce: When you say football, do you mean **soccer** or **rugger**, or both?

Nikolayev: I beg your pardon, I don't quite get you.

Pierce: There are two kinds of football. **Association** football, or soccer, played by teams of eleven with a round ball, and **rugby** or rugger, played by teams of fifteen with an **oval** ball.

Nikolayev: Oh, I see. In this country, when we say football, we always mean soccer. Rugby isn't so popular.

Donaldson: You don't play cricket or golf here, do you?

Rogov: Golf's **coming in.** There are even some golf clubs in big cities. As to cricket, **frankly**, most people don't know anything about it here. I don't know how it's played myself.

Donaldson: It's **pretty** difficult to describe. You have to see it played. By the way, a **single** game can last two days!

Rogov: Two days! That must be awfully **tiring!**

Donaldson: The players don't all play at the same time. Each team has eleven men, like in soccer, but there are always nine players waiting their turn and not playing in one of the **sides.** It's eleven against two all the time.

Nikolayev: That sounds pretty **unfair**, doesn't it?

Bentley: Oh, no! Cricket's the fairest game in the world. The players must never **lose their temper** or **complain**, even if there's a mistake. It's a good game, because it teaches you how to lose a game without losing your temper. In fact, it forms your **character.**

Donaldson: If someone **acts** unfairly, we often say, "It isn't cricket".

Nikolayev: That's very interesting. I wonder if they play cricket in the United States.

Bentley: I don't think so. Their national game's **baseball**, a most **exciting** game, requiring great skill.

Donaldson: But cricket's played in most other English—speaking countries in Asia and Africa and in **Australia** and **New Zealand as well**. I wonder if the other sports and games here are different from those we've got at home.

Nikolayev: I don't think so. In my opinion the **main** thing about sports and games in this country is that more and more people begin to realize their importance for health, and try to do something to **keep** themselves **fit**. Both adults and children **go in for** some kind of sport or another: swimming, **track and field athletics**, figure skating. **Bodybuilding**, **judo** and **karate** are becoming **increasingly** popular.

Bentley: And what's your favourite sport?

Nikolayev: **Gymnastics**. I started when I was very young, and I still go to the **gym** regularly and **practise**, **though** I **no longer** go in for in competitions. And what's yours?

Bentley: **Jogging**. I **run** my six miles every morning, and find that's enough to keep me fit.

Learn there words:

this country	эта страна, наша страна и т.д.(страна, где происходит разговор)
fan	болельщик
soccer [´sɔkə]	футбол *(разг.)*
Syn. **(association) football**	
rugger [´rʌgə]	рэгби *(разг.)*
Syn. **rugby**	
oval [´əuvl] *adj*	овальный
come in *v*	зд. входить в моду
Syn. **come into fashion**	
frankly [´fræŋklı] *adv*	откровенно;зд.откровенно говоря
Syn. **frankly speaking**	

Frankly, I didn't enjoy the party at all.

pretty *adv* — зд. довольно-таки (разг)

single *adj* — один, одиночный, отдельный, единый

There isn't a single ticket left. — Не осталось ни одного билета

a single room — номер на одного человека

tiring [´taɪərɪŋ] *adj* — утомительный

side *n c* — зд. спортивная команда

Syn. **team**

temper *n c* — нрав, характер

a sweet (bad) temper — хороший (плохой) характер

to lose one's temper — выйти из себя

to keep one's temper — сдерживаться, владеть собой

complain [kəm´pleɪn] *v* — жаловаться

to complain **to** sb **of** sth — жаловаться кому-л. на что-л. (о нездоровье и т.п.)

He never complains.

They complained to the manager of the poor service at the hotel (They complained that the service was poor). — Они пожаловались управляющему на плохое обслуживание в отеле.

We have nothing to complain of. — Нам не на что жаловаться.

act *v* — 1. действовать, поступать

He acted like a true friend.

2. играть (на сцене)

Who acted Hamlet?

baseball [´beɪsbɔːl] *n* — бейсбол (национальная американская игра)

exciting [ɪk´saɪtɪŋ] *adj* — волнующий, возбуждающий

an exciting film (story, event, etc.)

complicated [ˈkɔmplɪkeɪtɪd]	сложный
a complicated situation (rule, etc.)	
Australia [ɔsˈtreɪljə]	Австралия
New Zealand [ˈnjuːˈziːlənd]	Новая Зеландия
as well	а также
main *adj*	главный
the main thing	главное
the main points	основные моменты
the main idea	основная мысль

fit *adj*	1. пригодный
He isn't fit for that job.	Он не годится для этой работы.
He isn't fit to be a manager.	
Do as you think fit.	Поступайте, как считаете нужным.
	2. здоровый, годный к какой-либо деятельности по здоровью
He isn't fit for military service.	Он не пригоден для военной службы.
to keep fit	держаться в хорошей форме
go in for sth	заниматься чем-л.
go in for sport(s)	заниматься спортом

Для вашего сведения: названия некоторых видов спорта

track and field athletics [æθˈletɪks]	легкая атлетика
bodybuilding [ˈbɔdɪbɪldɪŋ]	атлетическая гимнастика
judo [ˈdʒuːdəu]	дзюдо
karate [kəˈrɑːtɪ]	карате
gymnastics [dʒɪmˈnæstɪks]	гимнастика (общий термин)

rhythmic [ˈrɪðmɪk]

gymnastics   художественная гимнастика

jogging [ˈdʒɔgɪŋ]   бег трусцой

---

increase [ɪnˈkriːs] *v*   увеличивать, увеличиваться

    to increase speed (prices, etc.)

    Business has increased.   Деловая активность уве
                                       личилась.

increase [ˈɪnkriːs] *n*   рост, увеличение

    There was an increase in prices last month.

increasingly [ɪnkˈriːsɪŋlɪ] *adv*   (все) больше и больше

gym *nc*   спортзал

practise [ˈpræktɪs] *v*   зд. тренироваться, упраж
                                        няться

though [ðəu] *conj*   хотя

no longer   больше не ...

    I no longer go in for sport (= I don't go in for sport any longer)

EXERCISES

 1

Подберите в тексте английские эквиваленты.

    вы имеете в виду футбол или регби, или и то и другое • извините, я не совсем вас понимаю • гольф входит в моду • что касается крикета ... • откровенно говоря • интересно, как в него играют? • это должно быть ужасно утомительно • как в футболе • звучит довольно несправедливо • если кто-то поступает несправедливо • большое мастерство • а также в Австралии и Новой Зеландии • отличаются от тех, которые есть у нас дома • начинают понимать их значение • занимаются тем или иным видом спорта • становятся все более и более популярными • какой ваш любимый вид спорта? • тренируюсь • больше не принимаю участия • держать себя в форме •

2

Ответьте на вопросы.

1. Do you think sports and games are an interesting topic for conversation?
2. Do you agree that the most popular games in this country are football and ice–hockey? What about other games?
3. Why do you think rugby is less popular in this country than association football?
4. Which of you has ever tried to play golf? Do you think it'll become a popular game here? Why?
5. Was the information about cricket new to you, or had you heard of the game before?
6. What do you think of the role of sports and games in character training?
7. What is more important for character training — to win, or to learn how to be a good loser?
8. Do all games require great skill?
9. Is cricket only played in England? Where else is it played?
10. Do you agree that many people in this country realize the importance of sports and games for their health?
11. What kinds of sports are becoming increasingly popular in this country?
12. Do you think that an athlete must necessarily go in for competitions?
13. What do you think of bodybuilding?
14. Why are judo and karate becoming increasingly popular? What about jogging ?

— 280 —

3

Прочитайте вслух примеры на новые слова.

1. Frankly, I don't like the fashion that is coming in. Do you?
2. Frankly, I find long discussions pretty tiring.
3. He lost his temper, and frankly, it was pretty awful!
4. Nothing would have happened if you hadn't lost your temper.
5. I wonder if I'll ever learn to keep my temper!
6. If you have anything to complain of, tell the hotel manager.
7. They complain that the equipment is giving a poor performance.

8. They complain that the decision was unfair.
9. It's a fair price, isn't it?
10. I admit he acted fairly.

11. What exciting news!
12. It was an exciting event.
13. We wouldn't have troubled you if it hadn't been so complicated.
14. If they hadn't acted unfairly, they wouldn't have found themselves in such a complicated situation.
15. I wonder if that piece of equipment is very complicated to operate.
16. We were very impressed by her skill as a tennis coach.
17. He realized that he was no longer fit to do such hard work.
18. Everybody realized that the problem was very complicated.
19. I'll be very happy if your plan is realized.
20. I believe in your skill as a businessman, so do as you think fit.
21. The doctor said that I was fit to go in for any kind of sport.
22. If I didn't go jogging regularly, I wouldn't be able to keep fit.
23. If you don't practice your English regularly, you will never learn to speak it.
24. My coach said I must increase the number of daily exercises gradually.
25. Our business contacts are gradually increasing.
26. There is a slight increase in business.
27. Jogging is becoming increasingly popular.

Заполните пропуски артиклями. Предварительно выучите данные после текста слова.

Football

It is generally considered that ... birthplace of football is England, where it is so popular. But that isn't quite so. ... similar game was played nineteen hundred years ago by Roman **soldiers**, who even had ... set of rules for it.

In England football was first played in the **Middle Ages** by teams formed of whole villages, and there were no very clear rules for ... game. Very often ... number of people playing on each side exceeded ... hundred. ... players were allowed to **attack** both ... ball and their opponents, so ... football match was often considered ... very convenient way of settling conflicts between ... villagers, who were, naturally, doing their best to beat each other as hard as they could! This often led to **injuries**, and several times **laws** were passed to **prohibit** ... game.

In ... nineteenth century there was already more order in it, and in 1863 ... group of Englishmen met to form ... football association which set strict rules for ... game. It would only be fair to say that ... association formed in England over ... hundred years ago is ... grandparent of ...International Football Association (F.I.F.A.), which exists now and **runs** ... World Cup competitions every four years.

In 1963 ... match between ... England team and the World was held to celebrate ... centenary of Association football. ... goalkeeper in that match was Lev Yashin, ... famous Russian footballer.

Learn these words:

soldier [´səuldʒə] *n*	солдат
the Middle Ages	средние века
attack [ə´tæk] *v*	нападать на, атаковать
injure [´ɪndʒə] *v*	повредить, ушибить, поранить
Syn. **hurt (hurt, hurt)**	ушибить

John fell down from the tree and injured his leg.

injury [´ɪndʒərɪ] *n*	повреждение, травма

He has several serious injuries.

law [lɔː]	*n*	закон, право (*юр.*)
civil law		гражданское право
to pass a law		принять закон
to break the law		нарушить закон
lawyer [´lɔːjə] *n c*		адвокат, юрист
company lawyer		юристконсульт
prohibit [prə´hɪbɪt] *v*		запрещать

Syn. **forbid (forbade, forbidden)**

run *v*	*зд.* организовывать, управлять, руководить
the World	*зд.* сборная мира
celebrate [ˈselɪbreɪt] *v*	праздновать, отмечать
centenery [senˈtiːnərɪ] *n c*	столетие, столетняя годовщина

5

Прочитайте вслух примеры на новые слова.

1. He wouldn't have been injured if he'd been more careful.

2. I wonder how seriously he was injured.

3. Did you hurt yourself?

4. Did you hurt your leg?

5. We would have protested if they had acted against the law.

6. I doubt whether everything was done according to the law.

7. The law passed by Parliament [ˈpɑːləmənt] was published by several newspapers.

8. I wonder what made them break the law?

9. I don't think it's a lawful decision.

10. I suggest talking to a lawyer.

11. Every businessman should know civil law.

12. Why do you think he decided to give up medicine and study law?

13. It's the law of nature.

14. I wonder which of them will take over and run the company.

15. The exhibition is run on a commercial basis.

16. Let's celebrate the occasion, shall we?

17. It's a national holiday, so it's celebrated by most people in this country.

Согласны ли вы или не согласны со следующими утверждениями? Дайте развернутые ответы. Используйте выражения из правой колонки.

1. Going in for sports and games is the best way to keep yourself fit.	Well, I'm afraid your idea of this kind of sport isn't right.
	Believe it or not, some people find ...
2. It's definitely better to choose one kind of sport and become very skilled at it than to go in for several kinds without any particular success.	I quite agree with you, I couldn't agree more ...
	My own opinion is that ...
	Well, yes and no. On the one hand ..., and on the other ...
3. More and more teachers realize the importance of sports and games for character training, so physical training is becoming increasingly popular in schools.	I don't think you are right.
	Well, it all depends.

4. Bodybuilding is a very dull kind of sport. It isn't harmless, and last but not least, it makes the human body unnatural and ugly.

5. Going to a stadium to watch sporting events is just a waste of time. It's equally interesting and exciting to watch them on the telly !

6. When you are losing a game, the worst thing you can do is to lose your temper.

7. Judo and karate are very dangerous kinds of sports, because they may lead to serious injuries.

8. Success in sports depends on the athlete alone. The coach can do nothing if the athlete has't got the necassary qualities.

9 The good thing about tennis is that you can play it at any time of life. The longer you don't give up playing it the better you feel.

10. Jogging is no longer as popular as it used to be, because many people complain that it does them more harm than good.

Unit 12

GRAMMAR

23. <u>Конструкция "сложное дополнение" (косвенный падеж + инфинитив).</u>

23.1. После глаголов, выражающих желание (пожелание) **want, would like** может употребляться сложное дополнение, которое состоит из *существительного + инфинитив с частицей to* или *личного местоимения в косвенном падеже + инфинитив с частицей to.*

1. I **want my son to be** a lawyer.	Я хочу, чтобы мой сын стал юристом.
2. We had least of all **wanted anyone to be injured** in the match.	Нам меньше всего хотелось, чтобы кто-нибудь получил травму во время матча.
3. We **would like them to enjoy** their stay in our city.	Мы хотели бы, чтобы они получили удовольствие от пребывания в нашем городе.
4. I'd **like him to come** here for his holiday.	Мне бы хотелось, чтобы он приехал сюда в отпуск.

Обратите внимание на то, что после глаголов, выражающих желание, сложное дополнение переводится на русский язык придаточным предложением, начинающимся с союза "чтобы".

23.2. К группе глаголов, после которых может употребляться сложное дополнение, в котором инфинитив имеет частицу to, относится также глагол **expect** [ɪkˈspekt] *ожидать, рассчитывать, полагать.*

1. Nobody **expected them to arrive** at such an early hour.	Никто не ожидал, что они прибудут в такой ранний час.

2. We **expect the probem to be solved** in the near future.	Мы ожидаем, что проблема будет решена в ближайшем будущем.

Наряду со сложным дополнением, после глагола **expect** может в большинстве случаев употребляться и придаточное предложение:

> We expected them to win the game = We expected (that) they would win the game.

ПРИМЕЧАНИЕ: Глагол **expect** не следует смешивать с глаголом **wait** *ждать,* выражающим не предположение, а физическое состояние ожидания:

I had expected him at ten, but he was half an hour late, and I had to wait.	Я ждал (ожидал) его в десять часов, но он опоздал на полчаса и мне пришлось подождать.

EXERISES

Прочитайте вслух и переведите.

1. I want my son to go in for sports.
2. I don't want you to take so much trouble.
3. I would like you to practise your English every day.
4. I don't think he wanted Bob to lose his temper, he simply wanted him to play according to the rules.
5. We want our contacts to increase in the near future.
6. The manager doesn't want his assistants to do so much routine paper-work any longer.
7. We are friends, and I naturally want him to be perfectly frank with me.
8. The Director General wants us to compare all those projects and say what we think of them.
9. I didn't expect the discussion to be so tiring.
10. Frankly, we had expected them to find a better place for the exhibition.
11. Everybody expected the talks to be a success.
12. We didn't expect the matter to be so complicated.

Перефразируйте, как показано в образце.

Дано: I want to have a good holiday (my children).

Требуется: I want my children to have a good holiday.

1. I don't want to waste so much time on this useless work any longer (my assistant).
2. I'd like to be absolutely frank with him (you).
3. I want to be as fair as possible (them).
4. My friend wants to begin jogging regularly (his elder son).
5. I want to make all the arrangements in good time (the managers).
6. I'd like to leave a message with the secretary (Mr. Bentley).
7. They wanted to fulfil all their obligations (their counterparts).
8. She wanted to impress the public (her article).

Выберите правильное слово.
   EXPECT or WAIT?

1. I wonder if you are (expecting, waiting for) any more visitors this afternoon.
2. Frankly, I had (expected, waited for) better progress.
3. None of us (expected, waited for) such great success.
4. I'm afraid you'll have to (expect, wait) a little.
5. I didn't (expect, wait) that he would lose his temper.
6. He said he couldn't afford (to expect, to wait) any longer.
7. Why do you think we had to (expect, wait for) their answer so long?
8. She's (expecting, waiting for) a baby at the beginning of March.
9. He suggested (expecting, waiting) till eleven, and then going home if they didn't come.

Перефразируйте, как показано в образце.

Дано: We didn't expect that the game would be so tiring.

Требуется: We didn't expect the game to be so tiring.

1. We didn't expect that the matter would be so complicated.

2. Why do you think nobody expected that the exhibition would attract so many visitors?
3. Nobody expected that such an enormous sum would be offered for the picture at the auction.
4. Nobody expected that the situation would be so dangerous.
5. Nobody expected that so much damage would be done by the flood.
6. We didn't expect that the weather would be so changeable.
7. We expect that the time and date will be convenient for everybody.
8. I didn't expect that they would quarrel over such an unimportant thing.

5

Переведите на английский язык.

1. Конечно, я хочу, чтобы моя команда победила своих соперников, но я понимаю, что их шансы (chances) равны.
2. Я хочу, чтобы вы поместили этот стенд на переднем плане фотографии.
3. Спросите посла, хочет ли он, чтобы прием состоялся на следующей неделе.
4. Нам бы хотелось, чтобы время и место собрания устраивало всех.
5. Мне бы хотелось, чтобы все победители в соревнованиях были приглашены на прием.
6. Никто не ожидал, что фильм будет иметь такой большой успех.
7. Откровенно говоря, я не ожидал, что его выступление (performance) произведет на меня впечатление, но я должен признать, что он лучший пианист на этом конкурсе.
8. Никто из нас не ожидал, что обе команды будут играть одинаково хорошо.
9. Мы ожидаем, что посетители особенно заинтересуются нашими последними моделями.
10. Никто не ожидал, что решение будет таким несправедливым.

GRAMMAR
(continued)

24. Сложное дополнение после глаголов восприятия.

24.1. Основными глаголами восприятия являются **see** в значении *видеть* и **hear** в значении *слышать*. После этих глаголов употребляется сложное дополнение, которое может состоять из *существительного + причастие I* или *местоимения в косвенном падеже + причастие I.*

1. I **saw him running.**	Я видел, как он бежал.
2. We **saw her crossing** the street.	Мы видели, что она переходит улицу.
3. I **saw him leaving** the house.	Я видел, что он выходит из дому.
4. I **heard him speaking** on the phone.	Я слышал, как он разговаривает по телефону.

Как видно из примеров, этот оборот переводится на русский язык дополнительным придаточным предложением, начинающимся с союзов *как* или *что*.

24.2. Сложное дополнение после глаголов этой группы может также состоять из *существительного или местоимения в косвенном падеже + инфинитив без частицы to:*

1. We **saw him leave** the house.	Мы видели, что он вышел из дому.
2. I **heard him make arrangements** for his journey.	Я слышал, как он договорился о своей поездке.

Инфинитив в этом обороте показывает, что действие было воспринято *полностью.*

Сравните:

I **saw** him **change** the wheel.	Я видел, как он *сменил* колесо (т.е. я видел действие полностью).
I saw him **changing** the wheel.	Я видел, *как (что)* он *меняет* колесо (т.е. я видел незавершенный процесс)

24.4. Сложное дополнение после глаголов **see** и **hear** возможно только в том случае, когда они выражают непосредственное восприятие действия органами чувств.

В тех случаях, когда **see** означает *увидеть - понять,* а **hear** *услышать - получить сведения, известия,* после них употребляются дополнительные придаточные предложения:

1. I see that the design is more reliable.	Я вижу (понимаю), что эта конструкция более надежна.
2. I heard that he was ill.	Я слышал (узнал, имею сведения), что он болен.

24.5. Сложное дополнение может употребляться и после глаголов **watch** - *наблюдать*, **notice** - *заметить*, **feel** - *чувствовать*, **listen** - *слушать* и некоторых других.

1. The reporter **watched them arranging** the exhibits.	Репортер наблюдал, как они расставляли экспонаты.	— 292 —
2. He **felt** the car **skidding**.	Он почувствовал, что машина буксует.	
3. Nobody **noticed her come** into the room.	Никто не заметил, как она вошла в комнату.	
4. We **listened to Alice playing** the piano.	Мы слушали, как Алиса играет на рояле.	

EXERCISES.

Прочитайте вслух и переведите.

1. When I entered the gym, I saw a group of girls practising without their coach.
2. I've never seen him lose his temper.
3. I've never heard her complain.
4. I heard them quarrelling, and decided to go up and ask what the matter was.
5. I heard that Helen was a good pianist, but I've never heard her play the piano.
6. We saw that the conversation was growing tiring and decided to stop before it was too late.
7. We watched the coach giving last-minute instructions to the players.
8. We saw the policeman go up to the driver and say something to him.
9. I've never heard him say anything unfair.

10. We heard that after the last injury he·was no longer fit to take part in serious competitions.
11. I didn't notice you come in.
12. I noticed that he wasn't particularly interested in the conversation.

2

Соедините два предложения в одно, как показано в образце.

1.

Дано: Jane was waiting for somebody. I saw her.
Требуется: I saw Jane waiting for somebody.
1. They were playing tennis. Their coach watched them.
2. Helen was playing the guitar. We listened to her.
3. Alice was talking to a colleague in Spanish. I heard it.
4. Bill Blake was changing money in a bank. The detective saw it.
5. Jill was parking her car. I saw it.

2.

Дано: Someone locked the front door. I heard it.
Требуется: I heard someone lock the front door.
1. She came in. I didn't hear it.
2. He went out. Nobody noticed it.
3. Jeff signed all the documents. Everybody saw this.
4. Jane congratulated Anne and Tom on their success. We all heard it.
5. Jill parked her car in Albert Road. I saw it.

3

Прочитайте вслух и перескажите.

A Joke

A little boy showed his father a new penknife. He said he had found in the street.

"Are you sure it was lost?" the father asked.

"Of course, it was lost!" the boy answered. "I saw a man looking for it."

Переведите на английский язык.

1. Я слышал, как он играет на гитаре.
2. Я слышал, что он хороший гитарист.
3. Мы видели, как он танцует.
4. Мы видели, что он профессиональный танцор.
5. Я видел, как он моет свою машину.
6. Я вижу, что ты помыл машину.

TOPICS FOR DISCUSSION and NEW WORDS

A Running Commentary.

Hello! I'm Harry Fennell with Sports **Update.**

We're now taking you to the Alexandra Park Sports Centre for the match between Orient and Arsenal that most football fans are **looking forward to.** The **commentary** will be given by Martin Shaw. Martin?

M.S. Hello, Harry! We're just waiting for the teams to come out. And here they are. You can see Larry O'Neil, the

Orient captain, leading the team. They are followed by Arsenal, with Bobby King, their captain, at their head. Both teams are in equally good form, and keep on **improving.**

Now you can watch the players **warming up ...**

The stadium is full. Each fan naturally expects his team to win.

You can hear the **referee blow** his **whistle.** The **kick–off** at last! Harry Grant takes the ball **forward.** I can see Dick Hunt trying to **intercept** him, but with no success.

Now Arsenal's **centre–forward** has the ball. You can see him trying to take the ball down the field. Oh, he doesn't notice an Orient **back** running up to him from **behind**!

He may lose the ball! He passes it to Bobby Hurst. I wonder why? What does he want Bobby to do? He's too far off to have a **chance** of scoring. But Bobby acts without **hesitation**! Oh, what a magnificent kick! What a beautiful goal! Frankly, I didn't expect Bobby to score at such a **distance! Good for him! Well done**, Bobby!

Arsenal have **opened the score.** You can hear the **crowd** shouting.

Learn these words:

update [´ʌpdeɪt]

последние сообщения (телевиз.)

Alexandra [ˌælɪgzɑːndrə]

Александра (женск. имя)

Orient [´ɔːrɪənt]

Ориент (назв. футбольного клуба)

Arsenal [´ɑːsɪnl]

Арсенал (назв. футбольного клуба)

Martin Shaw   [´mɑːtɪn´ʃɔː]

Larry O'Neil   [´lærɪəu´niːl]

look forward (to) *v prep*

с нетерпением ожидать чего—л.

I'm looking forward to the trip.
I'm looking forward to seeing you.
We are looking forward to hearing from you soon.

С нетерпением ждем от вас известий.

We are looking forward to an early reply.

Ждем скорого ответа *(заключит. фразы письма)*

commentary [´kɔməntrɪ] *n c*

комментарий

They are giving a running commentary **on** the match.

Матч транслируется по радио.

improve [ɪm´pruːv] *v*

улучшать, улучшаться

Your English is improving.
I'm doing my best to improve my English.
The weather's improving.

improvement [ɪmˈpruːvmənt] *n*   улучшение

There has been an improvement in the country's economy.

warm up   разогревать (ся), *зд.* разми—
                                     наться

They are warming up.   У них разминка.

referee [ˌrefəˈriː]   *n c*   судья (*спорт.*)

whistle [wɪsl] *v*   свистеть

whistle *n c*   свисток

The referee blew his whistle.   Судья дал сигнал.

to blow (blew, blown) [bləu,   дуть
blu:, bləun]
The wind was blowing, but it wasn't
cold.

Внимание: для любителей футбола.

kick *n c*   удар ногой

a free kick   свободный удар (спорт.)

a penalty kick   штрафной удар

a kick—off   первый удар по мячу

kick *v*   ударить ногой

He kicked the ball over the sideline (... за боковую линию)
He kicked the ball above (over) the   (... выше ворот)
goal
He kicked the ball into his own goal. (... в свои ворота)

---

forward *adv*   вперед

Ant. **backward**   назад

forward *n c*   зд. нападающий (*спорт.*)

intercept [ˌɪntəˈsept] *v*   перехватить

back *n*   зд. защитник (*спорт.*)

behind [bɪˈhaɪnd] *prep adv*   сзади, позади

Ant. **in front of**

There's a garden behind the house.

chance [tʃɑːns] *n* 1. шанс, надежда

He didn't think he had any chance of success.

Do you think there's still a chance of coming to an agreement?

2. случай, случайность

a lucky (unexpected, rare) chance счастливый (неожиданный, редкий) случай

by chance случайно

We met quite by chance.

3. удобный случай, благоприятная возможность

— 297 —

Syn. **opportunity** [ˌɔpəˈtjuːnətɪ]

a chance (opportunity) to do sth (of doing sth) возможность что-л. сделать

to take a chance (an opportunity) to do sth (of doing sth) воспользоваться возможностью (удобным случаем) сделать что-л.

to give sb a chance (an opportunity) to do sth (of doing sth) дать кому-л. возможность сделать что-л.

to miss a (the) chance, an (the) opportunity of doing (to do) sth упустить возможност

He had a wonderful opportunity to improve (of improving) his English.

She takes every opportunity of practising the piano.

The children were given an opportunity to go in for any sport they liked.

I'm so sorry I missed the opportunity to speak to him.

hesitate [ˈhezɪteɪt] *v* колебаться (не решаться)

He hesitated before giving a definite answer.

Don't hesitate to ask me for help.

hesitation [ˌhezɪˈteɪʃn] *n u* колебание, нерешительность

He agreed without a moment's hesitation.

distance [ˈdɪstəns] *n* расстояние

What's the distance **between** the two cities (**from** London **to** Glasgow)?

It's some distance away.

It's **within** walking distance (**of** home, etc.)

You will be able to see the palace **at (from)** a distance of 20 miles.

Good for you (him, her)!	Молодец!
Well done!	Здорово! *(Восклицание одобрения)*
to open the score	открыть счет *(спорт.)*
shout v	кричать

"Help!" he shouted.

He shouted for help.

Don't shout at me!

He shouted something to me, but I couldn't hear, because of the noise.

EXERCISES

1

Подберите в тексте английские эквиваленты.

матч, которого все болельщики с нетерпением ждут • мы как раз ждем, когда появятся команды • А вот и они • Вы видите, как Ларри О.Нил, капитан Ориента, выводит свою команду • За ними следует Арсенал • Обе команды в одинаково хорошей форме и продолжают совершенствоваться • Каждый болельщик, естественно, ожидает, что победит его команда • Я вижу, как Дик Хант пытается перехватить его, но безуспешно • Он не замечает, что сзади к нему подбегает защитник Ориента • Он может потерять мяч! • Интересно, почему? • Он слишком далеко, чтобы иметь шанс забить гол • действует без колебаний • Откровенно говоря, я не ожидал, что он забьет гол с такого расстояния • Молодец! Здорово! • открыл счет.

2

Прочитайте вслух примеры на новые слова.

1. I'm looking forward to my summer holiday.
2. We're looking forward to seeing you in Moscow.

3. We're looking forward to new contracts with your company.
4. Please turn on the radio! They're giving a running commentary on the contest.
5. I'd like you to listen to the commentary on the match this evening. It'll be given by our best sports commentator.
6. I'm happy to hear that his health is improving.
7. We all expect the situation to improve in the future.
8. We'd like you to improve the design a little.
9. They want us to make some improvements in the design.
10. I didn't notice much improvement, to say the least.
11. When I left the house, I felt a strong wind blowing.
12. Nobody expected him to kick the ball into his own goal.
13. He could have scored if he hadn't kicked the ball over the goal.
14. I don't think the team has much chance of winning.
15. What do you think is our chance of winning that contract?
16. Frankly, the chances are a hundred to one against us.
17. If, by any chance, you find yourself in a difficult situation, don't hesitate to ask me for help.
18. I wouldn't trouble you again if it weren't my only chance of settling the matter.
19. It would be fair to say that each of us has every opportunity to improve his or her English.
20. It's the chance of a lifetime.
21. I'm so sorry I had no opportunity to discuss the matter again.
22. If he'd been given an opportunity to learn to play the piano when he was a child, he'd have become a good pianist.
23. It was a wonderful opportunity, and he didn't hesitate to take it.
24. It was a rare opportunity, and I took it without hesitation.
25. I could see them shouting something, but I couldn't hear a word at such a distance.
26. I was told that some distance behind the church there was a beautiful lake.
27. Don't you think the picture looks better from a distance?
28. Looking back over a distance of forty years, we can say that we could've done better if we'd had more opportunities.

3

Повторите, используя подсказанные слова.

1. We are looking forward to **seeing you in St. Petersburg.**

   • hearing from you soon • establishing business relations with your company • doing more business with you in the future • setting up a joint venture with your company • meeting your

specialists •

2. This is an excellent opportunity to **sign new contracts**.
• improve your position on our market • solve the problem easily
• settle the matter quickly • meet the representatives of the
leading research institutes •

3. He didn't hesitate to **join us**.
• support our ideas • offer us his help • agree to our proposal
• give answers to all our questions • ·

4. I'm sorry I had no opportunity to **see him again**.   — 300 —
• discuss the matter with a lawyer • compare the two offers
carefully • study the matter more carefully •

5. We expect them to increase the order.
• improve the design • make some more improvements soon •
give us another chance • take part in the fair •

Подберите подходящие ответные реплики к высказываниям,
данным в колонке слева. Продолжите мысль.

1. When people have a chance to get a better-paid job, they never hesitate to give up their old one and accept the offer.	Good for you!
2. I began jogging regularly, and I feel a definite improvement in my health.	Well done, Tommy!
3. You can see Tom Clark finishing the long distance race: It's a new world record!	Congratulations!
4. What do you think is the right time for a child to begin learning a foreign language?	It depends. On the one hand ... on the other hand ...

5. I want to go into business, but I wonder if at my time of life (and I'm forty) I have any chance of success.

Well, I'm not absolutely sure ...

6. If you have an opportunity of giving up your professional job and going into business, you must do so without hesitation.

If I had to make a decision like that, I should think twice before ...

What makes you think so?

7. My son has been admitted to the Law faculty at the University.

I don't think you're right. It depends whether you like your profession or only work for money ...

Ответьте на вопросы.

1. Would you call yourself a football (hockey) fan?
2. Do you like watching sporting events with a commentary or without one? Why?
3. Which of our sports commentators do you think is best? Why?
4. Do you look forward to important matches?
5. Do you play any games like football, hockey, basketball, etc?
6. Do you think there's always a risk of an injury during these games?
7. Do you think you have enough out-of-door exercise, or do you spend most of your time indoors?
8. If a famous coach found that there might be a future for your child in professional sport, would you allow your child to take the chance, or would you hesitate? Why?
9. Which do you think is better – to be a professional in sports (music, dancing, acting, etc.) or an **amateur**? Give your reasons.

---

amateur [´æmətə]   любитель, не профессионал

Unit 13

GRAMMAR

25. Настоящее время группы Perfect Continuous (Present Perfect Continuous)

25.1 Эта временная форма образуется из Present Perfect вспомогательного глагола be и причастия I основного глагола:

Утвердительная форма:

I've been waiting [aıv bın ʹweıtıŋ]
He's been waiting [hi· z bın ʹweıtıŋ]

Вопросительная форма:

Have you been waiting? [ʹhæv ju bın ʹweıtıŋ]

Отрицательная форма:

I haven't been waiting [aı ʹhævnt bın ʹweıtıŋ]
She hasn't been waiting [ʃi ʹhæznt bın ʹweıtıŋ]

Вопросительно–отрицательная:

Haven't you been waiting? [ʹhævnt ju bın ʹweıtıŋ]

25.2 Present Perfect Continuous употребляется, когда речь идет о действии, которое началось в прошлом и все еще продолжается или только что закончилось:

1. We've been learning English for six months.	Мы занимаемся английским языком шесть месяцев.
2. How long have you been waiting?	Сколько времени вы ждете (прождали)?

3. I haven't been waiting long.

Я недолго жду.

Как видно из примеров, на русский язык эта временная форма в большинстве случаев переводится глаголом в *настоящем* времени и реже в прошедшем времени.

25.3. В высказываниях со сказуемым в Present Perfect Continuous обычно указывается *отрезок времени*, в течение которого продолжается (или продолжалось) действие. Обстоятельства времени чаще всего вводятся предлогами **for** *в течение* и **since** [sɪns] *с, с тех пор, как* и отвечают на вопрос **how long**? *сколько времени, как долго*? **Since (ever since)** может быть и наречием со значением *с тех пор*.

1. I've been looking for my telephone book for over an hour!

Я ищу свою записную книжку больше часа!

2. They've been quarrelling for such a long time!

Они так долго ссорятся!

3. How long have they been practising today?

Сколько времени они тренируются сегодня?

4. They've been arranging the new exhibits since early this morning.

Они с самого утра расставляют новые экспонаты.

5. He took over as Director General ten years ago, and has been running the firm successfully since then.

Он стал генеральным директором десять лет тому назад, и с тех пор успешно руководит фирмой.

6. They met at the last film festival and have been working together ever since.

Они познакомились на последнем кинофестивале, и с тех пор работают вместе.

25.4. Present Perfect Continuous может употребляться с наречиями **lately** [ˈleɪtlɪ] и **recently** [ˈriːsəntlɪ], которые переводятся на русский язык *(в) последнее время*.

1. They've been doing a lot to improve the quality recently.

В последнее время они многое делают, чтобы улучшить качество.

| 2. We've been trying to increase our international contacts lately (recently). | В последнее время мы стараемся расширить наши международные связи. |

ПРИМЕЧАНИЯ:

1. Слово **lately** может употребляться только с временами группы **Perfect** и **Perfect Continuous**. Слово **recently** может употребляться и с прошедшим временем группы **Simple** в значении *недавно, не так давно*:

1. I **haven't seen** him lately (recently).	В последнее время я его не вижу (не видел).
2. He **left** recently.	Он уехал недавно.
3. I **saw** him recently.	Я не так давно его видел.

2. Помимо перечисленных обстоятельств времени, с **Present Perfect Continuous** могут употребляться любые обстоятельственные слова, обозначающие отрезок времени, продолжающийся до момента речи:

| 1. It's been raining **all day (long)!** | Весь день идет дождь! |
| 2. He's been trying to keep fit **all his life**. | Он всю жизнь старается держаться в форме. |

25.5. Глаголы, которые не могут обозначать процесса и поэтому не употребляются в продолженных формах, во всех перечисленных случаях (24.2; 24.3; 24.4) употребляются в **Present Perfect**:

1. We've **been** friends since childhood.	Мы дружим с детства.
2. I've **known** him for a long time.	Я давно его знаю.
3. I **haven't seen** you for ages.	Я тебя целую вечность не видел.

Среди этих глаголов есть однако и такие, которые можно употребить в **Present Perfect Continuous** в некоторых случаях:

| 1. He **hasn't been feeling** well lately. | Он неважно себя чувствует в последнее время. |
| 2. I've **been wanting** to introduce you to each other for a long time. | Я давно хочу (хотел) вас познакомить. |

25.6. Сравнение Present Perfect и Present Perfect Continuous.

В большинстве случаев Present Perfect употребляется, когда речь идет о *законченном* действии, а Present Perfect Continuous - когда речь идет о действии *продолжающемся*.

1. We **have studied** your offer carefully, and are prepared to meet your specialists.

Мы тщательно **изучили** ваше предложение и готовы встретиться с вашими специалистами.

2. We **have been studying** your offer carefully, and hope that we will be ready to meet your specialists in the near future.

Мы тщательно **изучаем** ваше предложение и надеемся, что будем готовы встретиться с вашими специалистами в ближайшем будущем.

— 305 —

ПРИМЕЧАНИЕ: Если в предложении со сказуемым в Present Perfect указан *отрезок времени*, оно с некоторыми глаголами может быть близким по значению аналогичному предложению со сказуемым в Present Perfect Continuous. К таким глаголам относятся **live, work, teach, want** и некоторые другие:

1. I've taught (I've been teaching) English **all my life.**

Я всю жизнь преподаю английский.

2. He's lived (he's been living) here **since childhood.**

Он живет здесь с детства.

25.7.
Когда речь идет о длительном действии, продолжавшемся до определенного момента в прошлом, употребляется прошедшее время группы Perfect Continuous - Past Perfect Continuous:

We **had been driving** for about two hours **when we realized** that we were going in the opposite direction.

Мы ехали около двух часов, когда поняли, что едем в противоположную сторону.

Разница между Past Perfect Continuous и Past Perfect аналогична разнице между Present Perfect Continuous и Present Perfect.

25.8.
Времена группы Perfect Continuous не имеют форм пассивного залога. Русским предложениям типа:

итайте диалог. Разыграйте аналогичные ситуации,
няя выделенные слова словами, данными в скобках.

Inviting a Friend to Come Round.

Hello, Bill! What a pleasant surprise!

Oh, Alan, hello! Glad to see you too!

I haven't seen you for ages. Where have you been keeping yourself?

I've been to Canada on business. By the way, if you**'ve nothing planned** for Saturday evening, I'll be very glad if you could come and see me at my place.

Is it going to be a party?

Well, no, not really. Just a few friends who'll come round to see me. You know most of them. I'm sure they'll all be very pleased if you join us.

Thank you ever so. I'd be pleased to come.

Till Saturday, then. Bye!

Bye!

(•are not doing anything on Saturday evening • have nothing arranged for Saturday evening • have no plans for Saturday evening•)

6

азыграйте следующие эпизоды.

1. Вы хотите познакомить вашего зарубежного партнера со спе—циалистом, который будет работать в вашем совместном пред—приятии. Спросите вашего партнера, есть ли у него свободная минутка. Скажите, что вы хотите познакомить его с одним из лучших специалистов в данной области. Ваш собеседник много слышал об этом специалисте, с тех пор, как он работает в России. Он будет рад с ним познакомиться. Представьте их друг другу.

2. Вы встретили вашего зарубежного коллегу, работающего в нашей стране по контракту, с которым вы давно не виделись. Спросите, где он пропадал. Если у него нет определенных планов на субботний вечер, пригласите его к себе домой.

Дом строится с прошлого года. Мне сказали, что дом строится с прошлого года.

соответствуют английские предложения в активном залоге:

They *have been building* the house since last year.
I was told **they** *had been building* the house since last year.

EXERCISES

1

Прочитайте вслух и переведите, обращая внимание на употребление времен.

– 306 –

1. They've been building those pavilions for a very long time.
2. He's been learning Japanese for a year. He's learnt to speak it a little, but he can't say he's learnt to read and write.
3. We've been looking for some exhibition grounds since last month, but we haven't found a suitable place yet.
4. The auction has been going on for two days, and most pictures have already been sold.
5. They've been trying to solve the problem since they began to work together, but with no success.
6. Thank you for this wonderful music centre. I've been wanting to have one for a long time!
7. So sorry I'm late! Have you been waiting long?
8. "How long have you been using your car?" "Well, since I bought it three years ago."
9. "How long have you known each other?" "Since we went to college."
10. I've always wanted to play tennis, but I could never afford to spend enough time to learn.
11. Hello, Bill! I haven't seen you for ages! Where have you been keeping yourself?
12. He hasn't called me lately.
13. I haven't seen her lately.
14. We haven't heard from them lately.
15. It happened quite recently.

2

Повторите, используя подсказанные слова.

1. We've been learning English **for six months**.

• for nearly half a year • for more than six months • since September • since last year • since we became students at this college •

2. He's been running the company **for ten years**.

• for a long time • since 1986 • since he took over as Director General•for over ten years • for more than seven years •

3. How long have you been **learning English**?

• working on your project • studying their offer • doing business with your counterparts • looking for people who would be interested in your ideas •

4. He hasn't been **waiting** long.

• working • practising • looking for a job • waiting his turn • waiting his chance •

5. There **have been some changes** recently.

• has been some improvement • has been an increase in business • has been some trouble with that equipment • have been some dramatic events •

6. I haven't **seen them** lately.

• heard from them • been to the theatre • been doing anything • been feeling well • had any trouble with my computer • had any friends round • read anything interesting in the papers •

7. I've been wanting to **talk to you about it** for a long time.

• discuss it with you • go to the theatre • go out • introduce you to each other•introduce you to a very good friend of mine •

8. I've known **it for a long time**.

• him for ages • them since we went to college together • her since childhood •

9. He said he **hadn't been waiting long**.

• had been trying to get through to us since morning • had been trying to establish business contacts with us for a long time •

3

Прочитайте вслух и переведите, обращая внимание на употребление Present Perfect Continuous и Present Perfect.

1. You've made good progress in your English lately.
2. You've been making good progress in your English lately.
3. Have you had any trouble with this equipment since you bought it?

---

4. I've been having a lot of tr⟨⟩ always something the matte⟨⟩
5. We've been doing our best to⟨⟩ we hope to attract new buye⟨⟩
6. We have improved the quality⟨⟩ looking forward to seeing you⟨⟩ interested in.
7. We've been making some chang⟨⟩ finished the work yet, it'll take⟨⟩
8. We've made some changes in t⟨⟩ so as to meet all your requirem⟨⟩
9. We've been trying to settle the⟨⟩ no success.
10. We are pleased to let you know t⟨⟩ successfully.

4

Прочитайте диалоги вслух и разыгр⟨⟩

1

A. I wonder if you've got a free moment n⟨⟩
B. Yes, why?
A. I want you to meet Peter Bennett. I've bee⟨⟩ to each other for a long time.
B. Oh, Peter! I've been looking forward to me⟨⟩ was here. What a lucky chance!
A. Yes, indeed! Don't let's miss it.
B. No!

2

A. Hello, Boris. Good to see you again. It's bee⟨⟩ talked last. How are things?
B. Not too bad, but we've been having a hard ti⟨⟩ going.
A. It's always hard to start a business venture,⟨⟩ done, isn't it?

Про⟨⟩
заме⟨⟩

5

A.
B.
A.
B.

A.
B.

A.
B.
A.

7

Прочитайте диалоги вслух. Выучите новые слова. Распределите роли и разыграйте в классе ситуацию: "Деловое совещание на совместном предприятии".

1

At a Joint Venture Meeting

Chairman: Well, if everybody's here, let's begin. As I'm sure all of you know, we have invited a team of experts to do some work for us. They've been doing some market research for our company, and today I'm happy to introduce to you Mr James Bennett who is going to tell us the results. James, let me introduce my colleagues: Nick Petrov, the Finance Director, Boris Nikulin, the Production Manager, Oleg Belov, the Sales Manager, Nina Izvekova, a design expert.

James Bennett : I'm very happy to meet you all. I've heard a lot about you from my chief, now we've met, and I hope what I'm going to say will be of interest to you. So let me begin. Our team got down to work three months ago, and all this time we've been trying to find out what kind of future this joint venture has. I must admit that before we started our **investigation** we'd only had a **general** idea of your economic problems, now it would only be fair to say we have a pretty good idea of your opportunities. I can't say that there aren't going to be any difficulties. **On the contrary**, a great effort will be required, but the effort's worth making, because there're a lot of chances for someone who woudln't hesitate to take risks. Let me give you some facts and figures ...

Learn these words:

chairman [ˈtʃɛəmən] *n c*	председатель, председательствующий
investigation [ɪnˌvestɪˈgeɪʃn] *n c*	исследование, расследование, изучение
The matter is under investigation.	Вопрос (дело) изучается.
investigate [ɪnˈvestɪgeɪt] *v*	исследовать, расследовать, изучать
to investigate a crime	расследовать преступление
to investigate (study) the market	исследовать (изучить) рынок

to investigate the situation	изучить ситуацию
general [´dʒenrəl] *adj*	зд. общий
to have a general idea of sth	иметь общее представление о чём—л.
in general	вообще
on the contrary	напротив, наоборот
quite the contrary	как раз наоборот

"You aren't impressed, I'm afraid."

"On the contrary, I find it all very interesting and unusual."

2

During the Break

A. Well, how did you like the report?

B. I think they've done a wonderful job. They've investigated everything very carefully and in such a short time, too! I was impressed.

A. I'm very pleased to hear that. I've been working with James for a long time. He's done some very important market research for the world's leading companies.

B. Then the work he's been doing for us isn't of particular interest to him, I suppose.

A. On the contrary, he's very interested. When he was offered to be head of the team, he agreed without any hesitation, because he'd always been interested in investigating the Russian market. By the way, he sounded very optimistic [ˌɔptɪ´mɪstɪk], didn't he?

B. Yes, very **encouraging** indeed. Oh, the break's nearly over. Let's go back to the conference room, shall we?

A. Yes, let's.

Learn these words:

encourage [ɪn´kʌrɪdʒ] *v*	ободрить, поощрить, поддержать, обнадежить

The prize encouraged him to work harder.

He was encouraged by his success.

encouraging *adj*	ободряющий, обнадеживающий

Переведите на английский язык.

1. – Сколько времени вы работаете над этим проектом? – Это не простой вопрос. Разрешите подумать. Мы начали прошлой весной ... Да, не менее года. Мы уже многое сделали, но придется сделать больше.

2. – У вас есть свободная минута? Я хочу познакомить вас с г–ном Кларком. – С Биллом Кларком? Я его очень хорошо знаю. Я знаю его много лет. Он здесь? – Да. – Я буду очень рад увидеть его. Мы не виделись целую вечность.

3. – Сколько времени вы здесь живете? – Всю свою жизнь. Я здесь родился и никогда больше нигде не жил – Разве вы не путешествовали? – Конечно, путешествовал, но этот город всегда был моим домом.

4. – Извините, я опоздал. Вы давно меня ждете? – Нет, я пришел только пять минут назад.

5. – Что случилось с Джеком? Я его не вижу в последнее время. – Ничего, он в отпуске с прошлой недели.

– 312 –

Unit 14

GRAMMAR

26. <u>Выражение долженствования в английском языке.</u>

26.1. Русскому глаголу *должен* соответствуют в английском языке н е с к о л ь к о глагольных форм, различающихся по значению. Некоторые из них вам известны. Давайте их вспомним.

Модальный глагол **MUST**

(Действие должно быть выполнено, потому что так считает сам говорящий)

1. I **must** tell you all about it.	Я вам все должен рассказать (*я считаю это обязательным*).
2. You **must** go and see his recent pictures.	Вы (непременно) должны пойти посмотреть его последние картины (*я вам настоятельно советую*).
3. You **must** settle it as soon as possible.	Вы должны это урегулировать как можно скорее (*я вам приказываю*).
4. You **mustn't** cross the road here.	Здесь нельзя переходить дорогу (*это запрещается*).
5. "**Must** I do it all today?"	— Я (обязательно) должен сделать все это сегодня?
"Yes, I'm afraid you **must**."	— Боюсь, что да.
"No, you **needn't**."	— Нет, не надо (*не обязательно, можете не делать*).

Модальный глагол **HAVE TO** (= have got to в настоящем времени для однократного случая)

(Действие приходится выполнять под давлением внешних обстоятельств).

1. I **have to** get up early, because I live far from here.	Я должен *(мне приходится)* рано вставать, потому что я живу далеко отсюда.
2. He was late, and we **had to** wait.	Он опоздал, и мы должны были *(нам пришлось)* подождать.
3. When you have a computer, you **won't have to** waste so much time.	Когда у вас будет компьютер, вы не должны будете *(вам не придется, не надо будет)* тратить столько времени.
4. It's a straight line, you **don't have to** change.	Это прямая линия, вам не надо пересаживаться.

ПРИМЕЧАНИЕ: В отрицательной форме близким по значению глаголу **have to** является глагол **need** + инфинитив с частицей **to** (отсутствие необходимости из-за внешних обстоятельств):

1. You **don't need to change** (=You don't have to . . .). It's a straight line.	Вам не нужно пересаживаться, это прямая линия.
2. I **didn't need to see** the doctor (= I **didn't have to**). It was a slight injury.	Мне не нужно было обращаться к врачу. Это была легкая травма.

Форма **needn't** + инфинитив *без* частицы **to** выражает отсутствие необходимости совершать действие, но не благодаря внешним обстоятельствам, а в виде р а з - р е ш е н и я .

1. You **needn't send** a telex. I'll call them.	Вы можете не отправлять телекс. Я им позвоню.
2. We **needn't hurry**. We've still got a lot of time.	Мы можем не торопиться. У нас еще масса времени.

Как видно из примеров, эта форма не имеет какого-либо вспомогательного глагола и употребляется только в н а с т о я щ е м времени.

EXERCISES

1

Прочитайте следующие объявления.

1. Notice in a picture gallery.

> CAMERAS AND UMBRELLAS MUST BE LEFT AT THE DESK

2. At the zoo (в зоопарке).

> **Visitors mustn't feed the animals**

3. Above petrol pump.

> *ALL ENGINES MUST BE SWITCHED OFF*

2

Выберите правильное слово.

1. There has been no rain for a week, but the forecast says the weather's going to be changeable, so I (must, have to) carry my umbrella all the time!
2. "I'm so sorry I (must, have to) put off our appointment again, I've still got a high temperature." "That's all right! You (must, have to) stay at home till you feel well enough to go out. Get well!"
3. You (must, have to) come and have a game of tennis with my son. You'll be impressed!
4. The buses were full, and we (must, had to) take a taxi.
5. I understand. You (mustn't, don't have to) translate.
6. You (must, have to) look both ways before crossing the road.
7. We'll book a room for you. You (mustn't, don't have to) look for a hotel.
8. We're going by an early flight, so I (must, have to) get up not later than six o'clock tomorrow morning.
9. You (mustn't, don't have to) drive so fast, there's a speed limit here.
10. You (mustn't, don't have to) drive so fast, we've still got a lot of time.

GRAMMAR
(continued)

26.2. Долженствование в виде с о в е т а, р е к о м е н д а ц и и по поводу того, что с л е д у е т сделать, выражается модальным глаголом **should** [ʃud] после которого идет инфинитив без частицы to:

1. You **should book** the seats in good time.	Вы должны *(вам надо бы, следует)* заказать билеты заранее.
2. He **shouldn't work** so hard.	Он не должен *(ему не следует, не надо бы)* так много работать.
3. You **should consult** [kən'sʌlt] a lawyer.	Вы должны *(я вам советую)* проконсультироваться у юриста.

26.3. После глагола **should** может идти *перфектный инфинитив*. В этом случае высказывание выражает с о ж а - л е н и е, у п р е к по поводу того, что б ы л о или н е б ы л о сделано:

1. You **should have thought** of it before [...ʃudəv...]	Вам надо было подумать об этом раньше.
2. They **shouldn't have quarrelled!**	Они не должны были *(им не надо было, не следовало)* ссориться.
3. **You should have consulted** a specialist.	Вы должны были (вам следовало) посоветоваться со специалистом.

26.4. Сходные с **should** значения передает модальный глагол **ought** [ɔːt], после которого идет инфинитив с частицей **to. Ought to** в несколько б о л ь ш е й степени, чем **should** подчеркивает *долг, обязанность*, однако **should** и **ought to** — близкие синонимы. Иногда ответ на высказывание, содержащее **ought to** , содержит **should** и наоборот.

1. "You **ought to** call them again." "Yes, I suppose I **should**."	— Вам надо бы позвонить им еще раз. — Да, пожалуй что надо!
2. "You **oughtn't to have spoken** about it. (You ought not to have spoken about it)". "You're right. I shouldn't have done it".	Вам не надо было *(не следовало)* об этом говорить. Вы правы, мне не следовало этого делать.

ПРИМЕЧАНИЕ: Как **should,** так и **ought to** выражают с о в е т , р е к о м е н д а ц и ю , но не т а к о й н а с т о й ч и в ы й совет, н е такую н а с т о я т е л ь н у ю рекомендацию, как **must:**

1. You should read it. It's very interesting.	Вам надо бы это прочитать *(следует, следовало бы).* Это интересно.
2. You must read it. It's just marvellous!	Вы обязательно должны это прочитать. Это просто великолепно!

EXERCISES

1

Прочитайте вслух и переведите.

1. I think you should see a lawyer.
2. You should consult a doctor.
3. You shouldn't hesitate!
4. He should be very careful with this equipment.
5. You ought to visit them more often.
6. You shouldn't agree!
7. You shouldn't have agreed!
8. She should have been an actress.
9. You ought to have told me all about it long ago.
10. You ought to have compared your chances before taking a decision.
11. I think you should have a preliminary exchange of opinions.

2

В ответ на высказывание дайте совет или рекомендацию, употребив *should* или *ought to.*

1. **Your friend:** I feel bad. I can't work any longer today.

   You: . . . .

2. **Your colleague:** I don't know what to do. The finance manager is out, and I don't understand some of the figures in this paper.

   You: . . . .

3. **Your friend:** I've got a ticket for a film tonight, but I've just remembered it's my aunt's birthday!

   You: . . . .

Скажите, что следовало и чего не следовало делать.

Дано: Jane was ill, but didn't stay at home.

Требуется: Jane should have stayed at home (ought to have stayed at home).

1. He didn't leave a message.
2. We didn't congratulate him.
3. The company didn't finance the construction.
4. We didn't see the cathedral.
5. They didn't replace the defective part in the machine.
6. They didn't introduce the changes gradually.
7. They didn't improve the design.
8. The tickets haven't been exchanged.
9. The seats haven't been booked.

— 318 —

4

Верите ли вы предсказаниям? Прочитайте гороскоп и обсудите эту тему в классе.

Horoscopes [´hɔrəskəups] for **the coming week**.

ARIES [´eəri:z]
(March 21 — April 21)

You may have an opportunity to change your place of work, but the change may be for the worse. You should think hard before taking a decision. You shouldn't tell anyone about possible offers of a new job

TAURUS [´tɔ:rəs]
(April 21 — May 21)

This is a week of success in business. You may have to risk your money. Don't hesitate! You may not have another chance like that, and you must take it!

GEMINI [ˈdʒemɪnɪ]
(May 22 — June 21)

You may meet someone you'll be impressed by. Be careful! You should spend more time at home with your family.

CANCER [ˈkænsə]
(June 22 — July 23)

You may have some financial problems at the beginning of the week. Don't be discouraged! You'll have to learn how to be a good loser, but you shouldn't lose hope. Things will improve towards the end of the week.

LEO [liːə]
(July 24 — August 23)

There may be an opportunity to travel. You should take it without hesitation. You may want to talk to someone about it. This is something you mustn't do, because your chance may be lost.

VIRGO [ˈvəːgəu]
(August 24 – September 2)

Someone may tell you that there's a chance to win a television quiz. You shouldn't believe it! Quizzes are not for you. But at the weekend you may be lucky at cards. You shouldn't miss your chance.

LIBRA [ˈliːbrə]
(September 24 – October 22)
(also called *the scales* or
the balance)

You shouldn't play football. You may have an injury. A drive to the country and a walk in a wood will do you good, but you shouldn't leave expensive things in your car. You may be sorry!

SCORPIO [ˈskɔːpɪəu]
(October 24 — December 21)

There may be problems at work, but you shouldn't take them close to heart. The situation will improve soon, you won't even have to put in any partcular effort.

SAGITTARIUS
[ˌsædʒɪˈteərɪəs]
(November 23 December 22)

This is an important moment in your personal life. You shouldn't change anything if you want to be happy. Think carefully before taking important steps.

CAPRICORN
[ˈkæprɪkɔːn]
(December 22 — January 20)

You may have some slight health problems. Don't overeat!
You should give up smoking and drinking. A holiday at the seaside would put you right.

AQUARIUS
[əˈkweərɪəs]
(January 21 — February 19)

If you find a large sum of money or a **diamond** ring, don't be surprised. This week begins a **period** of luck. It's a good time to start a business venture, and you should begin looking for a good partner.

PISCES [ˈpaɪsiːz]
(also called *the fish*)
(February 20 — March 20)

There may be changes in your working routine. You may have to do more than you used to. You shouldn't work too much. You should leave time for outdoor excercise and parties.

---

diamond [ˈdaɪəmənd]

бриллиант, алмаз

period [ˈpɪərɪəd]

период

5

Переведите на английский язык.

1. Вам надо бы проконсультироваться с кем-нибудь еще.
2. Ему надо бы поискать другую работу.
3. Вам не следует так поздно ложиться спать.
4. Нам не надо бы тратить так много времени попусту.
5. Вам не следует бросать спорт.
6. Вам давно надо было со мной поговорить.
7. Нам надо было ему позвонить и поздравить его.
8. Ему не надо было колебаться.
9. Билеты надо было заказать заблаговременно.
10. Ничего не надо было менять.
11. Этого случая не следует упускать.
12. Этот случай не надо было упускать.

321 —

GRAMMAR
(continued)

26.4. Долженствование, вытекающее из предваритель-
ной договоренности или заранее наме-
ченного плана, выражается глаголом **be** +
инфинитив с частицей **to**:

1. The expedition **is to start** in a week's time.	Экспедиция должна от-правиться через неделю *(это намечено по плану).*
2. The goods **are to be packed** in strong cases.	Товар должен быть упако-ван в крепкие ящики *(имеется такая догово-ренность).*
3. The president **is to make** a statement tomorrow.	Президент должен завтра сделать заявление.

ПРИМЕЧАНИЕ: Этот способ выражения долженствования не
употребляется, когда речь идет о расписании. Поэтому
об отправлении и прибытии поездов, самолетов и т.п. говорят:

> The train (plane) **arrives** at eleven или **is due** [dju:] to arrive
> at eleven.

26.5. Эта конструкция имеет только настоящее и
прошедшее время. В прошедшем времени после be
может употребляться как простой так и перфектный

инфинитив. Разница в значении видна из следующих примеров:

1. They **were to give** an answer yesterday.	Они должны были дать ответ вчера (говорящий не знает, был ли дан ответ, он только знает, что была такая договоренность).
2. They **were to have given** an answer yesterday.	Они должны были дать ответ вчера (говорящий считает, что обещание скорее всего не было выполнено).

26.6. Близким обороту **be to** способом выражения долженствования является оборот **be supposed to** [səˈpəusttə], который выражает долженствование в силу договоренности или обычаев.

— 322 —

1. Teenagers in this country **are supposed to know** how to earn their living.	Подросткам в этой стране полагается знать, как заработать себе на жизнь (таков обычай).
2. What kind of paperwork **are we supposed to do** during the tests?	Какие записи нам полагается вести во время испытаний (как мы договоримся)?
3. You **aren't supposed** to smoke here.	Здесь не положено курить (таково правило).

Следует иметь в виду, что так же, как и в русском языке, в одной и той же ситуации разными людьми могут быть выбраны различные формы долженствования в зависимости от того, какая из этих форм наиболее точно передает отношение говорящего к действию, которое должно быть выполнено.

EXERCISES

Прочитайте вслух и переведите.

1. The agreement is to be signed on the 22nd of September.
2. According to the contract the wooden parts were to be made of expensive wood.
3. All the machines are to be packed in strong cases.

4. They were to have come an hour ago. I wonder what happened.

5. Such documents are to be signed by Director General.

6. What are the children doing here at such a late hour? They are supposed to be in bed!

7. A secretary at that firm is supposed to be fluent in several foreign languages.

8. He didn't know he was supposed to work overtime if the job was urgent.

9. Am I supposed to consult anyone, or can I deal with matters like that myself?

2

Прочитайте отрывок из интервью при приеме на работу. Придумайте начало и конец интервью и разыграйте его.

A. So you'd like to have a secretarial job with this company. You've got a well–paid job. What makes you look for a new one?

B. Well, I'm only supposed to do the paper work. I don't mind it, but I'd prefer to work with people as well.

A. Do you know that a secretary here is supposed to be fluent in at least one foreign language?

B. Yes, I do. I've been learning French for two years, and I can speak Spanish a little.

A. Do you mind if you have to work overtime, sometimes?

B. Oh, it depends how often I'm supposed to work overtime.

A. Not more than twice a month, when the work's urgent.

GRAMMAR
(continued)

27. Оборот **have something done.**

Сравните:

1. Anne **made** herself a new dress.	Анна сшила себе новое платье (Она сделала это сама).
2. Anne **had** a new dress **made**.	Анна сшила себе новое платье (Ей сшили платье, это было сделано не ею самой, а кем–то для нее).

B. Yes, she hurt her leg badly yesterday and can't walk.

A. Too bad! Have any of you been to see her?

B. No, not yet. None of us knew. We only found out this morning when she rang from home.

A. How did it happen?

B. She **fell** somewhere near the office. Someone gave her a lift to the nearest hospital, and they gave her **first aid** and sent her home in an **ambulance**.

A. I wonder how she is now.

B. Her leg still hurts, but she's had an **X–ray**, and it shows the **bone** isn't **broken**.

A. Poor girl! Please give her my **sympathy**!

Learn these words:

1

consult *v*	1. проконсультироваться (у . . .); получить консультацию; обратиться к . . .

to consult a doctor (a lawyer, a specialist, etc.)

	2. посмотреть, справиться (по чему–л.)

to consult a dictionary (a map, etc.)

surgeon [´sɔːdʒən] *n c*	хирург
pain *n*	боль

I've got a pain in my leg (= My leg hurts).

stomach [´stʌmək] *n*	желудок

on an empty stomach
I have a pain in my stomach (=I have stomachache)

worry [´wʌrɪ] *v*	беспокоить (ся), волновать (ся)

What's worrying you?
Don't worry!

to be worried about sb/sth	беспокоиться, волновать– ся из–за кого–л., чего–л.

I'm worried about him.

I'm not worried (about it) at all!   Меня это не волнует!

Сравните:

worry — употребляется, когда речь идет о душевном волнении

trouble — употребляется в таком же значении и также по поводу неудобства, физического беспокойства

bother [ˈbɔðə] — употребляется по поводу незначительного неудобства

He was worried (troubled) by the news.

I won't trouble (bother) you if you're busy.

---

appendicitis [əˌpendɪˈsaɪtɪs] *n u*   аппендицит

diagnosis [daɪəˈgnəʊsɪs] *n c*   диагноз

confirm [kənˈfɜːm] *v*   подтверждать

Nothing has been confirmed yet.

operation *n c*   операция (*мед.*)

He's just had an operation.

operate
(on sb for sth) *v*   оперировать, прооперировать

He was operated on for appendicitis.   Его прооперировали по поводу апендицита.

condition [kənˈdɪʃn] *n*   1. состояние

Syn. state

The house is in terrible condition (in a terrible state).

2. условие

We can't agree to your conditions.

complication
[ˌkɔmplɪˈkeɪʃn] *n c*   осложнение

per cent [pəˈsent]   процент (сотая доля)

The prices have increased **by** 10 per cent.   Цены увеличились на 10 %.

insist [inˈsist] *v*   настаивать

We insisted on our conditions

We insisted that all the conditions of the contract (should) be fulfilled.

convince [kən'vɪns] v	убедить (*не употребляется перед инфинитивом*)

You should **try to convince** him that he isn't right.
We couldn't convince him **of his mistake.**

Syn. **to persuade** [pə'sweɪd]	убедить, уговорить (*может употребляться перед инфинитивом*)

They persuaded us **to join** them.	Они уговорили нас при— соединиться к ним.

convincing *adj*	убедительный

a convicing speech (fact, etc)

trip *n c*	поездка, путешествие

Syn. journey
a trip to the seaside,
a holiday (business, pleasure) trip
to make a trip to . . .
to go on a trip to . . .

advice [əd'vaɪs] *n u*	совет

I often go to him for advice.	Я часто обращаюсь к не— му за советом.
to give sb some (a piece of) advice.	Дать кому—либо совет.

care *n u*	забота

to take care of sb/sth	позаботиться о ком—либо, чем—либо

Take care! (Take care of yourself!)	Береги себя! (*часто упот— ребляется при проща— нии*)

2

fall (fell, fallen) v	падать, упасть

aid [eɪd] *n u*	помощь, (обычно со стороны более сильного)

first aid	первая (скорая) помощь
ambulance [´æmbjuləns]	машина скорой помощи
X–ray [´eksreı] *n*	рентген, рентгеновский снимок
to have an X–ray	сделать рентген
bone *n*	кость
break (broke, broken) *v*	ломать, сломать
sympathy [´sımpəθı] *n c*	сочувствие

EXERCISES

Прочитайте тексты вслух. Предварительно отработайте произношение следующих слов.

[ʌ]	[ɜː]	[s-z]
worry	surgeon	advice
consult	confirm	advise

[ɔ]		
operate	diagnosis	
bother	appendicitis	

Подберите в текстах английские эквиваленты.

1. Моя жена беспокоится • я давно должен был обратиться к хирургу • посмотрим, права ли жена • здесь чувствуется боль? • мы сделаем анализы • если мой диагноз подтвердится, я бы порекомендовал. . . • я должен уехать в командировку • в таком состоянии • я настоятельно советую вам • у вас могут быть осложнения • вы не на сто процентов уверены • я бы не настаивал • просто съели что–то • звучит достаточно убедительно • что мне делать с командировкой? • это то, что не входит в обязанности врачей • это единственный совет, который я могу дать • куда мне идти, чтобы сделать анализы? • она обо всем позаботится.

2. Почему не пришла? • она сильно ушибла ногу • не может ходить • кто–нибудь ее навещал? • мы узнали только сегодня

утром • кто—то подвез ее • оказали первую помощь • инте—
ресно, как она себя чувствует • передайте, что я ей сочувствую.

3 🔲

Прочитайте вслух примеры на новые слова.

1. How long have you been having pains?
2. I have a pain in my back.
3. I've been having toothache since morning.
4. If the pain's so bad, you should certainly see a doctor.
5. We are not supposed to start work before they confirm that they agree to all our conditions.
6. They are supposed to confirm their offer in writing.

— 330 —

7. You can take part in the quiz on one condition: that you don't consult anybody.
8. You aren't supposed to consult a dictionary during the exam.
9. The goods arrived in poor condition.
10. This car's in very good condition.
11. We don't expect any complications. We're one hundred per cent sure everything'll be okay.
12. We insist that you should confirm the arrangement by fax.
13. I'm sorry, but I have to insist on our conditions.
14. I wouldn't insist if the matter weren't urgent.
15. You should try to convince them that the changes are absolutely necessary.
16. It was hard to convince her that we couldn't afford to buy that house.
17. You should try to persuade her not to buy that car.
18. He convinced me that I wasn't right.
19. He persuaded me to go in for the competition.
20. I wouldn't have believed him if his story hadn't sounded so convicing.
21. People often go to him for advice.
22. Let me give you a piece of advice.
23. I wonder what's worrying you.
24. Why does he look so worried?
25. "I'm worried about it." "Don't worry! Everything will be all right."
26. How do I call an ambulance?
27. Where am I supposed to go for an X—ray?
28. You ought to have given him first aid.
29. The X—ray will show if the bone's broken.
30. My sympathy's with you.
31. Please give them my sympathy.
32. Take care of yourself.

33. The market will take care of itself.

4

Заполните пропуски предлогами.

1. I have a pain . . . my stomach. I'm one hundred per cent sure I haven't eaten anything that disagreed . . . me, so I'm a little worried . . . it.
2. He's been operated on . . . leg injury. The surgeon wouldn't have insisted . . . the operation if the X–ray hadn't shown that the injury was serious. There might have been complications . . . an operation.
3.
The inspection confirmed that part . . . the goods were . . . poor condition.
4. We wouldn't insist . . . those changes if the prices hadn't increased . . . 20 per cent.
5. He persuaded me to go to the old man . . . advice.
6. Don't trouble. I'll take care . . . it myself.

5

Заполните пропуски словами *worry, worried, trouble, bother*

1. There's no need to . . . He's in good condition now.
2. I wouldn't have . . . you if it weren't so important.
3. He was . . . about his financial position.
4. I'm busy. Don't . . . me!
5. Don't . . . I'm sure the situation will improve.
6. He didn't even . . . to say that he was sorry!
7. Don't . . . I'll try to convince them.

6

Выберите правильное слово.

1. Let's (consult, advise) a dictionary.
2. You ought to have (consulted, advised) him to (consult, advise) a lawyer.
3. If I were you, I'd (consulted, advised) a professional financier.
4. You wouldn't have lost your way if you'd (consulted, advised) the map.
5. I don't (consult, advise) you to put off talking to him.

Прочитайте рассказы и перескажите их.

1

A New Abbreviation

A famous American doctor came to England to study the latest methods. When he looked at the **charts**, he found that the system of **abbreviations** was **familiar** to him. They were the same as doctors used in the United States. He understood them all except for some charts marked GOK. He decided to consult a British colleague about it. "How am I supposed to understand this GOK?" he asked. "I see you have quite an **epidemic** of it! What does it stand for?" "Oh," the British doctor answered. "That's what we use when we don't know the diagnosis. It means God Only Knows."

— 332 —

Learn these words:

chart *n c*	диаграмма, таблица, *зд.* карта больного
abbreviation [ə‚briːviˈeiʃn] *n c*	сокращение
familiar [fəˈmiljə] *adj*	знакомый
mark *v*	помечать
epidemic [epiˈdemik] *n c*	эпидемия
God *n*	Бог, Господь

2

He Found a Way Out

It happened in a small American town during World War Two. A man didn't want to join the army. As he knew he didn't have any particular illness to complain of, he decided to tell the medical commission that he was **short-sighted**. When the day of the medical examination came, he told the medical officer that he could hardly see anything. "All right," said the officer, "I shall test your eyes."

There was a chart on the wall, and the officer asked the man to read the biggest letters first.

"What letters?" the man asked looking very surprised.

"The letters on the chart," the officer answered.

"What chart?" the man asked again looking still more surprised.

"The chart on the wall," the officer explained **patiently**.

"What wall?" the man asked again looking absolutely helpless.

That convinced the medical officer, and he wrote that the man wasn't fit for military service because of extremely poor **eyesight**. The man was very pleased, and decided to celebrate by going to the cinema in the evening. When the film was over, he saw that the man sitting next to him was the medical officer who had tested his eyes. At first he wanted to run away, but seeing that the officer had recognized him, he quickly turned to him and said, "Excuse me, madam, is this train going to New York?"

Learn these words:

short – sighted *adj*	близорукий
eyesight *n u*	зрение
patiently ['peɪʃntlɪ] *adv*	терпеливо

Unit 15

GRAMMAR

28. Будущее время группы Continuous (Future Continuous).

28.1. Future Continuous, как и другие времена этой группы, может обозначать незаконченный процесс, то есть показывать, что действие будет продолжаться в определенный момент в будущем.

– 334 –

1. Don't phone me at seven. They'll **be showing** my favourite film on the telly, and I'll **be watching**.	Не звоните мне в семь часов. По телевизору будут показывать мой любимый фильм, и я буду смотреть.
2. I'll **be waiting** for you near the underground station. Don't be late.	Я буду тебя ждать около станции метро. Не опаздывай.

28.2. Future Continuous употребляется также, когда речь идет о действиях, которые будут происходить в будущем, так как это уже намечено или решено:

1. We'll **be looking** at the situation in the Middle East tomorrow.	Завтра мы будем рассматривать положение на Ближнем Востоке (из сообщения о программе теле- или радиопередач)
2. I'll **be going** to the chemist's later. Shall I get you anything?	Я попозже пойду в аптеку. Вам что-нибудь купить?

В вопросах это время иногда употребляют, когда хотят выяснить планы собеседника, чтобы обратиться с просьбой.

"**Will** you **be using** your big
dictionary today?"

– Ты будешь пользоваться
своим большим словарем
сегодня?

" No, you can take it."

– Нет, можешь его взять.

28.3. Эта временная форма может также употребляться,
когда говорящий как бы даст свой прогноз по поводу
того, что будет происходить в будущем:

Computers **will be taking
decisions** for us in the
future.

В будущем решения за нас
будут принимать компью-
теры.

EXERCISES

Прочитайте вслух и переведите на русский язык.

1. I'll be waiting for you near the theatre.
2. I'll be seeing my consultant tomorrow morning.
3. We'll be looking forward to seeing you in Moscow soon.
4. You'll recognize me. I'll be wearing a white coat and a red hat, and I'll be holding a red handbag.
5. I'll be going to the post office soon. Do you need anything there?
6. We'll be living in a different world in the future: machines will be doing many jobs that are done by people today, we'll be travelling to other planets regularly, and someone from other planets will be visiting the Earth.

Прочитайте диалоги вслух и разыграйте их.

1

A. Will you be using your bike this afternoon?
B. No, you may have it till tomorrow morning.
A. Oh, thank you.
B. You're welcome.

You're welcome [ˈwelkəm]

Пожалуйста (один из вариан-
тов вежливого ответа на
благодарность за услугу)

A. I'll be going to the post office later. Shall I get you anything?
B. Yes, two large **envelopes**, and three small ones, if you don't mind.
A. Not at all.

---

envelope [ˈenvələup] *n с*   конверт

GRAMMAR
(continued)

29. <u>Союзы</u> **whoever** [huːˈevə] *кто бы ни;* **whatever**
[wɔtˈevə] *что бы ни;* **whichever** [witʃˈevə] *какой бы*
ни; **whenever** [wenˈevə] *когда бы ни;* **wherever**
[weərˈevə] *где бы ни.*

– 336 –

1. **Whoever** calls, tell them I'm out.	Кто бы ни позвонил, скажите, что меня нет.
2. Don't worry, **whatever** happens.	Не беспокойся, что бы ни случилось.
3. **Whichever** day you come, we'll be pleased to see you.	В какой бы день вы ни приехали, мы будем рады вас видеть.
4. **Whenever** we start talking about it, they disagree with us.	Когда бы мы ни заговорили об этом, они с нами не соглашаются.
5. People were friendly **wherever** we went.	Люди были дружелюбны, куда бы мы ни пошли.

Как видно из примеров, все перечисленные слова являются союзами, соединяющими два предложения.

ПРИМЕЧАНИЯ:

1. Каждый из перечисленных союзов имеет синоним, начинающийся со слов no matter (no matter what, who и т.д.)

No matter what happens, don't worry = **Whatever** happens, don't worry

2. Аналогичные мысли могут быть выражены в *двух самостоятельных* предложениях при помощи выражения It doesn't matter.

It doesn't matter what happens. Don't worry.

EXERCISES

1

Прочитайте вслух и переведите на русский язык.

1. Whoever told you that, didn't tell you the truth.
2. Whatever problems you have, you can always come to me for help.
3. Whichever language you decide to learn, be prepared to work hard.
4. It has the same result, whichever way you do it.
5. Wherever you go for a holiday, I'll be pleased to join you.
6. Whenever he went to London, he stayed at the Hilton.

2

Соедините два предложения в одно.

Дано: It doesn't matter **when** you come. You're always welcome.
Требуется: Whenever you come, you're always welcome.

1. It doesn't matter **what** they offer you. Think twice before you agree.
2. It doesn't matter **who** calls. Tell them that I'm busy.
3. It doesn't matter **which** shop you go to. You'll find that book on sale.
4. It doesn't matter **when** you come. We'll be waiting for you.
5. It doesn't matter **where** we go skiing. We always enjoy it.

3

Заполните пропуски союзами **whatever, whoever, whichever, whenever, wherever**.

1. ... model you choose, make sure that it's high quality.
2. ... insists on his version should explain his reasons.
3. ... he says is usually very convincing.
4. ... we went, we found friendly people.
5. ...you come to me for a consultation, you're always welcome.

4

Переведите на английский язык.

1. Не волнуйтесь, что бы ни случилось.

6

Повторите, употребляя подсказанные слова.

1. I'd like to reserve a **single room with bath overlooking the sea**.
   • a double rooom facing the park • a single room with shower • a double room with bath not .overlookiing the street • a table in your restaurant • a table for two on Saturday evening •
2. Unfortunately, **Mr. Bennett** isn't available at the moment.
   • the book you've ordered • the wine you want • a room like that • accommodation like that •
3. The hotel is situated **in a very quiet part near the sea**
   • in a quiet street • in a beautiful place • near an underground station •
4. Whenever you make a reservation there's always **a room available**.
   • accommodation • a table • convenient accommodation • a quiet room • a nice room facing the sea•
5. I haven't got **much luggage**.
   • any carry on luggage • any luggage to leave in the left–luggage office • any luggage to take from the left–luggage • the claim check for the smaller suitcase •

7

Прочитайте рассказ и перескажите его.

A Republican and a Democrat.

It isn't difficult to travel now. People can travel by train and by plane, and if they have cars, they can drive to any place they want. But over a hundred years ago it wasn't as easy to travel as it is now. Though there were trains at that time, people often used horses.

Here is a story about an American congressman who was travelling from New York to Washington on horseback. On his way he had to stop at a small hotel for the night. The owner of the hotel came out to meet him. The congressman asked if there was a room available till the next morning. "Certainly," the owner of the hotel answered. "But I want to know whether you are a Republican or a Democrat." "Why do you want to know it?" the congressman asked. "You see," the owner of the hotel explained, "I want to do my best for all my visitors. And I've heard that a Republican likes good accommodation

2. Какую бы комнату вы ни выбрали, вы будете себя чувствовать удобно.
3. Когда бы вы ни приехали, мы будем рады видеть вас.
4. Кто бы ни позвонил, скажите, что я очень занят.
5. Куда бы вы ни решили поехать в отпуск, мы только будем рады (довольны) присоединиться к вам.

5

Прочитайте диалоги вслух, выучите новые слова и разыграйте анологичные эпизоды.

1

Making Hotel Reservations by Telephone

Clerk: Centre Hotel. Good morning. Can I help you?

Lavrov: Good morning. I'd like to **reserve** a **single room** wiith **bath** beginning next Tuesday.

C. Name, please?

L. Victor Lavrov.

C. How long will you be staying, Mr. Lavrov?

L. I'll be staying for ten days. And one more thing. I'd like it to be a **quiet** room, not **overlooking** the street.

C. Just a moment ... Unfortunately, we haven't got any such **accommodation available** at the moment, but the hotel's **situated** in a very quiet part. I'm sure you'll enjoy your stay here whichever room you book.

L. Oh, thanks, I'll leave it to you, then.

C. Very good, sir. We'll be looking forward to seeing you with us next Tuesday.

2

Checking In

Receptionist: Good morning, sir. Can I help you?

Lavrov: My name's Victor Lavrov. I believe you have a room booked for me.

R. Just a second ... Yes, it's a single room with bath on the third floor **facing** the park. Just **bed and breakfast**, right?

L. Yes, that's right. What time's breakfast?

R. From 8 to 10, sir.

L. Would you call me at 7.45, please?

R. Certaily, sir. Just sign here.
L. (*Puts his signature.*) Is that all?
R. Yes, sir. Here's your key. Room 327 on the third floor. I'll have your **luggage** sent up.

Learn these words:

clerk [klɑːk] *n* — клерк, служащий, кассир в билетной кассе и т.п.

reserve [rɪˈzɜːv] *v* — оставить за собой, зарезервировать,

Syn. **to book** — забронировать, заказать заранее

to reserve a seat (a table in a restaurant, a room in a hotel)

reservation [ˌrezəˈveɪʃn] *n* — *зд.* предварительный заказ

My travel agents have made all the reservations for my journey

single *adj* — один, отдельный, одинокий, одиночный

There isn't a single ticket left. — Не осталось ни одного билета.

He's single = He's unmarried.

a single room — номер на одного в гостинице

a double room — номер на двоих в гостинице

bath [bɑːθ] *n* — ванна

quiet [kwaɪət] *adj* — тихий, спокойный

a quiet child (street, part, place, etc.)

overlook [əuvəˈluk] *v* — *зд.* выходить на . . ., с видом на . . .

Syn. **to face**

a room overlooking (facing) the sea — комната с видом на море

unfortunately [ʌnˈfɔːtʃənətlɪ] *adv* — к сожалению

Unfortunately, there was nobody to consult.

accommodation [əˌkɔməˈdeɪʃn] *n u* помещен

Accommodation is expensive here. — Жилі
The hotel has accommodation for 200 guests. — В гос мести цев.

available [əˈveɪləbl] *adj* — имеющийс

Is the manager available just now? — Можно вид дующего?

Fruit is always available in that shop. — В этом мага в продаже ф

receptionist [rɪˈsepʃənɪst] *n c* — администрато

situated [ˈsɪtjueɪtɪd] *adj* — расположенн

The house is situated near the seafront. — Дом располож от набережной

check *v* — проверить

to check figures (bills, engines, etc.)

check in — въехать в гостин регистрацию на

to check in at a hotel
to check out of a hotel

check *n c* — чек, талон

bed and breakfast — условия, на которы нице, помимо поме предоставляется за

signature [ˈsɪgnətʃə] *n* — подпись

luggage [ˈlʌgɪdʒ] *n u* — багаж

Syn. **(Am) baggage**

"Have you got much luggage?" "Yes, quite a lot."

the left-luggage office (= the left-luggage) — камера хранения
Syn. (Am) the baggage room
the carry on luggage — багаж, который авиапа жир берет с собой в са

a luggage (baggage) claim-check — талон для получения ба

for himself, and a Democrat is more interested in a warm place and good food for his horse." "Then," said the congressman, "I am a Republican and my horse is a Democrat."

Learn these words:

a Republican	[rɪˈpʌblɪkən]	республиканец
a Democrat	[ˈdeməkrət]	демократ
horse	[hɔːs] *n c*	лошадь
congressman	[ˈkɒŋgresmən] *n c*	конгрессмен

GRAMMAR
(continued)

30. Оборот **I'd rather** + инфинитив без частицы to

1. **I'd rather** stay at home.	Я лучше останусь дома.
2. **I'd rather** not go out today.	Мне бы лучше не выходить сегодня.
3. I'd rather read a book than watch that silly film.	Я уж лучше почитаю, чем стану смотреть этот глупый фильм.

Как видно из примеров, оборот **I'd rather** + инфинитив без частицы to употребляется с первым лицом и выражает *предпочтение*. Он является разговорным синонимом формы **I'd prefer to** *я бы предпочел*.

ПРИМЕЧАНИЕ. Кроме известных вам случаев употребления глагола prefer (I prefer tea. He preferred to go for a walk.

She prefers swimming to jogging), существует единственно возможное продолжение высказывания, начинающегося с **prefer** + инфинитив с частицей **to**:

1. He prefers **to walk rather than go** by bus.	Он предпочитает ходить пешком, а не ездить в автобусе
2. I'd prefer **to consult** someone else **rather than make** a mistake.	Я бы предпочел посоветоваться с кем-нибудь еще, чем сделать ошибку.

EXERCISES

Прочитайте вслух и переведите на русский язык

1. I'd rather reserve accommodation in a quiet place.
2. I'd rather leave it all to the travel agency.
3. I'd rather check out in the morning.
4. I'd rather check out a bit earlier than stay in the hotel till evening.
5. I'd rather check all the figures again than make a mistake.
6. I'd rather check it all myself than worry.
7. "Shall we go by train?" "Well, I'd rather go by car".

2

Перефразируйте, употребив оборот *I'd rather.*

Дано: I'd prefer to settle it today.
Требуется: I'd rather settle it today.

1. I'd prefer to check all the bills myself.
2. I'd prefer to book a room facing the park.
3. I'd prefer not to stay long.
4. I'd prefer to live a quiet life.
5. I'd prefer not to trouble anyone.
6. I'd prefer to make a reservation today.

3

Прочитайте вслух диалоги, выучите новые слова и разыграйте аналогичные эпизоды.

1

Booking Airline Tickets by Telephone

Travel Agency Clerk: Good morning. Can I help you?

Alexander Nikitin: I'd like to reserve a seat on a morning flight to Seattle [sɪˈætl] next Wednesday.

Clerk: I can offer you two flights: at 7.30 a.m. and at 10 a.m. Which would you prefer?

N. I'd rather go by the 7.30.

C. First class or economy?

N. Economy, please.

C. Okay. Anything else?

N. When is the plane due in Seattle?

C. At 12.30. There are no **delays** as a rule. Your name, address and telephone number, please.

N. (*Gives the information required*)

C. We'll **deliver** the ticket two days before your **departure**. Thank you for calling us.

2

Booking a Seat at a Booking office in London.

Clerk: Yes, sir?

Lavrov: I'd like to book a seat on an afternoon train to Glasgo.

C. **Single or return**?

L. Return, please.

C. That'll be fifty–seven pounds, sir.

L. There you are.

C. Thank you. Your train leaves at two twenty–five from Platform 6.

Learn these words:

delay [dɪˈleɪ] *n c*   задержка

    with 35 minutes' delay   с задержкой в 35 минут
    after an hour's delay   после часовой задержки

without delay	без задержки, без прово- лочек
a delay **in** payment (delivery, etc.)	задержка платежа (по- ставки и т.д.)
deliver [dɪˈlɪvə] v	доставлять, поставлять
to deliver letters (goods, etc.)	
booking office n c	железнодорожная или авиа- ционная касса
a box–office	театральная касса
single or return	в один конец или в оба (о билетах)
departure [dɪˈpɑːtʃə] n	отъезд, отправление
arrival [əˈraɪvl] n	прибытие
arrive [əˈraɪv] v	прибывать, приезжать

Внимание! предлоги:

| to arrive **at** a station (a port, an airport) | (имеется в виду пункт прибы- тия) |
| to arrive **in** Moscow (London, Sweden, etc.) | (имеется в виду город, стра- на и т.п.) |

| **platform** [ˈplætfɔːm] n c | платформа |

Прочитайте вслух и переведите на русский язык.

1. The plane landed after an hour's delay.
2. I hope there won't be another delay.
3. There was a delay in delivery.
4. I prefer to make arrangements with a travel agency rather than see to booking tickets and reserving hotel accommodation myself.
5. Which platform does the train leave from?
6. What time does the train arrive?
7. What time is the train due in London?
8. We got to the station half an hour before their arrival.
9. I'd rather get to the airport in good time before the departure.
10. The ship arrived at the port with two hours' delay.

11. We are all looking forward to your arrival in Moscow.
12. All the signatures were collected without delay.

Заполните пропуски предлогами.

1. The plane arrived ... the airport ... three hour's delay.
2. ... a short delay the plane landed.
3. All the documents will be signed ... delay.
4. Your train leaves ... platform 9.
5. When we arrived ... London, it was raining.
6. When the train arrived ... the station, we started looking ... our friend ... the passengers.

5

Заполните пропуски артиклями

Why do we call ... place where we get tickets ... booking office? ... answer can be found in ... old way of travelling. Before there were railways, people used to travel in **coaches**. On ... day of ... . departure they had to go to ... special office to reserve ... seat in ... coach. ... clerk entered ... passenger's name and ... place where he wanted to go in ... book. Soon ... **verb** "to book" entered ... English language and has remained in it since then.

coach	зд. карета, дилижанс
verb [vəːb]	глагол

GRAMMAR

31. Оборот had better + инфинитив без частицы to.

1. It's going to rain. **You'd better take** an umbrella.	Собирается дождь. Вы бы лучше взяли зонтик.
2. **I'd better go** now, or I'll be late.	Я уж лучше пойду сейчас, а то опоздаю.
3. We've almost run out of petrol. **We'd better stop** somewhere to fill up.	У нас почти кончился бензин. Нам бы лучше остановиться где-нибудь, чтобы заправиться.

Как видно из примеров, этот оборот выражает совет, предупреждение и близок по значению модальному глаголу should. Этот совет (предупреждение) относится к настоящему или будущему.

Отрицательная форма этого оборота - **had better not**

1. You look ill. **You'd better not go** to work.	Ты плохо выглядишь. Тебе бы лучше не ходить на работу.
2. "Will you join us?" "**I'd better not**, I've got a lot of work to do."	—Ты пойдешь с нами? – Пожалуй нет. У меня очень много работы.

EXERCISES

Прочитайте вслух и переведите.

1. You'd better make a reservation before it's too late.
2. You'd better hurry up. You may be late.
3. You'd better have all the documents signed without delay.
4. I'm not one hundred per cent sure it's the right thing to do, so I'd better keep quiet about it.
5. He'd better book any accommodation available before it's too late.
6. You'd better leave your luggage in the left–luggage office.
7. You'd better have the tickets delivered at your place.
8. You'd better not insist if you don't find it absolutely necessary.
9. She'd better book a return ticket.
10. You'd better not book a room facing the street.

2

Перефразируйте, как показано в образце

Дано: a) You should make a reservation.

b) You shouldn't hurry.

Требуется: a) You'd better make a reservation.

b) You'd better not hurry.

1. You should try to convince them.
2. You shouldn't do it in a hurry.
3. He should keep quiet.
4. He shouldn't put it off.
5. You should wait.
6. You shouldn't expect too much.

7. He should consult a specialist.

8. We shouldn't start work on an empty stomach.

9. They should confirm their offer in writing.

10. You shouldn't bother him with such silly questions.

GRAMMAR

32. Оборот **be used to, get used to** *привыкнуть, привыкать.*

1. I'm **not used to getting up** so early.	Я не привык так рано вставать.
2. It was difficult for him to drive in England, because he **wasn't used to** left-hand traffic.	Ему было трудно водить машину в Англии, потому что он не привык к левостороннему движению.
3. It took him some time **to get used to driving** on the left.	Ему понадобилось некоторое время,чтобы привыкнуть водить слева.

В обороте be (get) used to слово to является *предлогом*, поэтому после него может идти существительное, местоимение или герундий.

Оборот be (get) used to не следует путать с известным вам оборотом used to в котором слово to является *частицей* перед инфинитивом:

Сравните:

1. He's **used to travelling** a lot.	Он привык много путешествовать.
2. He **used to travel** a lot.	Он (когда-то) много путешествовал.

ПРИМЕЧАНИЕ. Оборот **be (get) used to** имеет синоним **be (get) accustomed to** [ə'kʌstəmd]

He's accustomed (used) to working hard.	Он привык много работать.

EXECISES

1

Прочитайте вслух и переведите на русский язык.

1. She's used to looking after little children.
2. I can't get used to this terrible noise!
3. I don't mind getting up early. I'm used to it.
4. People get used to living in better conditions very easily.
5. She's used to dealing with very difficult matters.
6. When you get used to the cold weather in this country, you'll even enjoy it.
7. This is the kind of work I'm accustomed to.

2

Повторите, используя подсказанные слова.

1. He's used to **getting up early**.

   • dealing with complicated problems • making decisions quickly • being patient with people • doing his job carefully • driving on bad roads •

2. It won't take you long to get used to **the new time**.

   • your new colleagues • the new place • the changes in the timetable • the new working routine • using this equipment • using the fax–machine • doing the paperwork •

3. It was difficult for me to get used to **the noise**.

   • the new flat • working late • driving on the left • teaching little children • working overtime • speaking English on the phone •

3

Заполните пропуски оборотом be (get) used to или used to.

1. It didn't take her long to ... working with a computer.
2. I'm not afraid of swimming in cold water. I ... to it.
3. When he was young he ... be a splendid athlete.
4. She isn't ... taking care of other people. It won't be easy for her to ... it.
5. At first he found it difficult to work overtime, but then he ... it.
6. He doesn't smoke any longer, but he ... smoke 20 cigarettes a day!

TOPICS FOR DISCUSSION AND NEW WORDS

Travelling by Air

The rules for passengers who are going abroad are similar in most countries, but sometimes there might be a slight difference in **formalities**.

If, for instance, you are supposed to begin with **going through the customs**, you'd better fill in the customs **declaration** before you talk to the customs officer. An experienced customs officer usually "**smells**" a **smuggler**, but he may ask any passenger routine questions, for instance, "Have you got anything to **declare?**" or "Any **spirits**, **tobacco**, presents?" The usual answers would be, "Yes, I've got some **valuables**, but I've put them all **down** in the declaration", or "I've got two blocks of cigarettes for my own use" or something of that kind.

Then you go to the **check–in counter** where your ticket is looked at, your things are **weighed** and **labeled**, a claim–check for each piece of luggage is **inserted** in the ticket and you are given a **boarding pass**, which has a seat number on it. Of course, if your luggage **weighs** more than 20kgs, you have to pay **extra**. The next formality is filling in the **immigration** form and going through passport control. The form has to be filled in in **block letters**. You write your name, **nationality**, **permanent** address and the purpose of your trip. In most countries there is also a **security check** when your carry–on luggage is inspected. This is an anti–**hijacking measure**, and anything that might be dangerous or **disturbing** to other passengers must be **handed** to one of the **crew** and only returned to the owner after the plane has **reached** its **destination**.

After fulfilling all these formalities you go to the **departure lounge** where you can have a snack, read a paper, buy something in the **duty–free** shop and wait for the **announcement** to **board** the plane.

Some of these formalities are repeated when you arrive at your destination. The customs declaration and the immigration form are often filled in **on board** the plane. At the airport you may be met by a specially trained dog who will make sure that you are not **carrying drugs**, and the immigration officer might want to know at whose **invitation** you are coming and whether you have a return ticket.

There is another **inconvenience** you have to be prepared for when travelling long distances by plane. It's the **jet–lag**, a difference between the time you are accustomed to and the new time.

At first you won't be feeling very well because of it, but don't worry — it won't take you long to get used to it.

difference ['dɪfrəns] *n*	разница

What's the difference **between** a mile and a kilometre?

formality [fɔ'mælɪtɪ] *n*	формальность
to go through *v*	проходить
to go through formalities	пройти формальности
customs ['kʌstəms] *n pl*	таможня
to go through the customs	пройти таможенный до- смотр
a customs duty (customs duties)	таможенная пошлина
a customs declaration [ˌdeklə'reɪʃn]	таможенная декларация
smell *v*	нюхать, пахнуть, зд. чувство- вать
smuggler ['smʌglə] *n c*	контрабандист
to smuggle sth in (into the country, out of the country)	что–либо провести контрабандой
declare [dɪ'kleə] *v*	заявить; объявить
to declare war on ...	объявить кому–л. войну
I declare the meeting open.	Объявляю собрание от- крытым.
Have you (got) anything to declare?	У вас есть что–л. для предъявления таможне?
spirits ['spɪrɪts] *n pl*	спиртное
Syn. **alcohol** ['ælkəhɔl] *n u*	алкоголь
tobacco [tə'bækəu] *n*	табак; табачные изделия
valuables ['væljuəblz] *adj*	ценности
valuable *adj*	ценный
a valuable thing (piece of advice)	ценная вещь (совет)
valuable experiece	ценный опыт

counter [ˈkauntə] *n c*   прилавок; *зд.* стойка

    a check-in counter   стойка регистрации
    the British Airways counter   стойка регистрации компании "Бритиш Эруэйз"

weigh [weɪ] *v*   весить; взвешивать

    It weighs a ton [tʌn]!   Это весит тонну!
    You must have your luggage weighed.   Вы должны взвесить свой багаж.

weight [weɪt] *n*   вес

label [ˈleɪbl] *n v*   бирка, ярлык;

    — 352

    to label   навесить бирку, наклеить ярлык

insert [ɪnˈsɜːt] *v*   вложить; *зд.* вклеить

board [bɔːd] *v*

    to board a ship (plane)   сесть на пароход (самолет, поезд)

    Your plane is called (to board).   На ваш самолет объявлена посадка.

    Your plane is boarding.   На ваш самолет идет посадка.

boarding pass *n c*   посадочный талон

extra [ˈekstrə] *adj*   дополнительный

    You'll be getting extra pay for overtime.   Вы будете получать дополнительную плату за сверхурочные.

    to pay extra   платить дополнительно, доплатить

immigration [ˌɪmɪˈgreɪʃn]   въезд в страну, иммиграция

    an immigration form   иммиграционный бланк

block letters   печатные буквы

passport control [ˈpɑːspɔːt kənˈtrəul]   паспортный контроль

nationality [ˌnæʃəˈnælɪtɪ] *n*   *зд.* гражданство или подданство

permanent [ˈpɜːmənənt] *adj*   постоянный

security [sɪˈkjuərətɪ] *n* безопасность; меры безопасности

the Security Council [ˈkaunsɪl] Совет Безопасности
a security check проверка безопасности

hijack (highjack) [ˈhaɪdʒæk] *v* угонять (*гл. образом самолеты*)

anti [ˈæntɪ] (Br), анти–, против(о)– (*приставка*)
[æntaɪ] (Am)
measure [ˈmeʒə] *n* 1. мера (веса и т.п.)

2. мера (мероприятие)

They took strong measures against hijacking.

disturb [dɪˈstɜːb] беспокоить

I hope the noise doesn't disturb you.
"Please don't disturb" "Просьба не беспокоить" *табличка (гл. образом в гостиницах)*

hand *v* вручить, сдать

You can hand the filled in form to the man at the desk.

crew [kru:] *n* экипаж, команда

destination [ˌdestɪˈneɪʃn] *n* место назначения

They arrived at their destination on time.

reach *v* достичь, добраться до (дотянуться до)

The ship reached the port of Корабль прибыл в порт
destination with a delay. назначения с опозданием.

I can't reach the top shelf. Я не могу дотянуться до верхней полки.

They reached an agreement. Они достигли соглашения.

departure lounge [laundʒ] *n* зап ожидания

duty *n* зд. пошлина

a customs duty таможенная пошлина
to pay duty on sth уплатить пошлину за что–л.

duty free (= not liable ['laɪəbl] to duty)	не подлежащий тамо— женному обложению
announcement [əˈnəʊnsmənt] *n*	объявление (*обычно устное*)
to make an announcement	сделать объявление
announce *v*	объявить, сделать объявление
It was announced on the radio.	Это было объявлено по радио.
carry [ˈkærɪ] *v*	нести, носить, везти
to carry sth in one's hands (arms)	
drug *n c*	лекарство, наркотик
drugstore [ˈdrʌɡstɔː] drug traffic	(Am) аптека торговля наркотиками
invitation [ˌɪnvɪˈteɪʃn] *n*	приглашение
at the invitation of ...	по приглашению
invite [ɪnˈvaɪt] *v*	приглашать

Syn. **ask**

How many people are you going to invite (ask) to dinner?

inconvenience [ˌɪnkənˈviːnɪəns] *n*	неудобство
to cause [kɔːz] sb inconvenience	причинить кому—л. неу— добство
jet–lag *n*	разница во времени при пе— релёте в разные часовые по— яса

Syn. **time lag**

EXERCISES

Прочитайте текст вслух. Предварительно отработайте произношение следующих слов.

[æ]	[ɜː]
formality	**insert**
valuables	**disturb**

— 354 —

tobacco	disturbing
hijack	permanent
invitation	boarding pass
immigration	customs duties
destination	passport control
declaration	departure lounge

355 —

Подберите в тексте английские эквиваленты.

Возможна небольшая разница в прохождении формальностей● прохождение таможни● заполнить таможенную декларацию● у вас имеется что—либо для предъявления таможне?● я записал их в декларацию● для личного пользования● что—нибудь в таком роде● стойка регистрации● талон для получения багажа вкладывается в билет● вам выдают посадочный талон.● вы должны оплатить отдельно● бланк надо заполнять печатными буквами.● гражданство.● постоянный адрес.● цель поездки.● проверка безопасности.● противоугонные меры.● должно быть сдано одному из членов экипажа и возвращено владельцу после того, как самолет достигнет места назначения.● ждать объявления о посадке на самолет.● когда вы прибудете на место назначения.● вы не везете наркотики.● есть еще одно неудобство, к которому вы должны приготовиться.● разница между привычным вам временем и новым.● сначала будете не очень хорошо себя чувствовать.● не беспокойтесь, вы быстро к нему привыкнете.

3

Ответьте на следующие вопросы. Суммируйте ответы в кратких сообщениях.

a. 1. Have you ever travelled long distances by plane?
2. When was it?
3. Where did you go?
4. How long did the journey take?
5. Did you enjoy your trip?
6. Was it a business trip or a pleasure trip?

b. 1. Have you ever had to go through the customs?
2. Did you have anything liable to duty?

3. Did the customs officer ask you to open your suitcases?
4. Did you carry any spirits, or tobacco for your own use?
5. How long did it take you to go through the customs and other formalities?

c. 1. What are you supposed to write in the immigration form?
2. Why does it have to be filled in in block letters?
4. Do you think a security check is a necessary measure? Why?
5. Do you think you would be allowed to carry a toy pistol (игрушечный пистолет) on the plane?

d. 1. What can passengers do in the departure lounge?
2. Do you always undestand the announcements made at the airport in Russian?
3. Where are the forms filled in before the arrival?
4. Why are specially trained dogs used at airports?
5. Have you ever seen such a dog?

e. 1. Which do you prefer — to travel by air or by land?
2. Do you like travelling, or would you rather not experience all the inconveniences of a long journey?
3. Have you ever experienced a jet–lag?
4. How long did it take you to get used to the new time?

f. 1. Do you like to live in hotels?
2. What kind of accommodation would you like to have in a hotel?

3. Tell us about the hotel you were really impressed by.

4 🎞

Прочитайте диалоги вслух и разыграйте аналогичные эпизоды.

1

A. Excuse me, could you tell me where the British Airways counter is?
B. Certainly. Can you see the escalator [´eskəleitə] over there?
A. The escalator? Yes.
B. Well, go up the escalator and you will see the counter you're looking for. You can't miss it.
A. Thanks a lot.
B. You're welcome.

2

Clerk: Will you put your bags on the **scales**?

Passenger: Shall I have my carry-on things weighed, too?

C. Yes, sir. I'm afraid you'll have to pay extra.

P. How much?

C. Fifty dollars, please.

P. Here you are.

C. Thank you. Where would you like to sit?

P. I'd rather have a window seat.

C. Smoking or nonsmoking?

P. Nonsmoking, please.

C. Okay. Here's your ticket. And hurry up. Your flight's now boarding at **Gate** 7.

---

scales *n pl*   весы

gate *n*   ворота; зд. выход

3

Passenger: I wonder why they aren't making any announcements about flight 25 to Moscow.

Clerk: Just a moment, ma'am. I'm sorry there will be a 45-minute delay, so your flight will be boarding in about an hour.

P. Oh, I can't find my claim-checks!

C. They are inserted in your tickets, ma'am.

P. Oh, thank you ever so.

C. You're welcome. Have a nice flight.

4

Going Through the Security Check.

Officer: Will you put all your carry-on luggage on the **belt**, sir?

Passenger: Okay.

O. Now go through here. Are you wearing any metal sir?

P. Metal? Yes, this watch.

O. Please take it off and step through here again. Now it's okay. Thank you. Here's your watch. Have a good flight.

P. Thanks.

---

belt *n c*   пояс; зд. лента конвейера

5

Заполните пропуски артиклями.

Fathers and Sons

... well-known American **millionaire** was travelling on business in England. He came to ... town, where he had been several times before, always staying in ... same hotel and in ... same room. Handing him ... key, ... receptionist said he could never understand why such ... rich and famous man always booked ... smallest and cheepest room they had. "I'm used to it," ... millionaire answered. It's ... nice quiet room, and I don't need ... larger one." "Well," said ... receptionist, "I must say your son isn't like you at all. He often stays with us, too, and always books ... most expensive room we have." "I haven't ... slightest doubt he does," said ... millionaire. "Don't forget that there's ... great difference between ... two of us. His father's ... rich man, and mine is not."

— 358 —

---

millionaire [ˌmɪljəˈnɛə] *n c*   миллионер

6

Представьте, что вы находитесь в данной ситуации. Разыграйте следующие эпизоды.

1. You must urgently fly from London to New York. Phone the travel agency or a booking office and book a seat on a plane.

   Give the date on which you want to leave London. If you want a return ticket, say so to the clerk. Say when you are planning to fly back to London.

2. You are at London airport. Ask someone how to get to the counter you want (you're flying by a British Airways plane). Thank the person who has shown you the way.

3. You are checking in at the British Airways counter. Unfortunately, you have excessive weight. Ask the agent how much you must pay extra. Ask him if the plane has been called yet, and which gate it is boarding at.

4. You are meeting a friend at an airport in Canada. The plane hasn't arrived on time. Ask the clerk at the inquiry office why there is a delay and how long it is going to be. Thank him for the information he gives you.

5. You are going through security check. You don't want to put your camera on the belt, because you're afraid the film might

be damaged. Ask the officer if he could check your camera by hand.

6. You are meeting your American counterpart at Moscow airport. You have come to meet him with a younger colleague. When your counterpart comes out to you, introduce them to each other. Your colleague will take you to the hotel where you have reserved a room. On the way to the hotel your counterpart may be interested in some buildings and monuments. Give explanations. Help him to check in at the hotel.

---

excessive [ɪkˈsesɪv]   лишний, чрезмерный

A Letter from the Author of this Book.

Dear Students,

Now the time has come to congratulate you again, because you have completed another important stage in your English. You are no longer beginners! You have practically covered all the essential rules of English grammar, and your vocabulary now exceeds 2,700 words. You have already learnt enough general English to begin specializing in the English of your profession. This is not a bad result, and you have every reason to be satisfied.

There is something, however, we must talk about very seriously. Unfortunately, there is no such thing as a stabilized state in your knowledge of the language. Like any activity requiring a skill, your ability to use English needs regular practice. You either go on acquiring knowledge, practising and making progress, or you begin to forget what you have learnt and lose the skills, and very quickly at that!

In other words, once you have started learning a foreign language, you shouldn't stop, otherwise, you risk forgetting a great deal of what you know.

Of course, it isn't always easy to find someone to speak to, but finding a good English book to read is no problem at all. When you read, you sometimes increase your vocabulary without any special effort on your part, but don't forget that a new word is always worth looking up in the dictionary, especially if you are going to use it in your own speech.

In addition to reading, which has always been a reliable way of increasing competence in a foreign language, there is something that only a modern learner can afford to do. It is listening to the radio and tapes and watching video films. These are opportunities not to be missed, because it is very important to learn to understand different varieties of natural spoken English, especially the two main ones – British and American.

When you find it difficult to understand a tape or a film, don't be discouraged. Play it again and again until you understand it better. Regular listening will improve your ability to understand other speakers.

And now a few words about writing. We don't write as much as our grandfathers used to, but writing is very important, particularly for a businessman. Technically, an exercise in writing is very simple. All you need is paper and pen and, if possible, someone to see if what you have written is correct.

If brief, you have every opportunity to keep up your English and improve it.

I wish you every success.

Natalya Bonk

---

essential [ɪˈsenʃl] *adj*		существенный, основной
vocabulary [vəˈkæbjulərɪ] *n*		словарь
activity [ækˈtɪvɪtɪ] *n*		деятельность
skill *n*		зд. навык

ability [ə´bɪlɪtɪ] *n*	способность
acquire [ə´kwaɪə] *v*	приобретать
otherwise [´ʌðəwaɪz] *adv*	иначе, в противном случае
a gret deal	многое
competence [´kɔmpətəns] *n*	компетенция
variety [və´raɪətɪ] *n*	вариант, разновидность
correct [kə´rekt] *adj*	правильный
in brief	вкратце, *зд.* короче говоря

Приложение

СПИСОК НЕПРАВИЛЬНЫХ ГЛАГОЛОВ

Инфинитив	Прошедшее время	Причастие 2
be	was	been
beat	beat	beaten
become	became	become
begin	began	begun
blow	blew	blown
break	broke	broken
bring	brought	brought
build	built	built
burn	burnt	burnt
buy	bought	bought
catch	caught	caught
choose	chose	chosen
come	came	come
cost	cost	cost
cut	cut	cut
deal	dealt	dealt
do	did	done
draw	drew	drawn

drink	drank	drunk
drive	drove	driven
eat	ate	eaten
feed	fed	fed
feel	felt	felt
fight	fought	fought
find	found	found
fly	flew	flown
forget	forgot	forgotten
freeze	froze	frozen
get	got	got
give	gave	given
go	went	gone
hang	hung	hung
have	had	had
hear	heard	heard
hold	held	held
hurt	hurt	hurt
keep	kept	kept
know	knew	known
lead	led	led
learn	learnt	learnt
leave	left	left
lend	lent	lent
let	let	let
lie	lay	lain
lose	lost	lost
make	made	made
mean	meant	meant
meet	met	met

– 364 –

put	put	put
read	read	read
ride	rode	ridden
ring	rang	rung
rise	rose	risen
run	ran	run
say	said	said
see	saw	seen
sell	sold	sold
send	sent	sent
set	set	set
shoot	shot	shot
sing	sang	sung
sit	sat	sat
sleep	slept	slept
smell	smelt	smelt
speak	spoke	spoken
spend	spent	spent
stand	stood	stood
steal	stole	stolen
swim	swam	swum
take	took	taken
teach	taught	taught
tell	told	told
throw	threw	thrown
understand	understood	understood
wake	woke	woken
wear	wore	worn
win	won	won
write	wrote	written

ТАБЛИЦА ВРЕМЕННЫХ ФОРМ

		PRESENT	PAST
SIMPLE	to write / to translate	1. I hardly ever **write** letters. 2. Alex often **writes** letters. 3. He usually **translates** business letters. 4. Do you **translate** letters? 5. **Does** he **translate** letters? 6. **Don't** you **write** letters occasionally?	1. I **wrote** a letter to a friend yesterday. 2. When **did** you **write** to him? 3. When **did** he last **write** to you? 4. Why **didn't** you **write** to him?
CONTINUOUS	to be writing / to be translating	1. "What **are** you **doing?**" "**I'm writing** a letter." 2. Alex **is translating** a letter, so he can't talk to you just now. 3. Для выражения будущего действия. "What **are** you **doing** tonight?" "**I'm going** to the cinema."	1. I **was writing** a letter when you came. 2. What **were** you **doing** when I came? 3. I **wasn't making** any calls at five o'clock.
PERFECT	to have written / to have translated	1. I've just **written** a letter to a friend. 2. **Has** he **answered** your letter yet? 3. I **haven't seen** him lately. 4. I **haven't seen** him for a long time. 5. I **haven't seen** him since we went to college.	1. I'**d written** all the letters when you came. 2. He said he'**d** already **translated** all the letters. 3. How many letters **had** you **translated** by the time the manager came?
PERFECT CONTINUOUS	to have been writing / to have been translating	1. I've **been writing** letters since morning. 2. What **have** you **been writing** all this time? 3. He's **been translating** books all his life. 4. How long **have** you **been translating** this article?	1. He said he'**d been looking** through the mail since morning. 2. We'**d been walking** through the forest for three hours when we realized that we'd lost our way.

АКТИВНОГО ЗАЛОГА.

FUTURE	FUTURE IN THE PAST
1. I think I'll **write** to him one of these days. 2. He'll probably **write** to me soon. 3. Just a moment! I'll **write** it down. 4. I'll **send** you a fax as soon as I make all the necessary arrangements. 5. I'll **call** you after I've seen everybody about it.	1. He said he'**d write** to us as soon as he got to London.
1. I'll **be waiting** for you at exactly ten. 2. **Will** you **be using** your computer this afternoon? 3. Tomorrow we'll **be looking** at the situation in Panama.	1. He said he'**d be waitihg** for you at exactly ten. 2. They said (on TV) they **would be looking** at the situation in Panama tomorrow.
(Употребляется сравнительно редко) 1. We'll **have written** all the most important letters by one o'clock (by the time you need them). 2. You'll understand the problem better after you'**ve studied** it more carefully.	1. They said they'**d have written** all the documents by the time you needed them next week. 2. He said you'**d understand** the problem better after you'**d studied** it more carefully.
(Употребляется сравнительно редко) 1. He'll **have been** working for an hour by the time we come to help him.	(Употребляется сравнительно редко) 1. He said he'**d have been** working for an hour by the time we came to help him.

ТАБЛИЦА ВРЕМЕННЫХ ФОРМ

		PRESENT	PAST
SIMPLE	to be written / to be translated	1. The mail **is** always **received** after 10 o'clock. 2. New houses **are** usually **built** on the outskirts. 3. All the contracts **are signed** by Director General. 4. This work **is done with** a very thin needle. 5. What **is** it made **of**? 6. He**'s** often invited to parties. 7. The boy **isn't** often given new toys.	1. America **was discovered** by Columbus. 2. I **was asked** to wait another week. 3. When **were** those houses **built**? 4. Who **was** the palace **designed by**? 5. We **weren't told** about it in time.
CONTINUOUS	to be being written / to be being translated	1. The event**'s being discussed** everywhere. 2. **Are** those houses still **being built**? 3. **Is** everybody being **served**? 4. Why **isn't** that lady **being served**?	1. The problem **was** still **being discussed** when the telephone rang. 2. **Were** those houses still **being built** when you visited the town last year?
PERFECT	to have been written / to have been translated	1. The contract **has** just **been signed**. 2. **Has** the doctor **been sent for**? 3. The problem **hasn't been solved** yet.	1. All the necessary documents **had been prepared** before the discussion started. 2. **Had** all the tickets **been sold** out when you came to the booking office?

ВНИМАНИЕ: Группа PERFECT CONTINUOUS в пассивном залоге отсутствует.

ПАССИВНОГО ЗАЛОГА.

FUTURE	FUTURE IN THE PAST
1. I think the answer **will be received** one of these days. 2. When **will** the work **be finished**? 3. How many people **will be invited**? 4. The problem **won't be solved** soon.	1. I thought the answer **would be received** last week. 2. I knew the problem **wouldn't be solved** soon.
не употребляется	*не употребляется*
1. The construction of the factory **will have been completed** by the time you arrive. 2. All the machines **will have been installed** by the time required by the Buyers.	1. They wrote the equipment **would have been delivered** and **installed** by the time required by the Buyers.

Алфавитный словарь-указатель

Уважаемые читатели!

СП "ПРИН-ДИ" готовит к выпуску учебник "Английский для международного сотрудничества. Курс для начинающих" Н.А. Бонк и И.И. Левиной, который представляет собой первую часть настоящей книги.

Планируется также выпуск фонозаписей для обеих частей учебника. "Английский для международного сотрудничества" в двух частях в сочетании с фонозаписями образует единый учебно-методический комплекс, рассчитанный на 400—500 часов аудиторной работы (8—9 месяцев). Курс обеспечивает практическое владение английским языком и может изучаться как под руководством преподавателя, так и самостоятельно.

По всем вопросам обращаться по адресу: Москва, 103489, а/я 83.

Н.А.Бонк

Английский для международного сотрудничества.
Учебник

Сдано в набор 25
Подписано к печати 1
Тираж 10
Тип. ИПО писателей. 3